For D<small>AD</small>,
Who also likes computing machines.

Lecture Notes in Computer Science

Edited by G. Goos and J. Hartm

336

Bruce R. Donald

Error

and I

Spring

Berlin Hei

Author

Bruce R. Donald
Department of Computer Science, Cornell University
4130 Upson Hall, Ithaca, NY 14853-7501, USA

This book is a revised version of a thesis submitted on June 30, 1987 to the Department of
Electrical Engineering and Computer Science at the Massachusetts Institute of Technology,
in partial fulfillment of the requirements for the degree of Doctor of Philosophy.

The book describes research done at the Artificial Intelligence Laboratory of the
Massachusetts Institute of Technology. Support for the Laboratory's Artificial Intelligence
research is provided in part by the Office of Naval Research under Office of Naval Research
contract N00014-81-K-0494 and in part by the Advanced Research Projects Agency under
Office of Naval Research contracts N00014-85-K-0124 and N00014-82-K-0334. The author
was funded in part by a NASA fellowship administered by the Jet Propulsion Laboratory. His
work on this book at Cornell has been funded in part by the Mathematical Sciences Institute,
and by the National Science Foundation.

CR Subject Classification (1987): I.2.9, I.3.5, F.2.1−2, I.2.8, J.6

ISBN 3-540-96909-8 Springer-Verlag Berlin Heidelberg New York
ISBN 0-387-96909-8 Springer-Verlag New York Berlin Heidelberg

Printing and binding: Druckhaus Beltz, Hemsbach/Bergstr.
2145/3140-543210

Preface

For the past six years, I have been interested in building robot planning systems that can function at the task-level. A task-level specification of a robot plan might have the form, *Put together this disk rotor assembly.* The planner is given geometric models of the parts, and geometric or analytic models of the robot dynamics. Beyond this, the specification, or input to the planner does not mention the specific kinematic and dynamic constraints that the robot must obey; these are determined by the planner using geometrical computation. Typically, there are additional constraints that the planner must also obey, for example, *Construct a robot plan that is robust in the face of uncertainty and error. Use compliant motion where appropriate to reduce uncertainty.* The goal of a task-level planner is to take a task-level specification and to produce a runnable robot program—one which is fully specified in terms of force-control, kinematics, and dynamics—that can accomplish the task.

Major advances in task-level planning can enable robotics to achieve its full potential in the assembly domain. Today, even existing robots cannot be exploited to their full capacity. For example, assembly tasks require compliant motion; however, compliance requires force-control, and such force-control motion strategies are quite difficult for humans to specify. Furthermore, robot assembly programs are very sensitive to the details of geometry. Finally, reprogramming a general purpose robot for a new assembly task can take time on the order of man-months. For these reasons, we have been working on the automatic synthesis of motion strategies for robots. Much work is required to reduce such current task-level technologies to practice.

Research in task-level planning is often characterized as *theoretical robotics.* There are several reasons for this; the first is that much of the work has been concerned with constructing a *theory* of planning. In other words, the computational problem "task-level planning" is not well-specified. Much of our work lies in specifying the computation precisely. Second, given some sort of decomposition of task-level planning into "planning problems", one is immediately driven to ask, *What are the algorithms for these problems? Can plans, in general, be computed? How efficiently can planning algorithms run?* Historically, the nature of these questions has led researchers to apply tools from theoretical computer science, computational geometry, and algebra. Much of this work, while foundational, must seem rather distant from the practitioner and the physical robot.

Recently, a great deal of attention has been focused on a particular robotics problem, called the find-path, or generalized movers' problem. In this problem, we ask the purely kinematic question, can a robot system be moved from one configuration to another, without colliding with obstacles? See figs. 1, 2. This is a nicely-defined mathematical problem, and, after much research, at this point its computational complexity is precisely known.

In fact, the neatness of this problem is deceptive, so much so that this formal problem has even been called "the" motion planning problem. From a task-level viewpoint, there

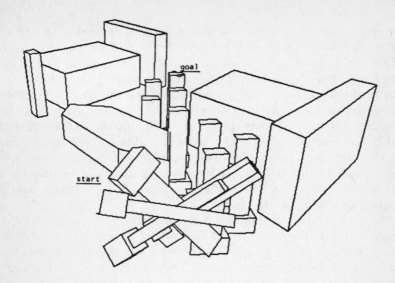

Figure 1: An example of a solution path for the classical find-path, or Movers' problem. This illustration is a "time-lapse" picture of a path found for a hammer-shaped object through a maze of polyhedral obstacles. From [Donald, 87a].

is much hidden in the statement "Can the robot system be moved...?" Specifically, the find-path problem assumes that the robot has a perfect control system that can exactly execute the plan, and that the geometric and analytic models of the robot and obstacles are exact.

In reality, of course, robot control systems are subject to significant uncertainty and error. Typical robots are also equipped with sensors—force sensors, kinesthetic position sensors, tactile sensors, vision, and so forth. However, these sensors are also subject to significant uncertainty. Finally, the geometrical models of the robot and the environment (parts, obstacles, etc.) cannot be exact—they are accurate only to manufacturing tolerances, or to the accuracy of the sensors used to acquire the models. Uncertainty is not a mere engineering detail; in particular, it is characteristically impossible to "patch" these perfect plans in such a way that they will function once uncertainty comes into play. Uncertainty is an absolutely fundamental problem in robotics, and plans produced under the assumption of no uncertainty are meaningless. What is needed is a principled theory of planning in the presence of uncertainty. Such a theory must not only be computational, but must also take uncertainty into account *a priori*. The overlap with exact motion planning algorithms can be stated roughly as follows: exact kinematic planning algorithms

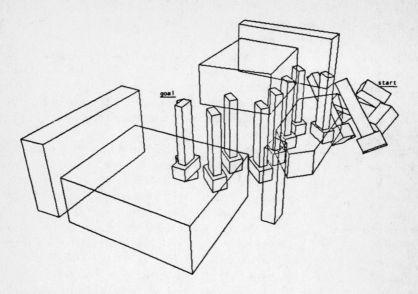

Figure 2: A different view of the solution path for the Movers' problem in fig. 1, with the obstacles "transparent" to allow us to view the rotations better.

provide a computational-geometric theory of holonomic constraints. In motion planning with uncertainty, we exploit compliant motion—sliding on surfaces—in order to effect a "structural" reduction in uncertainty. Such compliant motion plans can be synthesized from a computational analysis of the geometry of the holonomic constraints.

1   Uncertainty and Compliant Motion

Robots are subject to the following kinds of uncertainty:

1. Inaccuracy and errors in sensing,

2. Inaccuracy and errors in control,

3. Uncertainty about the geometry of the environment.

The last (3) is called "model error", and has received little previous attention. Model error arises because, in general, a robot can have only approximate knowledge of the shape and position of objects in the environment.

We now ask the question:

- How can robots plan and execute tasks (for example, a mechanical assembly using compliant motion) in the presence of these three kinds of uncertainty?

This is perhaps the most fundamental problem in robotics today. We call it the problem of *motion planning with uncertainty*.

In motion planning with uncertainty, the objective is to find a plan which is guaranteed to succeed even when the robot cannot execute it perfectly due to control and sensing uncertainty. With control uncertainty, it is impossible to perform assembly tasks which involve sliding motions using position control alone. To successfully perform assembly tasks, uncertainty must be taken into account, and other types of control must be employed which allow *compliant motion*.

Compliant motion occurs when a robot is commanded to move into an obstacle, but rather than stubbornly obeying its motion command, it complies to the surface of the obstacle. Work on compliant motion[1] attempts to utilize the task geometry to plan motions that reduce the uncertainty in position by maintaining sliding contact with a surface. Plans consisting of such motions can be designed to exploit the geometry of surfaces around the goal to guide the robot. By computing "preimages"[2] of a geometrical goal in configuration space, guaranteed strategies can be synthesized geometrically: We call this a *geometrical theory of planning*. The first results in this theory begin with Lozano-Pérez, Mason, and Taylor (or [LMT]), with subsequent contributions by Mason [Ma2], Erdmann [E] and Donald [D]. This research has led to a theoretical computational framework for motion planning with uncertainty, which we denote [LMT,E,D]. See [Buc, EM, Bro, CR] for other allied work.

The [LMT,E,D] framework begins by observing that the use of active compliance enables robots to carry out tasks in the presence of significant sensing and control errors. Compliant motion meets external constraints by specifying how the robot's motion should be modified in response to the forces generated when the constraints are violated. For example, contact with a surface can be guaranteed by maintaining a small force normal to the surface. The remaining degrees of freedom (DOF)—the orthogonal complement of the normal-space—can then be position-controlled. Using this technique, the robot can achieve and retain contact with a surface that may vary significantly in shape and orientation from the programmer's expectations. Generalizations of this principle can be used to accomplish a wide variety of tasks involving constrained motion, e.g., inserting a peg in a hole, or following a weld seam. The specification of particular compliant motions to achieve a task requires knowledge of the geometric constraints imposed by the task. Given a description of the constraints, choices can be made for the compliant motion parameters, e.g., the motion freedoms to be force controlled and those to be position controlled. It is common, however, for position uncertainty to be large enough so that the programmer cannot unambiguously determine which geometric constraints hold at

---

[1]See [Ma] for an introduction and survey.

[2]The *preimage* of a goal [LMT] is the set of configurations from which a particular commanded compliant motion is guaranteed to succeed.

any instant in time. For example, the possible initial configurations for a peg in hole strategy (see fig. 3) may be "topologically" very different, in that different surfaces of the peg and hole are in contact. Under these circumstances, the programmer must employ a combined strategy of force and position control that guarantees reaching the desired final configuration from all the likely initial configurations. We call such a strategy a *motion strategy*.

Motion strategies are quite difficult for humans to specify. Furthermore, robot programs are very sensitive to the details of geometry. For this reason, we have been working on the automatic synthesis of motion strategies for robots.

Note that compliant motion planning with uncertainty is significantly different from motion planning with perfect sensing and control along completely-known configuration space obstacle boundaries [Kou, HW, BK]. The first difference is physical:

- From a practical point of view, the motion-in-contact plans generated under the assumption of perfect control cannot ever be executed by a physical robot using position control alone.

The second difference is combinatorial:

- The planning of motions in contact with perfect control has the same time-complexity as planning free-space motions; that is, it can be done in time $O(n^r \log n)$ for r degrees of freedom and n faces or surfaces in the environment [C1]; the exponent is worst-case optimal. However, prior to this thesis, there are no upper bounds for planning compliant motions *with* uncertainty. However, for r fixed at 3, the problem is hard for non-deterministic exponential time [CR]. We show in chapter V that the planar case, somewhat surprisingly, turns out to be tractable.

The physical difficulty in fact motivates our work. This experimental viewpoint is manifest in chapters I–III. It is also possible to adopt a more theoretical perspective; in chapter V, we concentrate on the geometric and combinatorial aspects of the problem.[3]

2 Example: Synthesizing Guaranteed Plans

Error Detection and Recovery (EDR) strategies arose as a response to certain inadequacies in the "guaranteed success" planning model. Hence, in order to study EDR, it is first necessary to understand the structure of guaranteed compliant motion strategies, and how they may be synthesized. To this end, in the preface, we wish to give a flavor for the kinds of issues that arise in planning guaranteed motion strategies under uncertainty. We examine a very special case—the planar polygonal case. (That is, the workspace environment ("parts" and "obstacles") are polygonal). First, we will briefly develop a simple dynamic model that is adequate for this situation. Next, we carefully define the

---

[3]See also [Donald, 88b].

computational problem of synthesizing planar guaranteed strategies under uncertainty in sensing and control, and generalize our definition to include uncertainty in the shape of the parts and obstacles. Finally, we hint at the types of computational techniques employed.

For this very simple planning problem, we find that motion plans with a simple structure suffice. This permits us to illustrate by a specific example the situation that we will investigate later for fairly arbitrary plans. Together with the problem of constructing guaranteed compliant motion strategies under uncertainty, we will consider a rather restricted class of strategies, namely those that terminate by sticking on a surface.

2.1 Dynamic Model

Compliant motion is only possible with certain dynamic models. We will employ the generalized damper model [W, Ma]. We assume that the environment is polyhedral, and that it describes the configuration space of the robot, so that the robot is always a point. The planned path consists of r successive motions in directions $v_1, \ldots, v_r$. Each motion terminates when it sticks, due to coulomb friction, on some surface in the environment. Because of control uncertainty, however, the robot cannot move with precisely velocity v_i on the ith motion. Instead, it moves with velocity v_i^{free}, which lies in a cone of velocities $B_{ec}(v_i)$ about v_i. The boundaries of the cone form an angle of ϵ_c with v_i. ϵ_c is called the *control uncertainty*, and $B_{ec}(v_i)$ the *control uncertainty cone about* v_i. It is, in fact, equivalent to regard ϵ_c as specifying that v_i^{free} lies within a ball about v_i in velocity space.

For a compliant motion, the robot moves along an obstacle surface with a sliding velocity v_i^{slide} which is the projection onto the surface of the obstacle of some v_i^{free} in $B_{ec}(v_i)$. Under generalized damper dynamics, the motion of a polyhedral robot without rotations is completely specified by the motion of its reference point in configuration space. See fig 3.

The ith motion terminates by sticking on a surface when the velocity v_i^{free} in $B_{ec}(v_i)$ points into the negative coulomb friction cone on a surface (see fig. 4). Thus sticking on a surface can be non-deterministic. We will assume that motion i can terminate on any reachable surface for which some velocity $v_i^{free} \in B_{ec}(v_i)$ is inside the negative friction cone. Sticking termination is motivated by the fact that a robot with a force-sensing wrist can easily recognize sticking and robustly terminate the motion.

To test whether sticking is possible on some set of (say, goal) edges, we simply perform a geometric cone intersection on each edge. Sticking is possible when the intersection of the cone of velocity uncertainty and the negative friction cone have a non-trivial intersection. Since determining the possibility (or necessity) of sticking reduces to a simple cone intersection, which may be done in constant time per edge, in this preface we will focus on the more difficult issue of computing reachability. Representing friction in our planar polygonal configuration space is easy; see fig. 4. However, the more general question of representing friction in configuration spaces with rotations is subtle; see [E, BRS].

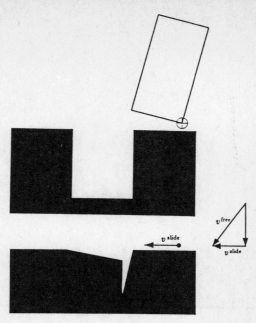

Figure 3: (a) Peg in hole environment. (b) Configuration space, showing the motion of the reference point during compliant motion.

While robust implementation of generalized damper dynamics is still a research issue, in our robotics laboratory we have recently implemented an experimental force-control system with this dynamic model to test our geometrical planning theories.

2.2   Definitions

We will regard the goal region G as a polyhedral region in configuration space. Since in general we cannot precisely know the initial configuration of the robot, we will also assume that the start region R is some polyhedral region in configuration space.

We now pose three problems (see fig. 6):

Problem 1: One-Step Compliant Motion Planning with Uncertainty. Given a polyhedral start region R, a polyhedral environment $\mathcal{P}$ of n vertices, control uncertainty ϵ_c, coefficient of friction μ, and a polyhedral goal G, find one commanded motion direction v such that under v, all possible motions from R terminate by sticking in G.

Problem 2: One-Step Compliant Motion Verification. Given $(R, \mathcal{P}, \epsilon_c, \mu, G)$ and v, verify that under v, all possible motions from R terminate by sticking in G.

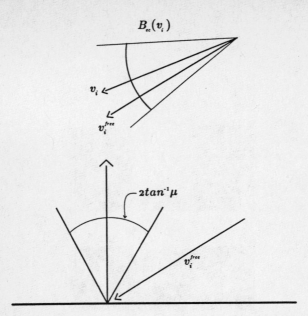

Figure 4: The control uncertainty cone B_{ec} about a nominal commanded velocity v_i. The coulomb friction cone edge makes an angle of $\tan^{-1}\mu$ with the normal. The velocity v_i^{free} will result in sliding on the surface.

Problem 3: Compliant Motion Planning with Uncertainty Given $(R, \mathcal{P}, \epsilon_c, \mu, G)$, and an integer r, find a sequence of r motions such that each motion terminates in sticking, and the final motion terminates in the goal. Or, if no such r-step strategy exists, then say so.

2.3 Model Error

We now introduce model error into the picture. How can compliant motion strategies be synthesized in the presence of sensing, control, and geometric model error, such that the strategies are guaranteed to succeed so long as the errors lie within the specified bounds? As an example, consider a peg-in-hole assembly with sensing and control uncertainty, with toleranced parts. We wish to synthesize a compliant motion strategy that is guaranteed to succeed so long as the parts lie within the specified tolerances, and the sensing and control errors lie within the specified bounds.

We can now state our fourth problem. We parameterize our family of geometries by the parameter space $\alpha_1, \ldots, \alpha_k$, so that $\mathcal{P}(\alpha_1, \ldots, \alpha_k)$ denotes a particular geometry, and each α_i lies within some given interval. Note that this parameterization need not be "continuous". We wish to find a plan which will succeed for all geometries $\mathcal{P}(\alpha_1, \ldots, \alpha_k)$.

Problem 4: Compliant Motion Planning with Uncertainty and Geometric Model Error Given $(R, \mathcal{P}(\alpha_1, \ldots, \alpha_k), \epsilon_c, \mu, G)$, and an integer r, find a sequence of r motions such that, for all possible values of $\alpha_1, \ldots, \alpha_k$, each motion terminates in sticking, and the final motion terminates in the goal. Or, if no such r-step strategy exists, then say so.

We have begun an attack on this problem by introducing additional dimensions to the configuration space; each dimension represents a way in which the parts could parametrically vary. We termed the product space of the motion degrees of freedom and the geometric model variational dimensions "generalized configuration space" and showed how to compute "preimages" [LMT,E] of a geometrical goal in this generalized configuration space. The preimage of a goal is the set of (generalized) configurations from which a particular commanded compliant motion is guaranteed to succeed. Using this technique, we have developed a framework for computing motion strategies that are guaranteed to succeed in the presence of sensing, control, and geometric model uncertainty. The motion strategies comprise sensor-based gross motions, compliant motions, and simple pushing motions.

2.4   Backprojections

We now sketch, for a specific example, a computational approach to the compliant motion planning problem with uncertainty. Later, we will mount a more systematic attack using similar, albeit considerably generalized methods.

Erdmann [E] has shown that in the plane, when G is a single edge of the polygonal environment $\mathcal{P}$, then the one-step verification problem (2) can be done in time $O((n + c)\log n)$, where c is the number of intersections encountered by a planar arrangement algorithm.

Erdmann's algorithm makes use of *backprojections*, which he defined as a simplified case of the [LMT] notion of geometrical preimages. The question of goal reachability from a start region can be reduced to deciding the containment of the start region within the backprojection of the goal.

The backprojection $B_\theta(G)$ of a goal G (with respect to a commanded velocity v_θ^*) consists of those configurations guaranteed to enter the goal (under v_θ^*).[4] That is, the backprojection is the set of all positions from which all possible trajectories consistent with the control uncertainty are guaranteed to reach G. See fig. 5. The terms "preimage" and "backprojection" come from viewing motions as "mappings" between subsets of configuration space. Hence the backprojection of a goal is the set of configurations from which a particular commanded compliant motion is guaranteed to succeed. [LMT]

---

[4]The star * denotes the ideal, or perfect control velocity. Henceforth, we will typically identify a commanded motion v_θ^* with its angular direction θ.

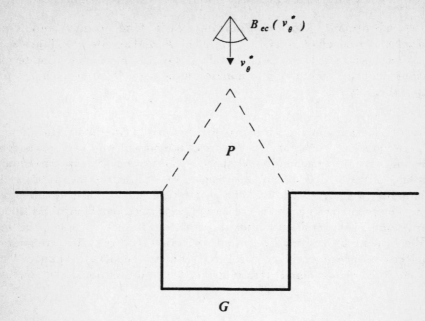

Figure 5: The goal is the region G. Sliding occurs on vertical surfaces, and sticking on horizontal ones. The commanded velocity is v_θ^*, and the control uncertainty is $B_{ec}(v_\theta^*)$. The *backprojection* of G with respect to θ is the region P.

envisioned a back-chaining planner that recursively computes preimages of a goal region. Successive subgoals are attained by motion strategies. Each motion terminates when all sensor interpretations indicate that the robot must be within the subgoal.

See fig. 6. Here is the key point about backprojections: Given $(R, \mathcal{P}, \epsilon_c, \mu, G, v_\theta^*)$, the one-step verification problem (2) reduces to testing set containment, i.e., that

$$R \subset B_\theta(G).$$

Erdmann showed that when G is a single edge of a planar environment $\mathcal{P}$, then $B_\theta(G)$ has size $O(n)$ and can be computed as follows (see fig. 7):

(a) Find all vertices in the environment where sticking is *possible* under v_θ^*.

(b) At each of these vertices, erect two rays, parallel to the two edges of the *inverted* velocity cone $-B_{ec}(v_\theta^*)$.

(c) Compute the arrangement from the environment plus these additional $O(n)$ constraints.

(d) Starting at the goal edge, trace out the backprojection region.

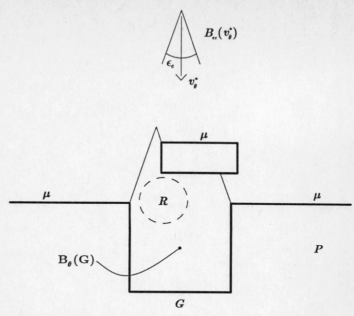

Figure 6: A compliant motion planning problem with goal G, start region R, control uncertainty ϵ_c, obstacles $\mathcal{P}$, and coefficient of friction μ. v_θ^* is a solution which is guaranteed to succeed.

An excellent exposition of Erdmann's algorithm can be found in [E]. With John Canny, we implemented a plane-sweep algorithm for backprojections from general polygonal goals. The idea is similar, and interested readers may find details in chapter V. While in general the complexity of these algorithms is $O((n+c)\log n)$, both methods take time $O(n\log n)$ and space $O(n)$ when the goal has $c = O(n)$ intersections with $\mathcal{P}$.

This sketch of the algorithm for verifying a compliant motion strategy gives some flavor for the kind of solution we desire. Consider the remaining problems. The trick to obtaining a computational solution to problem (1) lies in considering all possible backprojections (for all possible θ) simultaneously, and choosing θ that are suitable. In chapter V we show that it is possible to do this efficiently, and also provide exact algorithms for problems (3) and (4) as well.

Finally, we must note that there are many variants and facets of the guaranteed compliant motion planning problem; these we address later. For these problems, we also give computational approaches.

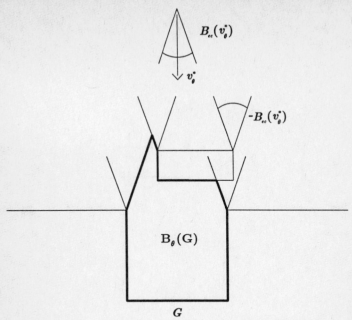

Figure 7: An illustration of Erdmann's algorithm for computing the backprojection $B_\theta(G)$ of a goal G in the plane.

3   Error Detection and Recovery

A task-level planning system requires a precise theory of Error Diagnosis and Recovery, and a method for generating sensor-based plans with built-in error detection and recovery. We call this the *Error Detection and Recovery (EDR) Theory*. I believe that the chief contribution of our work has been to define and develop a theory of EDR. Perhaps the simplest way to view EDR is as a generalization, or extension, of guaranteed geometrical planning theories. Of course, much work is required to make this notion precise, and useful; that is the bulk of this thesis. In effect, we shall propose a "new" theory of planning.

Our approach to EDR observes that there are certain inadequacies with the "guaranteed success" planning model. It is simply not always possible to find plans that are guaranteed to succeed. For example, if tolerancing errors render an assembly infeasible, the plan executor should stop and signal failure. In such cases the insistence on guaranteed success is too restrictive. For this reason we turn to EDR strategies. EDR plans will succeed or fail recognizably: in these more general strategies, there is no possibility that the plan will fail without the executor realizing it. The EDR framework fills a gap when guaranteed plans cannot be found or do not exist: it provides a technology for constructing plans that might work, but fail in a "reasonable" way when they cannot.

The key theoretical issue is: How can we relax the restriction that plans must be guaranteed to succeed, and still retain a theory of planning that is not completely *ad hoc*? We attempt to answer this by giving a constructive definition of EDR strategies. In particular, our approach provides a formal test for verifying whether a given strategy is an EDR strategy. The test is formulated as a decision problem about projection sets in a generalized configuration space which also encodes model error. Roughly speaking, the projection sets represent all possible outcomes of a motion (the *forward projection*), and weakest preconditions for attaining a subgoal (the *preimage*).

Given the formal test for "recognizing" an EDR strategy, we can then test the definition by building a generate-and-test planner. The generator is trivial; the recognizer is an algorithmic embodiment of the formal test. It lies at the heart of this research. A second key component of the planner is a set of techniques for chaining together motions to synthesize multi-step strategies. The planner, called LIMITED, synthesizes robot control programs with built-in sensor-based EDR.

While EDR is largely motivated by the problems of uncertainty and model error, its applicability may be quite broad. EDR has been a persistent but ill-defined theme in both AI and robotics research. We give a constructive, geometric definition for EDR strategies and show how they can be computed. This theory represents what is perhaps the first systematic attack on the problem of error detection and recovery based on geometric and physical reasoning.

4 Experimental Results

Since my Ph.D. thesis, my group at Cornell has implemented an experimental force-control system on our PUMA robot. In particular, we implemented an approximate generalized damper. Our PUMA 560 robot arm has a VAL-II controller, a Multibus-based 68000 computer system running NRTX (a real-time variant of UNIX) for real-time control, an Astek 6-axis force-sensing wrist, and a Monforte tool-changing gripper with finger positioning and sensing. We closed the servo loop outside of VAL-II to obtain a servo rate we estimate as approximately 20-30 hz. Probably due to the inherent passive compliance in the joints and wrist, the robot can maintain compliant contact between a (gripped) steel bolt and an aluminum surface at speeds of 1-3 inches per second.

This experimental system was sufficiently stable to perform experiments executing the plans generated by LIMITED. In particular, we executed the plans and we performed all the assemblies shown in chapter I, figs. 2-13. Again, the interesting thing about these plans is that they were generated by a machine, from task-level descriptions. Thus we were able to build a small slice of a task-level system, right down to the physical robot [Donald, 88a].

The peg-in-hole plans worked very well, even with tight (1 mm) clearances. The gear-meshing plans also worked, although we found it somewhat tricky to implement the failure mode analysis "oracle" that determines when sticking or breaking contact occurs using force- and position-sensing (chapter III). For both types of plans, we found that there were unmodelled effects (impact, bouncing) that could have an effect on plan execution, and unmodelled constants (the damping constants, the amount of force to maintain for sliding on a surface, the force termination thresholds) that must be chosen by the runtime executive. A more advanced planner would take these effects and constants into account. A more sophisticated runtime force-control plan executor might adaptively adjust these parameters to a local optimum. In addition, from an experimental viewpoint, much research is needed on the implementation and choice of termination predicates.

Work is underway!

Ithaca, 1988

Acknowledgments

I suspect that paradise is very much like the MIT AI Lab. Thanks to all the friends and scientists there who made this work possible. While tradition requires me to take responsibility for any remaining flaws, honesty compels me to share credit with them for whatever insight and clarity this thesis manifests.

I am deeply indebted to my supervisor, Tomás Lozano-Pérez, for his guidance, support and encouragement. Many of the key ideas in this thesis arose in conversations with Tomás, and this work would have been impossible without his help. Thanks for giving so much.

Rod Brooks and Eric Grimson were ideal thesis readers. Thanks for many useful comments and suggestions, and for your help and taste over my years at MIT.

Thanks to Patrick Winston for providing generous support and the unique environment of the AI Lab. Thanks for believing in me.

Mike Erdmann was always willing to talk about my work, and contributed many deep insights to the theory. Mike introduced me to the field of ultra-low energy computational physics, and provided valuable and insightful comments on a draft of this thesis. Thanks especially for your friendship, and for always being there for me.

Thanks to John Canny for collaborating on the plane-sweep algorithm, for helping with the complexity bounds, and for many discussions on robotics and computational geometry. John was extremely generous with his time and ideas, and I count myself lucky to have such a stellar mathematician as friend and collaborator.

Thanks to Steve Buckley for his friendship and for many discussions on robotics. Conversations with Steve, Russ Taylor, and Matt Mason helped me to formulate the EDR problem and focus my research. Steve, Randy Brost, and Margaret Fleck made many helpful suggestions on early drafts of this thesis. Thanks to Randy who believed in the EDR theory from day one. Thanks to John Reif, for his encouragement on this and stimulating collaboration on other work.

Many other scientists, machines, and friends have helped me over the last few years. Thanks to Sundar Narasimhan, Mike Caine, and Steve Gordon for talking so much about robotics with me. I am grateful to all the rest of the Girl Scouts for their friendship and uncritical support. Thanks to Jimi Hendrix for months of faithful and devoted crunching. I am grateful to Ms. Laura Nugent for pointing out the relevance of Tong's vector-bundle-valued cohomology [Gor] to this research. Thanks to Laura Radin for her friendship, and for feeding Mike and me more than we deserved.

A generous fellowship from NASA's Jet Propulsion Laboratory facilitated my research. Thanks to Carl Ruoff of JPL for his enthusiastic support of basic science, to Rich Mooney of Caltech for his enthusiastic support of Bruce Donald, and to Claudia Smith of MIT for waging many administrative battles on my behalf.

I thank the late Rick Jevon, my first scientist friend, for all he taught me about computers and life.

Thanks to my parents, for incalculable help over many years, and for your unconditional support.

Table of Contents

I. Introduction

1. Description of Problem and the Planner

Robots must plan and execute tasks in the presence of uncertainty. Uncertainty arises from sensing errors, control errors, and uncertainty in the geometric models of the environment and of the robot. The last, which is called *model error*, has received little previous attention. In this thesis we present a formal framework for computing motion strategies which are guaranteed to succeed in the presence of all three kinds of uncertainty. We show that it is effectively computable for some simple cases. The motion strategies we consider include sensor-based gross motions, compliant motions, and simple pushing motions.

We show that model error can be represented by position uncertainty in a generalized configuration space. We describe the structure of this space, and how motion strategies may be planned in it.

It is not always possible to find plans that are guaranteed to succeed. In the presence of model error, such plans may not even exist. For this reason we investigate *Error Detection and Recovery (EDR) strategies*. We characterize such strategies geometrically, and propose a formal framework for constructing them.

This thesis offers two contributions to the theory of manipulation. The first is a framework for planning motion strategies with model error. Model error is a fundamental problem in robotics, and we have tried to provide a principled, precise approach. The framework can be described very compactly, although many algorithmic and implementational questions remain.

The second contribution is a formal, geometric approach to EDR. While EDR is largely motivated by the problems of uncertainty and model error, its applicability may be quite broad. EDR has been a persistent but ill-defined theme in both AI and robotics research. Typically, it is viewed as a kind of source-to-source transformation on robot programs: for example, as a method for robustifying them by introducing sensing steps and conditionals. We take the view that if one can actually plan to sense an anomalous event, and to recover from it, then it is not an error at all. When such plans can be guaranteed, they can be generated by the [LMT] method. In our view of EDR, an "error" occurs when the goal cannot be recognizably achieved given the resources of the executive and the state of the world. The EDR framework fills a gap when guaranteed plans cannot be found or do not exist: it provides a technology for constructing plans that might work, but fail in a "reasonable" way when they cannot. This theory attempts a systematic attack on the problem of error detection and recovery based on geometric and physical reasoning.

1.1. Application and Motivation

1.1.1 A Simple Example

Consider fig. 1, which depicts a peg in hole insertion task. One could imagine a manipulation strategy derived as follows: The initial plan is to move the peg straight down towards the bottom of the hole. However, due to uncertainty in the initial position of the peg, the insertion may fail because the peg contacts to the left or right of the hole. Either event might be regarded as an "error." The "recovery" action is to move to the right (if the peg contacted to the left) and to move to the left (if the peg contacted to the right). Thus a plan can be obtained by introducing sensing steps and conditional branches.

Suppose that this conditional plan can be guaranteed—that is, it is a complete manipulation strategy for this simple task. In this case, it seems strange to view the contact conditions as "errors." We do not regard these events as "errors." Our reasoning is that if they can be detected and planned for, then they are simply events in a guaranteed plan.

We are interested in a different class of "errors." Now suppose that there is uncertainty in the width of the hole. If the hole is too small, we will consider this an error, since it causes all plans to fail. Similarly, if some object blocks the hole, and cannot be pushed aside, this is also an error, since it makes the goal unreachable. If either error is possible, there exists no guaranteed plan, for there is no assurance that the task can be accomplished. Since no guaranteed plan can be found, we are left with the choice of giving up, or of considering a broader class of manipulation strategies: plans that might work, but fail in an "reasonable" way when they cannot. Specifically, we propose that EDR strategies should achieve the goal when it exists and is recognizably reachable, and should signal failure when it is not. For example, an EDR strategy for the peg-in-hole problem with model error might attempt to achieve the insertion using compliant motion, but be prepared to recognize failure in case the hole is too small. Below, we describe how an implemented planner, called LIMITED, synthesizes such strategies. LIMITED is an implementation of the EDR theory in a restricted domain.

1.1.2 Application: Planning Gear Meshing

We must stress that EDR is not limited to problems with model error. There are many applications in which the geometry of the environment is precisely known, but in which guaranteed plans cannot be found, or are very difficult to generate. We now describe such a situation.

An interesting application domain for EDR is gear meshing. It is an example where EDR is applicable even though the shape of the manipulated parts is precisely known. Let us consider a simplified instance of this problem. In fig. 2 there are

Fig. 1. The goal is to insert the peg in the hole. No rotation of the peg is allowed. One can imagine a strategy which attempts to move straight down, but detects contact on the top surfaces of the hole if they occur. If the peg sticks on the top surfaces, the manipulator tries to move to the left or right to achieve the hole. Are these contact conditions "errors"? We maintain that they are not, since they can be planned for and verified.

two planar gear-like objects, A and B. The task is to plan a manipulation strategy which will mesh the gears. The state in which the gears are meshed is called the *goal*.

We will consider two variants of this problem. In the first, we assume that the manipulator has grasped A, and that neither A nor B can rotate. However, A can slide along the surfaces of B. In the second, B is free to rotate about its center, but this rotation can only be effected by pushing it with A. In both cases, the initial orientation of B is unknown. We regard A as the moving object and B as the environment; hence *even though the shape of B is precisely known, we choose to view the uncertainty in B's orientation as a form of model error*. In the first case, the system has only two degrees of motion freedom. In the second, there are

Fig. 2. Geometric models of two gear-like planar objects A and B. A is grasped and can translate but not rotate. B can rotate about its center if pushed. The orientation of B is unknown. The task is to generate a motion strategy to mesh the gears.

three degrees of motion freedom, one of which is rotational, since B can be pushed. We distinguish between the rotation and non-rotation variants of the problem in order to highlight the additional techniques our planner employs when rotations are introduced.

In both variations, there is uncertainty in control, so when a motion direction is commanded, the actual trajectory followed is only approximately in that direction. There is also uncertainty in position sensing and force sensing, so that the true position and reaction forces are only known approximately. The magnitude of these uncertainties are represented by error balls.

In general, a commanded motion of A may cause A to move through free space, and contact B, possibly causing B to rotate. Our EDR theory is a technique for analyzing these outcomes geometrically to generate strategies that achieve the goal when it is recognizably reachable, and signal failure when it is not.

In an experiment, the EDR theory in the gear domain was applied using the planner, LIMITED, as follows. Consider the problem of meshing two planar gears, under uncertainty as above. Suppose that gear B can rotate passively but has unknown initial orientation, as above. Suppose that A has been gripped by a robot. The initial position of A is uncertain. The robot can impart either pure forces (translations), or pure torques (rotations) to A. The planner can choose the direction of translation or rotation. Can a multi-step strategy of commanded translations and rotations be found to mesh the gears?

LIMITED was able to generate an EDR strategy for this problem. The characteristics of the experiment are:

- There are three degrees of motion freedom (two translational and one rotational) for A.
- There is one degree of rotational model error freedom (the orientation of B).
- It is possible to push B to change its orientation.
- There is sensing and control uncertainty.
- The geometry of the gears is complicated—they have many edges.
- Quasi-static analysis [Mason] is used to model the physics of interaction between the gears.

Thus we have a kind of four-degree of freedom planning problem with uncertainty and pushing. To generate multi-step EDR strategies under pushing, LIMITED employed the EDR theory together with a technique called *failure mode analysis*.

Now, there may exist a guaranteed strategy to mesh the gears. For example, experimental evidence suggests that for involute teeth gears, almost any meshing strategy will succeed. For other gear shapes perhaps some complicated translation while spinning A will always succeed. I don't know if there is such a guaranteed strategy for this case. It seems difficult for a planner to synthesize such guaranteed strategies, or even to verify them, if they exist at all.

A person might try to solve this problem with the following motion strategy:

- *Ram the gears together. See if they mesh.*

Or, somewhat more precisely,

- *Ram A into B. If they mesh, stop. If they jam, signal failure and try again.*

Probabilistically, this is a rather good strategy. It is certainly very simple, and probably easier to generate than a guaranteed strategy. If vision can be used to sense whether A and B are meshed, then it is an EDR strategy with just one step.

Suppose, however, that vision is poor, or that the gears are accessible to the robot gripper, but not to the camera. This means that position sensing will be very inaccurate, and hence may be of no use in determining whether the gears are successfully meshed. This will often be the case in practice. In this case, force sensing must be used to disambiguate the success of the motion (meshing) from failure (jamming in an unmeshed state). If the robot has force sensing, then it might use the following two-step EDR strategy:

- *Ram the gears together. Spin them to see whether they meshed.*
  Or, again more precisely,
- *Ram A into B. Next, spin A. If A and B break contact, or if the gears stick (don't rotate), then signal failure. Otherwise, signal success.*

This strategy is essentially the one that LIMITED generates. The plan is

Motion 1: *Command a pure translation of A into B.*[1]
  Terminate the motion based on force-sensing when sticking occurs (when there is no motion).
Motion 2: *Command a pure rotation of A.*
  If breaking contact or sticking occurs, signal failure. Otherwise, signal success.

In this plan, motion (1) does not terminate distinguishably in success (meshed) or failure (jammed). That is, after motion (1) terminates, the plan executive cannot necessarily recognize whether or not the gears are meshed. LIMITED predicts this, and generates motion (2), which disambiguates the result of motion (1). The generation of the second, disambiguating motion involves the use of *failure mode analysis. Breaking contact* and *sticking* are examples of failure modes. The second motion is generated so that from any unmeshed state resulting from motion (1), all possible paths will terminate distinguishably in a failure mode. Failure mode analysis is a robust subtheory of EDR by which LIMITED generates multi-step strategies under pushing.

1.1.3 Experiment: Peg-in-Hole with Model Error

This section describes a plan that was generated by LIMITED for a peg-in-hole problem with model error. It gives the flavor of how EDR strategies work. Since pushing motions are not involved here, LIMITED does not use failure mode analysis to solve this problem.

Another peg-in-hole problem is depicted in fig. 3. Again, as in fig. 1, there is uncertainty in the width of the hole; that is, the width is known to lie within some given interval. In addition, there are chamfers on the sides of the hole. The depth of the chamfers is also unknown, but we are given bounds on the depth. Finally, the exact orientation of the hole is uncertain. The geometry of the hole is input to the planner as a set of parametrically defined polygons. They are defined by a

---

[1]LIMITED generates the actual force vector.

three parameter family, for *width* of the hole, *depth* of the chamfers, and *orientation* of the hole. An associated bounding interval is also input for each parameter. The geometry of the peg is input as a polygon.

In this problem, the width of the hole may be smaller than the width of the peg. Thus there can exist no strategy that is guaranteed to succeed for all geometric uncertainty values. However, assume that the assembly—the hole geometry— is inaccessible to robust vision or position-measuring devices. In particular, the measurement error will typically determine the model error bounds, which in this example are large for the purpose of illustration. *Thus it is not a priori possible to measure the dimensions ahead of time to determine whether or not the assembly is feasible.* Instead, the best we can hope for is an EDR strategy: a strategy that takes some action in the world to attempt the assembly, but whose outcome can be recognizably diagnosed as success or failure by the run-time robot executor.

The peg is allowed to translate in the plane. Its motion is modeled using generalized damper dynamics. This permits sliding on surfaces about the hole. Friction is modeled using Coulomb's law. With these dynamics and *perfect* control, the peg would exhibit straight-line motions in free space, followed by sliding motions in contact, where friction permits. Here, however, there is control uncertainty, which is represented by a cone of velocities. Motions in free space fan out in a kind of "spray." Again, sliding is possible on surfaces, but so is sticking, depending on the effective commanded velocity at a given instant. (In this case, we say sliding is *non-deterministic*). The size of the control uncertainty cone of velocities is an input to the planner. Whether sticking may occur on an edge may be computed by intersecting the friction cone with the *negative* control uncertainty cone.

It is possible to sense the position of the peg and the forces acting on it. This information is only approximate. The error bound on the position sensor readings is input to the planner as the radius of a disc.

LIMITED generates plans using a configuration space representation of the constraints [Lozano-Pérez]. In the plane, one imagines shrinking the moving object to a point, and correspondingly "growing" the obstacles. The point must be navigated through free-space, sliding on surfaces, and so forth, into the hole. Fig. 4 shows configuration spaces for different parametric variations of model error. Notice that when the "real" hole is too small for the peg to fit, then there is simply no hole at all in the corresponding configuration space. Each frame in fig. 4 is called a "slice;" a slice represents a cross-section where the model error parameters are constant. To synthesize an EDR strategy, LIMITED must in some sense consider all such slices. In practice LIMITED works by constructing a finite, although typically large number of slices. We will show how in many cases, only a low polynomial number need be considered. LIMITED begins by considering a small number of slices, and generates a tentative motion strategy. This strategy must pass a test—which we call the EDR test—to be recognized as an EDR strategy. One of the chief goals of this thesis is to derive this test, and to make it formal and algorithmic. Next, LIMITED attempts to "generalize" the strategy by considering successively more slices. The strategy is modified so that it passes the EDR test in all slices. The number of slices considered is the *resolution* of the planning. This approach is called *multi-resolution* planning.

Let's consider an EDR plan that LIMITED computed for this problem. Figs. 5-13 show the plan graphically. Qualitatively, the plan may be described as follows:

- *(1) First, move left and slightly down. The motion will terminate on the left side of the hole, on the left chamfers, or overshoot the hole entirely. Where the motion terminates depends both on the trajectory evolution within the control uncertainty, and on the actual geometry of the hole. The motion may, however, slide down the left edge of the hole all the way into the goal. However, this sliding is non-deterministic, and the motion may stick anywhere along that edge. Since the first motion may terminate arbitrarily close to the goal region, LIMITED predicts that the run-time executive system cannot necessarily distinguish whether or not the first motion failed to achieve the goal.*

- *(2) The termination regions from motion (1) are taken as the start regions for a new motion. Next, try to recover by commanding a motion straight down and slightly to the right. This motion may achieve the goal, or may undershoot it, or may overshoot it. The second motion terminates when the peg sticks on a surface. If such a termination surface is outside the goal, it is called a* failure region. *LIMITED calculates that after the second motion, the failure regions are distinguishable from the goal regions. Hence after the second motion, the run-time executive can recognize whether or not the plan has failed.*

Finally, since LIMITED is a forward-chaining planner, it is possible to take the failure regions from motion (2) and plan a third recovery motion. Thus, roughly speaking, in the EDR framework, *recovery* actions are planned by forward-chaining from the failure regions of the previous motion. When the failure regions are potentially indistinguishable from the goal (using sensors), then the recovery action must satisfy the formal EDR test when executed from the *union* of the goal and the previous failure regions. For example, when we view motion strategies as "mappings" between subsets of configuration space, then typical "robust" recovery actions are EDR plans in which the goal is a "fixed point."[2] Motion (2) is an example of such a one-step EDR plan.

Figs. 5–13 show the plan in just four different slices, to give a flavor for the plan. The rest of the slices may be found later in the thesis. Fig. 5 shows the configuration spaces of the four slices. The goal region here is shaded black. Note that in one slice, the goal disappears. The initial uncertainty in the position of the

---

[2] That is, when motion (2) originates in the goal, it also terminates recognizably in the goal.

peg is represented by constraining the reference point (the point to which the peg has been shrunk) to lie in one of the start regions in fig. 6.

Figs. 7–8 represents the *forward projection* of the first motion. This region is the outer envelope of all possible trajectories evolving from the start regions. It is the set of all configurations that are reachable from the start regions, given the commanded velocity and control uncertainty cone.

Fig. 9 shows the termination regions for motion (1). The termination regions outside the goal are not necessarily distinguishable from the goal.

Figs. 10–11 show the forward projection of the second motion.

Fig. 12 shows the termination regions for the second motion.

Fig. 13 shows the size of the position sensing uncertainty ball. The goal and the failure regions in fig. 12 are distinguishable using sensors.

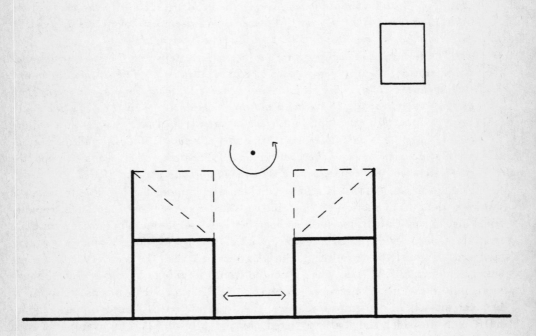

Fig. 3. A peg-in-hole environment with model error. The width of the hole (α_1), depth of chamfer (α_2), and orientation of the hole (α_3) are the model parameters. The hole is allowed to close up.

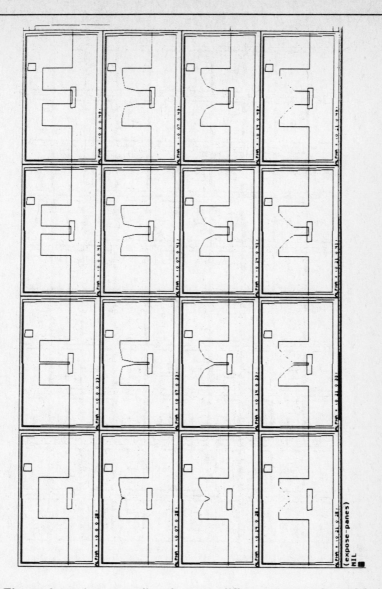

Fig. 4a. The configuration space slices for many different parametric model error values. These configuration spaces were generated for the peg-in-hole problem with model error depicted in fig. 3. Fig. 4a shows a few slices taken at constant orientation, whereas in fig. 4b, more slices are shown at various orientations.

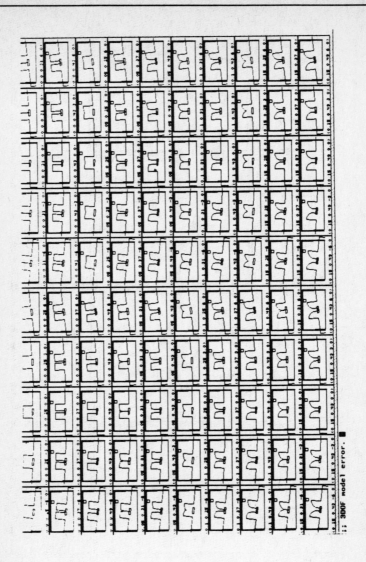

Fig. 4b.

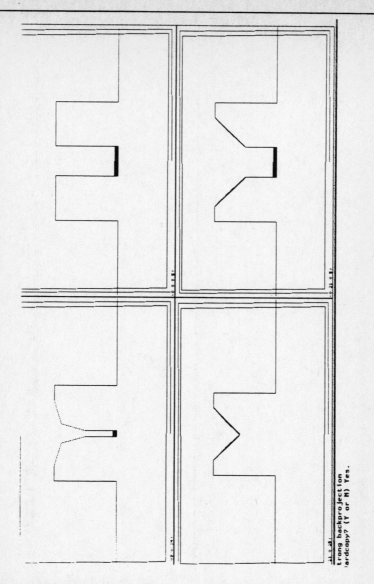

Fig. 5. 4 configuration space slices for the peg-in-hole with model error problem. The goal region is shaded black. In one slice, the goal vanishes.

14

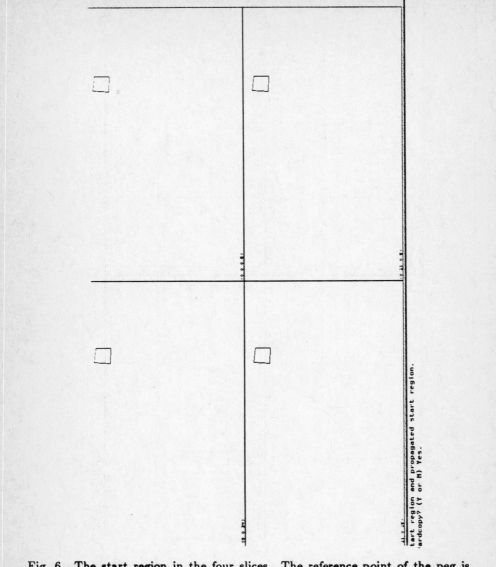

Fig. 6. **The start region** in the four slices. **The reference point of the peg is** known to start within this region.

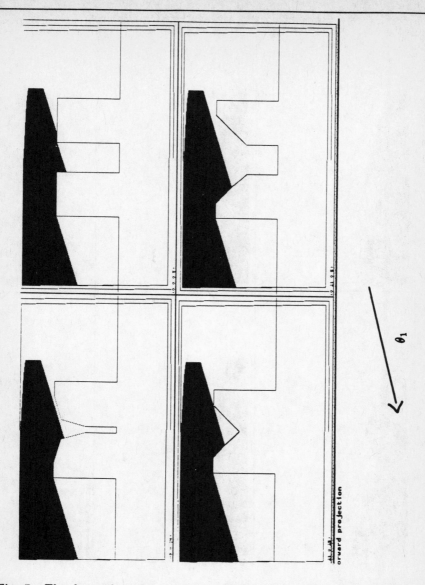

Fig. 7. The forward projection of the first motion. This region is the outer envelope of all possible trajectories evolving from the start regions. It is the set of all configurations that are reachable from the start regions, given the commanded velocity and control uncertainty cone.

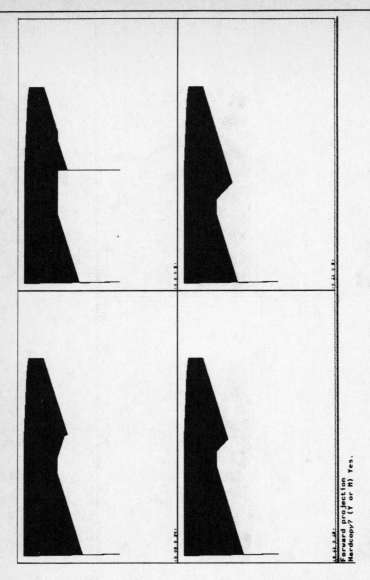

Fig. 8. The forward projection of the first motion, shown without the obstacles.

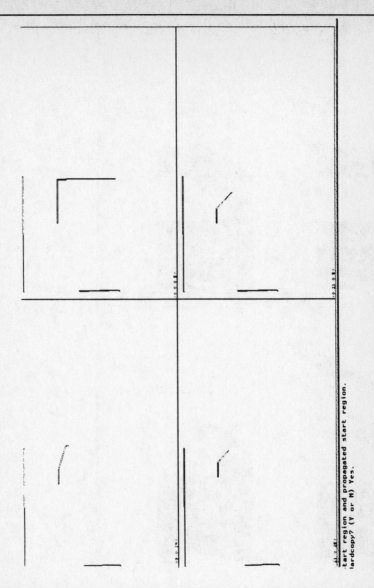

Fig. 9. The termination regions from the first motion. These regions are configurations where the motion finishes.

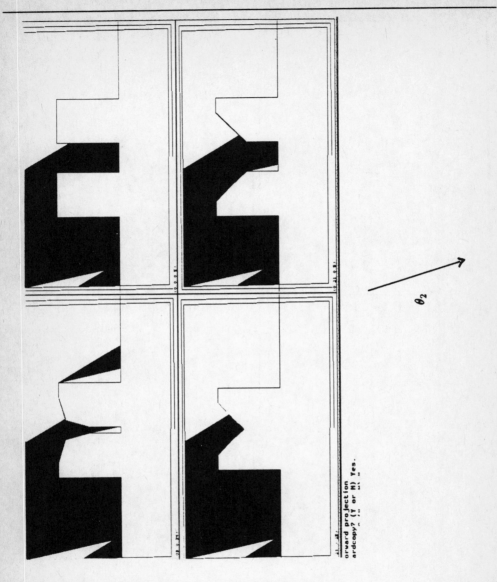

Fig. 10. The forward projection of the second motion.

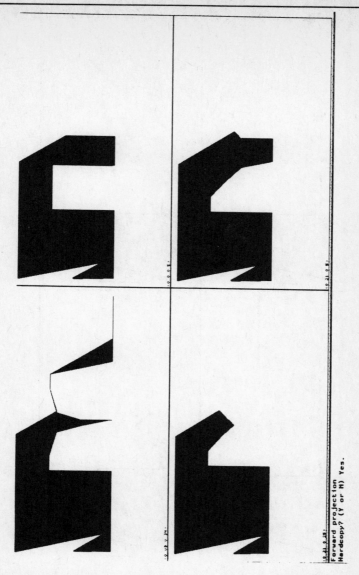

Fig. 11. The forward projection of the second motion, shown without the obstacles.

20

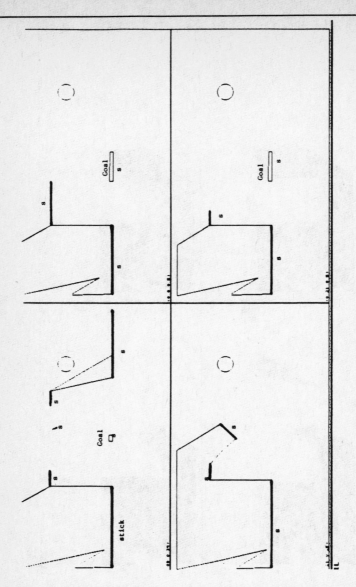

Fig. 12. The termination regions for the second motion. These are edges in configuration space where sticking can occur.

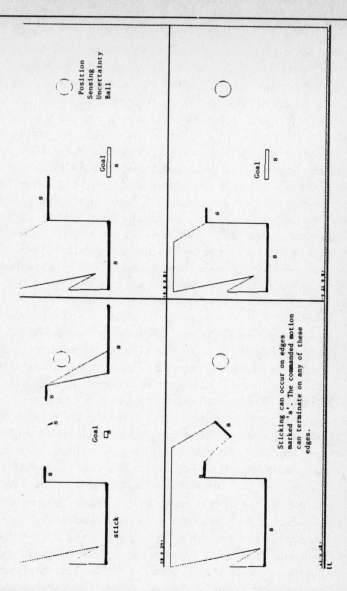

Fig. 13. The failure regions and the goal are distinguishable, even given the sensing uncertainty. The disc indicates the magnitude of the position sensing uncertainty.

1.2. Research Issues

The gross motion planning problem with no uncertainty has received a great deal of attention recently. In this problem, the state of the robot may be represented as a point in a configuration space. Thus moving from a start to a goal point may be viewed as finding an arc in free space connecting the two points. Since the robot is assumed to have perfect control and sensing, any such arc may be reliably executed once it is found. In particular, given a candidate arc, it may be tested. That is, motion along the arc may be simulated to see whether it is collision free. For example, an algebraic curve may be intersected with semi-algebraic sets defining the configuration space obstacles. In the presence of uncertainty, however, we cannot simply simulate a motion strategy to verify it. Instead, we need some technique for simulating *all* possible orbits, or evolutions of the robot system, under any possible choice of the uncertain parameters. With sensing and control uncertainty, the state of the robot must be viewed as a subset of the configuration space. Motions, then, can be viewed as mappings between these subsets. Of course there are many such subsets! From this perspective, it is clear that a chief contribution of [LMT] has been to identify and give a constructive definition for a privileged class of subsets, called *preimages*, and show that it is necessary and sufficient to search among this class. This framework appears very promising for planning guaranteed motion strategies under sensing and control uncertainty. The [LMT] framework assumes no model error. In this thesis, we reduce the problem of planning guaranteed strategies with sensing, control, *and geometric model* uncertainty to the problem of computing preimages in a (higher dimensional) generalized configuration space. [3]

This is an interesting and useful result; previously, there was really no systematic theory of planning in an environment whose geometry is not precisely known. However, I do not think that it is the main point of this thesis. This is because there are certain inadequacies with the planning model. The insistence that strategies be guaranteed to succeed is too restrictive in practice. To see this, observe that guaranteed strategies do not always exist. In the peg-in-hole problem with model error (figs. 3–13) there is no guaranteed strategy for achieving the goal, since the hole may be too small for some model error values. For these values the goal in configuration space does not exist. Because tolerances may cause gross topological changes in configuration space, this problem is particularly prevalent in the presence of model error. More generally, there may be model error values for which the goal may still exist, but it may not be reachable. For example, in a variant of the problem in fig. 3, an obstacle could block the channel to the goal. Then the goal is non-empty, but also not reachable. Finally, and most generally, there may be model error values for which the goal is reachable but not *recognizably* reachable. In this case we still cannot guarantee plans, since a planner cannot know when they have

---

[3] We use the terms model error and model uncertainty interchangeably.

succeeded.

These problems may occur even in the absence of model error. However, without model error a guaranteed plan is often obtainable by back-chaining and adding more steps to the plan. In the presence of model error this technique frequently fails: in the peg-in-hole problem with model error, this technique will not work since no plan of any length can succeed when the hole closes up.

This is why we investigate EDR strategies, and, in particular, attempt to formalize EDR planning. The key theoretical issue is: How can we relax the restriction that plans must be guaranteed to succeed, and still retain a theory of planning that is not completely *ad hoc*? We attempt to answer this by giving a constructive definition of EDR strategies. In particular, this approach provides a formal test for verifying whether a given strategy is an EDR strategy. The test is formulated as a decision problem about projection sets in a generalized configuration space which also encodes model error. Roughly speaking, the projection sets represent all possible outcomes of a motion (the *forward projection*), and weakest preconditions for attaining a subgoal (the *preimage*).

Given the formal test for "recognizing" an EDR strategy, I then tested the definition by building a generate-and-test planner. The generator is trivial; the recognizer is an algorithmic embodiment of the formal test. It lies at the heart of this research. A second key component of the planner is a set of techniques for chaining together motions to synthesize multi-step strategies. The planner is a forward-chaining, multi-resolution planner, called LIMITED. LIMITED operates in a restricted domain. Plans found by LIMITED in experiments are described above, and in chapters II and III.

Finally, let me suggest that a new framework—the EDR framework— for planning with uncertainty may be justified not only by the restrictiveness of the guaranteed-success model, but also by the hardness of the problem. The gross motion planning problem without uncertainty may be viewed, under some very general assumptions, as a decision problem within the theory of real closed fields. This gives a theoretical decision procedure with polynomial running time once the degrees of freedom of the robot system are fixed [SS]. However, no such theoretical algorithm is known for the general compliant motion planning problem with uncertainty. Furthermore, the lower bounds for computing guaranteed strategies even in 3D are dismal: the problem is known to be hard for exponential time [CR]. At this point it is unknown whether EDR planning is more efficient than guaranteed planning. However, there is some experimental evidence leading one to conjecture that certain problems requiring very complicated, exponential-sized guaranteed plans may admit very short EDR plans.

However, the motivation for this thesis is not complexity-theoretic. Instead, the chief thrust is to show how to compute motion strategies under model error (and sensing and control uncertainty), using a formal and constructive definition of EDR strategies. The first goal was a precise geometric characterization of EDR planning—when one thinks. about it, it is in fact somewhat surprising that such a thing should exist at all! But in fact it does, as we shall see. The second goal was to test this characterization by building a planner. Thus it was necessary to devise implementable algorithms to construct the geometric projection sets and decide questions about them. Therefore, this thesis and LIMITED contain a mixture of precise combinatorial algorithms and of approximation algorithms. We indicate which algorithms are exact and give combinatorial bounds. We also identify the approximation algorithms, and indicate the goodness of the approximation and whether it is conservative. Much work, or course, remains in developing better algorithms for EDR planning, and in testing out the plans using real robots.

1.3. Review of Previous Work

Broadly speaking, previous work falls the following categories: Algorithmic motion planning, Compliant motion planning with uncertainty, Model Error, and Error detection and recovery.

1.3.1 Algorithmic Motion Planning

In algorithmic motion planning, (also called the piano movers' problem, or the find-path problem) the problem is to find a continuous, collision-free path for a moving object (the robot) amidst completely known polyhedral or semi-algebraic obstacles. It is assumed than once such a path is found, it can be reliably executed by a robot with perfect control and sensing. Many algorithms employ configuration space, [Lozano-Pérez, Arnold, Abraham and Marsden, Udupa]. [Lozano-Pérez and Wesley] proposed the first algorithms for polygonal and polyhedral robots and obstacles without rotations. These results were later extended by [Lozano-Pérez 81, 83] to polyhedral robots which could translate and rotate. [Brooks 83] designed a find-path algorithm based on a generalized-cone representation of free-space. Brooks later extended this method for a revolute-joint robot. [Donald 84,85,87] developed a motion-planning algorithm for a rigid body that could translate and rotate with six degrees of freedom amidst polyhedral obstacles (the so-called "classical" movers' problem). [Lozano-Pérez 85] reported another 6DOF algorithm for 6-link revolute manipulators. [Canny 85] developed an algebraic formulation of the configuration-space constraints, which led to a very clean collision-detection algorithm. All of these algorithms have been implemented.

There are many theoretical results on upper and lower bounds for the find-path problem, see [Yap] for a good survey article. These results begin with [Lozano-Pérez and Wesley], who give the first upper bounds: they give efficient algorithms for planning in 2D and 3D in the absence of rotations. [Reif 79] obtained the first lower bounds, demonstrating the problem to be $\mathcal{PSPACE}$-hard when the number of degrees of freedom are encoded in the input specification of the problem. [Hopcroft, Joseph, and Whitesides] and [Hopcroft, Schwartz, and Sharir] have also given intersesting lower bounds for motion planning. [Schwartz and Sharir] gave a very general theoretical algorithm for motion planning via a reduction to the theory of real closed fields. The algorithm is doubly-exponential in the degrees of freedom, but polynomial in the algebraic and geometric complexity of the input. Over the next five years, there were many papers reporting more efficient special-purpose motion planning algorithms for certain specific cases; see [Yap] for a survey. To date the fastest general algorithm is due to [Canny, 87], who gives a generic motion planning algorithm which is merely singly-exponential in the degrees of freedom. For a motion planning problem of algebraic complexity d, geometric complexity n, and with r degrees of freedom, Canny's algorithm runs in time $(d^{O(r^2)} n^r \log n)$ which is within a log factor of optimal. While none of these theoretical algorithms have been implemented, Canny's is conjectured to be efficient in practice as well.

One might ask whether exact algorithms for motion plannning can ever be utilized after uncertainty in sensing and control are introduced. The answer is a qualified "yes." In particular, the Voronoi diagram has proved to be useful for motion planning among a set of obstacles in configuration space (see [Ó'Dúnlaing and Yap 82; Ó'Dúnlaing, Sharir, and Yap 84; Yap 84], and the textbook of [Schwartz and Yap 86] for an introduction and review of the use of Voronoi diagrams in motion planning). The Voronoi diagram, as usually defined, is a *strong deformation retract* of free space so that free space can be continuously deformed onto the diagram. This means that the diagram is complete for path planning, i.e. Searching the original space for paths can be reduced to a search on the diagram. Reducing the dimension of the set to be searched usually reduces the time complexity of the search. Secondly, the diagram leads to robust paths, i.e. paths that are maximally clear of obstacles. Hence Voronoi-based motion planning algorithms are relevant to motion planning with uncertainty. [Canny and Donald] define a "Simplified Voronoi Diagram" which is still complete for motion planning, yet has lower algebraic complexity than the usual Voronoi diagram, which is a considerable advantage in motion planning problems with many degrees of freedom. Furthermore, the Simplified diagram is defined for the 6D configuration space of the "classical" movers' problem. For the 6DOF "classical" polyhedral case, [Canny and Donald] show that motion planning using the Simplified diagram can be done it time $O(n^7 \log n)$.

Many additional robotics issues are discussed in [Paul; Brady *et al.*].

1.3.2 Compliant Motion Planning with Uncertainty

This section reviews previous work on planning compliant motions which are guaranteed to succeed even when the robot system is subject to sensing and control uncertainty. All of this work assumes perfect geometric models of the robot and obstacles.

Work on compliant motion can be traced to [Inoue, Whitney, Raibert and Craig, Salisbury]. This work in force control attempted to use the geometric constraints to guide the motion. By cleverly exploiting the task geometry, placements far exceeding the accuracy of pure position control can be achieved. [Mason 83] develops spring and damper compliance models, and gives an extensive review of research in compliant motion. [Simunovic, Whitney, Ohwovoriole and Roth, Ohwovoriole, Hill and Roth] have all considered frictional constraints, as well as jamming and wedging conditions. [Erdmann], [Burridge, Rajan and Schwartz] have considered algorithmic techniques for predicting reaction forces in the presence of friction. [Caine] has considered manual techniques for synthesizing compliant motion strategies, generalizing the methods of [Simunovic, Whitney]. [Mason, 82] has developed a way to model pushing and grasping operations in the presence of frictional contact. [Peshkin] has extended this work. [Brost] has further developed techniques for predicting pushing and sliding of manipulated objects to plan squeeze-grasp operations. In addition, Brost is currently investigating the application of EDR techniques to the squeeze-grasp domain.

Early work on planning in the presence of uncertainty investigated using skeleton strategies. [Lozano-Pérez 76] proposed a task-level planner called LAMA which used geometric simulation to predict the outcomes of plans, and is one of the earliest systems to address EDR planning. [Taylor] used symbolic reasoning to restrict the values of variables in skeleton plans to guarantee success. [Brooks 82] later extended this technique using a symbolic algebra system. [Dufay and Latombe] implemented a system which addresses learning in the domain of robot motion planning with uncertainty.

[LMT] proposed a formal framework for automatically synthesizing fine-motion strategies in the presence of sensing and control uncertainty. Their method is called the *preimage* framework. [Mason, 83] further developed the preimage termination predicates, addressing completeness and correctness of the resulting plans. [Erdmann] continued work on the preimage framework, and demonstrated how to separate the problem into questions of *reachability* and *recognizability*. He also showed how to compute preimages using backprojections, which address reachability alone, and designed and implemented the first algorithms for computing backprojections. [Erdmann and Mason] developed a planner which could perform sensorless manipulation of polygonal objects in a tray. Their planner makes extensive use of a representation of friction in configuration space [Erdmann]. [Buckley] implemented a multi-step planner for planning compliant motions with uncertainty in 3D without rotations. He also developed a variety of new theoretical tools, including a combined spring-damper dynamic model, 3D backprojection and forward projection algorithms, and a finitization technique which makes searching the space of commanded motions more tractable.

[Hopcroft and Wilfong] addressed the problem of planning motions in contact, and proved important structural theorems about the connectivity of the 1-edges of configuration space obstacle manifolds. [Koutsou] has suggested a planning algorithm which plans along 1-edges. Other planning systems for compliant motion have been developed by [Turk], who used backprojections, [Laugier and Theveneau], who use an expert system for geometric reasoning about compliant motion, and [Valade].

Recently, there has been some theoretical work on the complexity of robot motion planning with uncertainty. [Erdmann] showed the problem to be undecidable when the obstacles are encoded as a recursive function on the plane. [Natarajan] has shown the problem to be $PSPACE$-hard in 3D for finite polyhedral obstacles. [Canny and Reif] have demonstrated that in 3D the problem of synthesizing a multi-step strategy is hard for non-deterministic exponential time; in addition, they proved that verifying a 1-step strategy is NP-hard.

1.3.3 Model Error

There is relatively little previous work on planning in the presence of model uncertainty. [Requicha] and [Shapiro] address representational questions of how to model part tolerances, and mathematical models for variational families of parts. [Buckley] considers some extensions of his planner to domains with model uncertainty. [Brooks 82] developed a symbolic algebra system which can constrain the variable values in skeleton plans, and introduce sensing and motion steps to reduce these values until the error ranges are small enough for the plan to be guaranteed. Some of the variables in these plans can represent model error—particularly, the position of objects in the workspace—and hence his planner can reason about motion planning in the presence of model uncertainty.

Work on manipulator pushing and sliding [Mason, Peshkin] and squeeze-grasping [Brost] may be viewed as addressing model error where the error parameters are the position and orientation of the manipulated part. The *operation space* of [Brost] is a clever example how to model actions with uncertain effects, and objects with uncertain orientation, in the same space. [Durrant-Whyte] considers how to model geometric uncertainty probabilistically, and how to propagate such information in applications related to motion planning.

[Lumelsky] considers the following problem: suppose that a robot has a 2D configuration space, perfect control and sensing, the obstacles are finite in number, and each obstacle boundary is a homeomorphic image of the circle. Then a collision free-path may be found by tracing around the boundary of any obstacles encountered when moving in a straight line from the start to the goal. At each obstacle boundary encountered, there is a binary choice of which way to go, and the move may be executed with perfect accuracy. Lumelsky also demonstrates complexity bounds under these assumptions, and has considered configuration spaces such as the plane, the sphere, the cylinder, and the 2-torus. While it is not clear how this technique can extend to higher-dimensional configuration spaces, it is useful to compare Lumelsky's approach as an example of how to exploit a useful geometric primitive (wall-following). See also [Koditschek] for extensions to this approach using potential fields. The *potential-field* approach to collision avoidance, as formulated by [Khatib], also can deal with uncertain obstacles, and gross motions around these obstacles can often be synthesized in real time. [Brooks 85] has described a map-making approach for a mobile robot in a highly unstructured environment— i.e., amidst unknown obstacles. His approach allows the robot to aquire information about the position and shape of these obstacles as the robot explores the environment. [Davis] has addressed the mobile robot navigation problem amidst partially unknown obstacles using an approximate map.

There is almost no work on planning compliant motions or assemblies in the presence of model error.

1.3.4 Error Detection and Recovery

There has been almost no formal analysis of the EDR problem. STRIPS [Fikes and Nilsson] has a run-time executive (PLANEX) which embodied one of the first systems addressing EDR. STRIPS' triangle tables may be viewed as a kind of forward projection. [Ward and McCalla; Hayes] have presented research agendas for error diagnosis and recovery in domain-independent planning. [McDermott] has stressed the importance of EDR in plan execution and sketched an approach based on possible worlds. [Srinivas] described a robot planning system for a Mars rover which could detect certain manipulation errors and recover. [Gini and Gini] have described a view of EDR based on a predetermined list of high-level error types. The domain-independent planning literature [Chapman] is relevant to the history of EDR; for example, the planner of [Wilkins] has an error recovery module in which the executor can detect inconsistencies in the set of logical propositions representing the world state. At this point, an operator can intervene and type in new propositions to disambiguate the state and aid recovery. The robots described by [Brooks 85] have an EDR flavor—they are not required to achieve a particular goal, but merely to attempt it until some other goal takes a higher priority.

Portions of the material in this thesis have been presented in [Donald 86a,b].

[Brost] is employing these EDR techniques in his research on planning squeeze-grasp operations.

1.4. Map of Thesis

Here is an outline of the remainder of the thesis. The thesis is divided into six roman-numeral *chapters*. A parallel arabic *section*-numbering scheme permits finer-grain cross-references. *Starred* (*) sections subsections may be skipped at first reading if desired.

Chapter II presents the basic issues in EDR. It begins with a discussion of planning with model error. We introduce a generalized configuration space with non-holonomic constraints as a key tool. EDR is defined, and given a geometrical characterization. Experiments, implementation, and computational complexity are discussed. Chapter II intends to provide a slice of all the most interesting aspects of this work, while striving for a somewhat informal style of presentation. The end of the chapter hints at the theoretical issues to come.

The chapters III—V, can be read independently if desired.

Chapter III describes the construction of multi-step strategies in some detail. Here, we discuss planning using preimages, "push-forward" algorithms, and failure-mode analysis. These techniques are then unified by introducing the "weak" EDR theory. Weak EDR is a theory which defines certain laws of composition on motion strategies. It provides a new framework for studying multi-step strategies; we use it to derive properties of multi-step EDR plans.

In chapter IV, the EDR theory is applied to the problem of planning sensing and motion for a mobile robot navigating amidst partially unknown obstacles. We show how the EDR theory, and generalized configuration space in particular, can be used to generate strategies in the mobile robot domain.

Chapter V describes implementational and complexity-theoretic issues. We discuss methods for limiting search in an EDR planner. To this end, we introduce a combinatorial object call the *non-directional backprojection*, and analyze its complexity. Our analysis leads to efficient algorithms for certain subproblems in EDR planning. In particular, we give an efficient algorithm for planning one-step (guaranteed) strategies in the plane. By using results from computational algebra, we show that planning a guaranteed planar multi-step strategy with sticking termination can be decided in time polynomial in the geometric complexity, and roughly singly-exponential in the number of steps in the plan.

Chapter VI contains conclusions and suggestions for future work.

All readers should be able to read through chapter II. At that point the remaining topics can be selected as the reader's taste and preference dictate. I feel the most interesting and important subsequent material is on the weak EDR theory (in the multi-step strategy chapter III). However, readers interested in computational complexity might prefer chapter V, while moboticists might skip to chapter IV.

The thesis contains three thematic lines of development. The first is *theoretical robotics*, by which we mean the theory of manipulation and geometrical planning. This line is strong in chapters II and III. Readers who have seen some of this thesis material at conferences [D] will find altogether new material in sections 7–15. This line of development contains the following topics:

- *Model error* is discussed in detail in sections 2, 6, 9, 11, and 13.
- The *basic EDR theory* is discussed in sections 3–5, and 7–10.
- *Failure-Mode Analysis* comes up in section 11.
- *The Weak EDR Theory* makes its debut in section 12.

The second theme is *complexity and algorithmic issues*. These are stressed in sections 6 and 14.

The third theme is *applications, implementation, and experiments*. These are described in sections 6, 7, 10, 11, 13, and 14.1.

II. Basic Issues in Error Detection and Recovery

This chapter presents an overview of our theory and experiments in EDR. It attempts to deliver a slice of all the most interesting aspects of the work, while striving for a non-demanding style of presentation.

We begin by showing how to represent model error, and explore the physics of generalized configuration space. Using this representation, we next present the basic theory behind constructing both guaranteed strategies and EDR plans in the presence of sensing, control, and model uncertainty.

The implementation of LIMITED is then discussed, along with experiments in EDR planning.

The chapter closes by proving complexity bounds for EDR planning, and with an introductory discussion of deeper EDR-theoretic issues. For interested readers, these discussions are continued and elaborated in considerable detail in chapters V and III, respectively.

2. Basic Issues in Error Detection and Recovery

2.1. Simple Example of Model Error

We will begin developing the EDR theory by examining some very simple planning problems with model error. Of course, this does not mean that EDR is limited to situations with model error.

Example (1). Consider fig. 14. There is position sensing uncertainty, so that the start position of the robot is only known to lie within some ball in the plane. The goal is to bring the robot in contact with the right vertical surface of A.

We will simplify the problem so that the computational task is in configuration space. This transformation reduces the planning task for a complicated moving object to navigating a point in configuration space. Consider fig. 15. The configuration point starts out in the region R, which is the position sensing uncertainty ball about some initial sensed position. To model sliding behavior, we will assume Coulomb friction and generalized damper dynamics, which allows an identification of forces and velocities. Thus the commanded velocity v_0 is related to the effective velocity v by $f = B(v - v_0)$ where f is the effective force on the robot and B is a scalar. Given a nominal commanded velocity v_0^*, the control uncertainty is represented by a cone of velocities (B_{ec} in the figure). The actual commanded velocity v_0 must lie within this cone.[1]

The goal in fig. 15 is to move to the region G. Now, with Coulomb friction, sticking occurs on a surface when the (actual) commanded velocity points into the friction cone. We assume the friction cones are such that sliding occurs (for all possible commanded velocities in B_{ec}) on all surfaces save G, where all velocities stick. We will assume that the planner can monitor position and velocity sensors to determine whether a motion has reached the goal. Velocity sensing is also subject to uncertainty: for an actual velocity v, the sensed velocity lies in some cone B_{ev} of velocities about v.

Now we introduce simple model error. The shape of A and B are known precisely, and the position of A is fixed. However, the position of B, relative to A is not known. B's position is characterized by the distance α. If $\alpha > 0$ the goal is reachable. But if $\alpha = 0$, then the goal vanishes. No plan can be guaranteed to succeed if $\alpha = 0$ is possible. Suppose we allow α to be negative. In this case the blocks meet and fuse. Eventually, for sufficiently negative α, B will emerge on the other side of A. In this case, the goal "reappears," and may be reachable again.[2] Let us assume that α is bounded, and lies in the interval $[-d_0, d_0]$.

---

[1] See [Mason 81] for a detailed description of generalized damper dynamics.

[2] This model is adopted for the purposes of exposition, not for physical plausibility. It is not hard to model the case where the blocks meet but do not fuse.

Our task is to find a plan that can attain G in the cases where it is recognizably reachable. Such a plan is called a *guaranteed strategy in the presence of model error*. But the plan cannot be guaranteed for the α where the goal vanishes. In these cases we want the plan to signal failure. Loosely speaking, a motion strategy which achieves the goal when it is recognizably reachable and signals failure when it is not is called an *Error Detection and Recovery (EDR) strategy*. Such strategies are more general than guaranteed strategies, in that they allow plans to fail.

Before we attack the problem of constructing guaranteed strategies and EDR strategies (both in the presence of model error) let us consider the examples we have seen so far. Although in these examples model error has been represented by a kind of parametric "tolerancing", the planning framework can represent arbitrary model error. For example, we could represent CAD surfaces with real coefficients, and allow the coefficients to vary. Discrete and discontinuous model error may also be represented. Finally, note that we permit gross topological changes in the environment—for example, the goal can vanish.

2.2. Representing Model Error

To represent model error, we will choose a parameterization of the possible variation in the environment. The degrees of freedom of this parameterization are considered as additional degrees of freedom in the system. For example, in fig. 15, we have the x and y degrees of freedom of the configuration space. In addition, we have the model error parameter α. A coordinate in this space has the form (x, y, α). The space itself is the cartesian product $\Re^2 \times [-d_0, d_0]$. Each α-*slice* of the space for a particular α is a configuration space with the obstacles A and B instantiated at distance α apart. Fig. 15 is such a slice.

More generally, suppose we have a configuration space C for the degrees of freedom of the moving object. Let J be an arbitrary index set which parameterizes the model error. (Above, J was $[-d_0, d_0]$). Then the *generalized configuration space* with model error is $C \times J$. One way to think of this construction is to imagine a collection of possible "universes", $\{ C_\alpha \}$ for α in J. Each C_α is a configuration space, containing configuration space obstacles. The ambient space for each C_α is some canonical C. $C \times J$ is simply the natural product representing the ambient space of their disjoint union. There is no constraint that J be finite or even countable. In fig. 3, C is again the cartesian plane, and J is a three-dimensional product space. One of the J dimensions is circular, to parameterize the angular variation represented by α_3.

In fig. 16 we show the generalized configuration space for example (1). Note that the goal in generalized configuration space becomes a 2-dimensional surface,

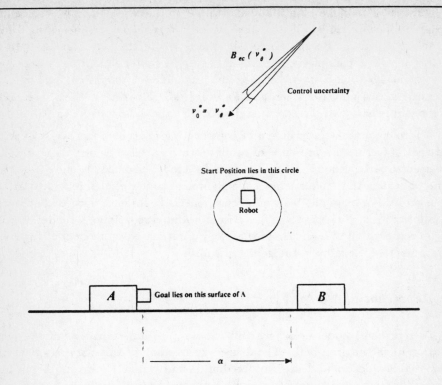

Fig. 14. The goal is to bring the robot into contact with the right vertical surface of A. (For example, the "robot" could be a gripper finger). There is position sensing uncertainty, so in the start position the robot is only known to lie within some uncertainty ball. There is also control uncertainty in the commanded velocity to the robot. It is represented as a cone, as shown.

and the obstacles are 3-dimensional polyhedra. Note that the goal surface vanishes where A and B meet.

Given a configuration space corresponding to a physical situation, it is well known how to represent motions, forces, velocities, and so forth in it (eg., see [Arnold]). The representations for classical mechanics exploit the geometry of differentiable manifolds. We must develop a similar representation to plan motions, forces, and velocities in generalized configuration space . Henceforth, we will denote the generalized configuration space $C \times J$ by $\mathcal{G}$. We develop the following "axioms" for "physics" in $\mathcal{G}$.

(1) At execution time, the robot finds itself in a particular slice of $\mathcal{G}$, (although it

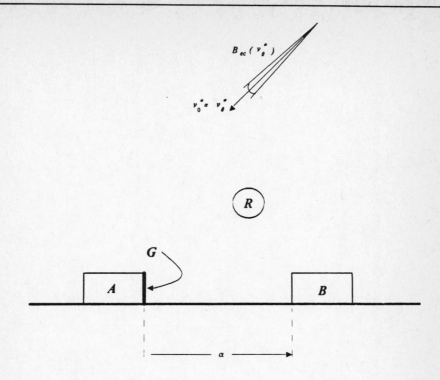

Fig. 15. The equivalent problem in configuration space. The blocks A and B, the distance between the blocks α, and the commanded velocity $v_\theta = v_0^*$ with control error cone $B_{ec}(v_0^*)$. The position of A is fixed.

may not know which). Thus we say there is only one "real" universe, α_0 in[3] J. This α_0 is fixed. However, α_0 is not known *a priori*. Thus all motions are confined to a particular (unknown) α_0-slice, such as fig. 15. This is because motions cannot move between universes. In fig. 16, any legal motion in $\mathcal{G}$ is everywhere orthogonal to the J-axis and parallel to the x-y plane.

(2) Suppose in any α-slice the position sensing uncertainty ball about a given sensed position is some set B_{ep}. The set R in fig. 15 is such a ball. We cannot sense across J: position sensing uncertainty is infinite in the J dimensions.[4] Thus the position sensing uncertainty in $\mathcal{G}$ is the cylinder $B_{ep} \times J$. In figs. 15,16, this simply says that x and y are known to some precision, while α is unknown. The initial position in fig. 15 is given by $R \times [-d_0, d_0]$. This cylinder

---

[3] α_0 is a point in the multi-dimensional space J.

[4] One generalization of the framework would permit and plan for sensing in J. In this case one would employ a bounded sensing uncertainty ball in the J dimensions.

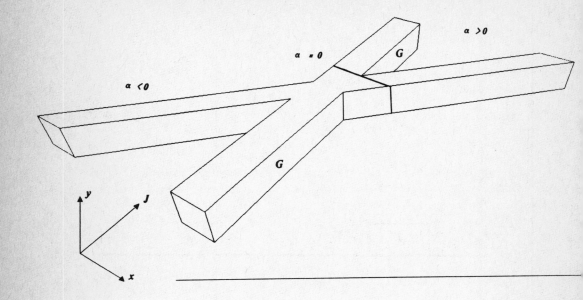

Fig. 16. The generalized configuration space obstacles for example (1). The generalized configuration space is three dimensional, having x and y degrees of motion freedom, and an α degree of model error freedom. Legal motions are parallel to the x-y plane, and orthogonal to the J axis.

is a 3-dimensional solid, orthogonal to the x-y plane and parallel to the J-axis in fig. 16.

(3) Suppose in the configuration space C, the velocity control uncertainty about a given nominal commanded velocity is a cone of velocities B_{ec}. Such a cone is shown in fig. 15. This cone lies in the *phase-space* for C, denoted TC. (Phase space is simply Position-space × Velocity-space. A point in phase space has the form (x, v), and denotes an instantaneous velocity of v at configuration x). Phase space represents all possible velocities at all points in C. The phase space for $\mathcal{G}$ is obtained by indexing TC by J to obtain $TC \times J$. All velocities in generalized configuration space lie in $TC \times J$. For Ex. (1) $TC \times J$ is $\Re^4 \times [-d_0, d_0]$. The generalized velocity uncertainty cones are two-dimensional, parallel to the x-y plane, and orthogonal to the J axis.

(4) Generalized damper dynamics extend straight-forwardly to $\mathcal{G}$, so motions satisfy $f = B(v - v_0)$ where f, v, and v_0 lie in $TC \times J$. Thus friction cones from configuration space (see [Erdmann]) naturally embed like generalized velocity cones in $TC \times J$.

These axioms give an intuitive description of the physics of $\mathcal{G}$. A formal axiomatization is given in an appendix. We have captured the physics of $\mathcal{G}$ using a set of *generalized uncertainties*, friction, and control characteristics (1-4). These axioms completely characterize the behavior of motions in $\mathcal{G}$.

2.3. Representing Pushing Operations in Generalized Configuration Space

By relaxing axiom (1), above, we can consider a generalization of the model error framework, in which pushing motions are permitted, as well as compliant and gross motions. We relax the assumption that motion between universes is impossible, and permit certain motions across J. Consider example (1). Observe that a displacement in J corresponds to a displacement in the position of the block B. Thus a motion in J should correspond to a motion of B. Suppose the robot can change the position of B by pushing on it, that is, by exerting a force on the surface of B. The key point is that pushing operations may be modeled by observing that commanded forces to the robot may result in changes in the environment. That is, a commanded force to the robot can result in motion in C (sliding) as well as motion in J (pushing the block). Let us develop this notion further.

Our previous discussion assumed that motion across J was impossible. That is, all motion is confined to one α-slice of generalized configuration space. In example (1), this is equivalent to the axiom that B does not move or deform under an applied force. Such an axiom makes sense for applications where B is indeed immovable, for example, if A and B are machined tabs of a connected metal part. However, suppose that B is a block that can slide on the table. See fig. 17. Then an applied force on the surface of the block can cause the block to slide. This corresponds to motion in J. In general, the effect of an applied force will be a motion which slides or sticks on the surface of B, and which causes B to slide or stick on the table. This corresponds to a coupled motion in both C and J. When the motion maintains contact, it is tangent to a surface S in generalized configuration space.

Our goal is to generalize the description of the physics of $\mathcal{G}$ to permit a rigorous account of such motions. This model can then be employed by an automated planner. *Such a planner could construct motion strategies whose primitives are gross motions, compliant motions, and pushing motions.*[5]

---

[5] Our model of pushing is less general than [Mason, 82], since it requires knowledge of the center of friction. See an appendix for details.

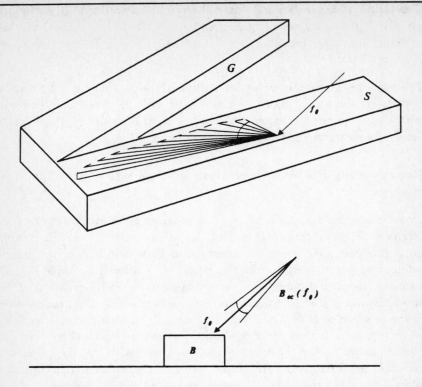

Fig. 17. A force f_θ applied to the top surface of B can cause sliding (or sticking) on the top of B, coupled with motion of B on the table. This corresponds to a pushing motion in $\mathcal{G}$. By giving the right geometric structure to the surface S, we can predict the resulting cone of motions in $\mathcal{G}$, given a commanded velocity f_θ subject to control uncertainty. A planner could generate a motion along S in order to plan pushing operations.

The description of the physics should embrace the following observations:

The phase space for C corresponds to forces exerted at the center of mass of the robot. The phase space for J corresponds to forces acting at the center of mass of B. When pushing is allowed, the phase space for generalized configuration space is not $TC \times J$ but $TC \times TJ$. In the pushing application, all forces are exerted in C, but may be "transferred" to J via the contact. In other words, the applied forces we consider will have zero component along J. However, they may result in a motion in J, via the transferred pushing force.

In free space, or on surfaces generated by immovable objects, all differential motions lie within one α-slice. This is because objects can only be pushed when the robot is in contact with them.

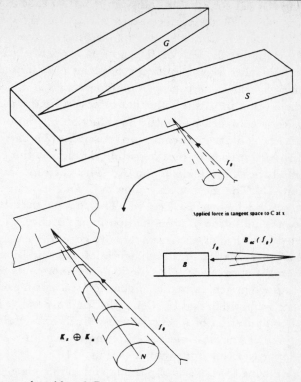

Applied force in tangent space to C at x

$B_{ac}(f_a)$

Fig. 18. Pushing on the side of B can cause B to slide, even in the absence of friction. This behavior can be modeled by giving the surface S a normal which points across J. The surface can exert reaction forces along this normal. Thus, applying a force in C results in a reaction force with a J component. The resulting motion moves across J, tangent to S. That it, it pushes the block. Friction can also be introduced on S. A picture of the friction cone developed in an appendix is shown. It represents the range of reaction forces the surface S can exert.

Along surfaces generated by objects that can be pushed, the differential motions are tangent to the surface in $\mathcal{G}$, and may move along J as well as C. See fig. 17.

A motion in free space corresponds to a gross motion. A motion on a surface staying within one α-slice corresponds to a compliant motion. A motion on a surface which moves across J corresponds to a pushing motion.

Configuration space surfaces share many properties with real space surfaces. When pushed on, they push back. In particular, they have a normal. In the absence of friction, they can exert reaction forces only along this normal direction. We must define what the normals to generalized configuration space surfaces are. For example, see fig. 18. The normal is transverse to J, so that even when the applied force lies exclusively in C, the surface exerts a reaction force with a J component. Thus the resultant force can cause a motion across J, tangent to S. In fig. 18 this implies that pushing on the side of B results in a transferred force to J, causing B to slide. In generalized configuration space, this is simply viewed as applying a force to a surface S, which exerts a reaction force across J. Since the resultant force is across J, the motion in $\mathcal{G}$ will be in that direction (under damper dynamics).

The physics is complicated by the introduction of friction. Given an applied force, one of four qualitative outcomes are possible. (1) The motion may slide in C and J. This corresponds to pushing while sliding[6] at the point of contact. (2) The motion may stick in C and slide in J.[7] This corresponds to pushing with no relative motion. (3) The motion may slide in C and stick in J. This corresponds to compliant motion in one α-slice. (4) The motion may break contact. This corresponds to the initiation of gross motion in one α-slice.

In order to generalize physical reasoning to generalized configuration space, we must provide a generalization of the configuration space friction cone [Erdmann] for generalized configuration space. The friction cone represents the range of reaction forces that a surface in generalized configuration space can exert. A picture of this generalized cone is shown in fig. 18. Using the friction cone, it is possible to specify a geometrical computation of reaction forces. Such an algorithm is necessary for a planner to predict the possible resulting motions from an uncertainty cone of commanded applied forces. For example, see fig. 17.

By characterizing the physics of pushing and sliding via geometrical constraints in generalized configuration space, it appears that a unified planning framework for gross-, compliant-, and pushing motions emerges. However, certain aspects of the physics require elaboration and simplification before a practical planner for pushing operations can be implemented; see an appendix for details.

*2.3.1 Example: The Sticking Cone

This starred subsection may be skipped at first reading.

As an example of how a planner could reason about friction in generalized configuration space, see fig. 19. Here we take the configuration spaces of the robot and of B to be cartesian planes. (See fig. 14 to recall the definition of the robot and B). Assume that we can apply a two dimensional force f_c on the robot, and a two dimensional force f_j at the center of mass of B. (This assumption is for the sake of discussion; in pushing applications, f_j would be zero). The friction cone

---

[6] Or rotating.

[7] This outcome is not possible in the example with block B, since if B moves, this causes motion in C and in J.

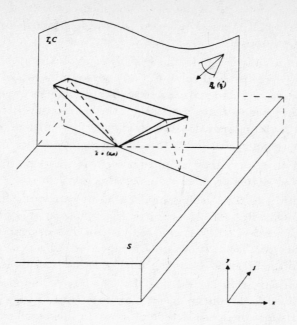

Fig. 19. Assume a fixed, negative normal force at the center of mass of B. The 3D force space at $\bar{x}$ represents the product of the 2D forces f_c that can be exerted by the robot on the surface of B, with the 1D tangential forces f_j that can be exerted at the center of mass of B. An applied force (f_c, f_j) in the cone represents a combination of forces that causes no motion in $\mathcal{G}$, that is, neither sliding on the surface of B, nor of B on the table. Note that the cone in $\mathcal{G}$ is skewed out of the embedded tangent space to C at x. This is because when a force f_c is applied in the friction cone on the top surface of B, the block B can slide unless an opposing force is exerted tangentially at the center of mass of B. By intersecting the sticking cone with the negative velocity cone, we can determine whether sticking is possible on S.

in generalized configuration space will then be four-dimensional. This is hard to draw; we have selected a fixed, negative normal component for f_j. The 3D force space at the point of contact $\bar{x}$ represents the product of the 2D forces that can be exerted by the robot on the surface of B, with the 1D tangential forces that can be applied at the center of mass of B. An applied force (f_c, f_j) in the negative of the cone in fig. 19 represents a combination of forces that causes no motion in $\mathcal{G}$, that is, neither sliding on the surface of B, nor of B on the table. Note that the cone in $\mathcal{G}$ is skewed out of the embedded tangent space to C at x (denoted $T_x C$ in the figure). This is because when a force f_c is applied in the friction cone on the top surface of B, the block B can slide unless an opposing force is exerted tangentially at the center of mass of B.

Let us call the cone in fig. 19 the *sticking cone* $\mathcal{K}$. Using the sticking cone, we can now specify a geometrical computation to determine when sticking occurs at $\overline{x}$, assuming generalized damper dynamics: Simply intersect the negative velocity control uncertainty cone $-B_{ec}(v_0^*)$ with $\mathcal{K}$. If the intersection is trivial, then sticking cannot occur. If the intersection is non-trivial, then sticking can occur. If the negative velocity cone lies inside $\mathcal{K}$, then sticking must occur.

This shows that the computation to determine whether sticking is possible at a point reduces to simple geometric cone intersection.

Now we return to the pushing application, by restricting the applied force f_j in J to be zero. See fig. 19. Assume it is impossible to apply force at the center of mass of B. Therefore, the velocity cone is two dimensional and lies entirely in the tangent space to C at x; it has no J component. This two-dimensional cone is intersected with the 3D cone $\mathcal{K}$ to determine whether sticking is possible at $\overline{x}$.

Let us emphasize that by insisting that the force f_j applied in J be zero, we obtain a two-dimensional control uncertainty cone, even though generalized configuration space has four degrees of freedom. Thus, in the model error framework, the generalized control uncertainty can be viewed as a *non-holonomic constraint*. Holonomic constraints are constraints on the degrees of freedom of the moving object(s); non-holonomic constraints are constraints on their differential motions. Holonomic constraints can be captured by surfaces in (generalized) configuration space. To capture non-holonomic constraints geometrically, we must introduce constraints in the phase space. This viewpoint is developed in an appendix, where we provide a more rigorous account of the construction of normals, friction cones, sticking cones, and the computation of reaction forces in generalized configuration space.

2.4. Guaranteed Plans in Generalized Configuration Space

A motion strategy [LMT] is a commanded velocity (such as v_0^* in fig. 15) together with a *termination predicate* which monitors the sensors and decides when the motion has achieved the goal. Given a goal G in configuration space, we can form its *preimage* [LMT]. The preimage of G is the region in configuration space from which all motions are guaranteed to move into G in such a way that the entry is recognizable. That is, the preimage is the set of all positions from which all possible trajectories consistent with the control uncertainty are guaranteed to reach G recognizably. For example, see fig. 20. The entry is recognized by monitoring

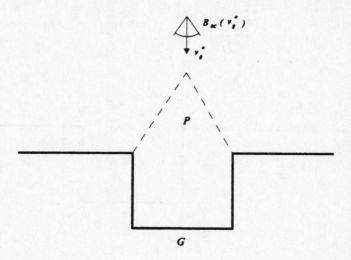

Fig. 20. The goal is the region G. Sliding occurs on vertical surfaces, and sticking on horizontal ones. The commanded velocity is v_θ^*, and the control uncertainty is $B_{ec}(v_\theta^*)$. The *preimage* of the G with respect to θ is the region P.

the position and velocity sensors until the goal is attained. Fig. 20 is a *directional* preimage: only one commanded velocity v_θ^* is considered. Here all preimage points reach the goal recognizably under this particular v_θ^*. The *non-directional* preimage is the union of all directional preimages.

We envision a back-chaining planner which recursively computes pre-images of a goal region. Successive subgoals are attained by motion strategies. Each motion terminates when all sensor interpretations indicate that the robot must be within the subgoal. [LMT,E] provide a formal framework for computing preimages where there is sensing and control uncertainty, but no model error. In particular, [Erdmann] shows how *backprojections* may be used to approximate preimages. The backprojection of a goal G (with respect to a commanded velocity v_θ^*) consists of those positions guaranteed to enter the goal (under v_θ^*). Recognizability of the entry plays no role. Fig. 21 illustrates the difference between backprojections and

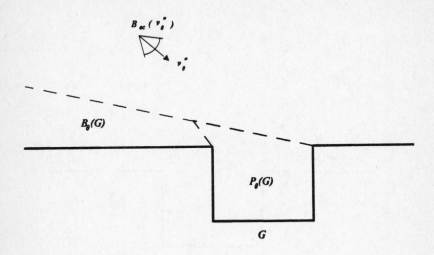

Fig. 21. Here, the radius of the position sensing uncertainty ball is twice the width of the hole. Sliding occurs on all surfaces under the control velocities shown. The preimage of the goal under commanded velocity v_θ^* is $P_\theta(G)$. The backprojection $B_\theta(G)$ strictly contains this preimage: while all points in the backprojection are guaranteed to reach G, the sensing inaccuracy is so large that the termination predicate cannot tell whether the goal or the left horizontal surface has been reached. Only from the preimage can entry into G be recognized.

preimages. Here the radius of position sensing uncertainty is greater than twice the diameter of the hole. Sliding occurs on all surfaces. Furthermore, we assume that the robot has no sense of time (i.e., no clock)—for example, it might be equipped with a contact sensor that only fires once. The back projection $B_\theta(G)$ strictly contains the preimage $P_\theta(G)$: while all points in the backprojection are guaranteed to reach G, the sensing inaccuracy is so large that the termination predicate cannot tell whether the goal or the left horizontal surface has been reached. Only from the preimage can entry into G be recognized.

Preimages provide a way to construct guaranteed plans for the situation with

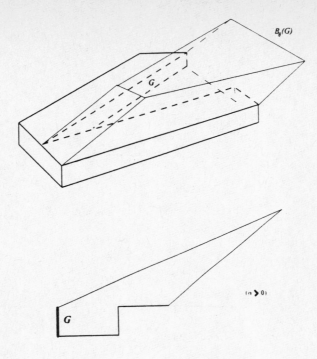

$B_\theta(G)$

G

$(\alpha > 0)$

G

Fig. 22. The backprojection of the goal surface G in generalized configuration space for commanded velocity v_θ^* is denoted $B_\theta(G)$. Here is the backprojection for α positive. A typical α-slice of the backprojection is shown below.

no model error. Can preimages and backprojections be generalized to situations with model error? The answer is yes. Consider fig. 15,16. The goal in generalized configuration space is the surface G (which has two components). The start region is the cylinder $R \times J$ (where J is $[-d_0, d_0]$). The generalized control and sensing uncertainties in $\mathcal{G}$ are given by the physics axioms above. These uncertainties completely determine how motions in generalized configuration space must behave. We form the backprojection of G under these uncertainties. The backprojection has two components, shown in fig. 22,23. It is a three-dimensional region in $\mathcal{G}$ of all triples (x, y, α) that are guaranteed to reach G under the control uncertainty shown in fig. 15. Equivalently, we can view it as all points in $\mathcal{G}$ guaranteed to reach G under the generalized uncertainties that specify $\mathcal{G}$'s physics. Note that backprojections do not "converge to a point" along the J axis (compare fig. 20). This is because there is perfect control along J, and the commanded velocity along J is zero. This is why

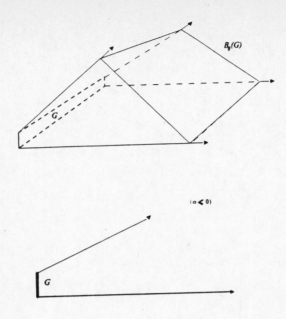

Fig. 23. The backprojection of the other component of G. A typical α-slice for α negative is shown below. The backprojection in $\mathcal{G}$ of the entire goal surface is the union of the backprojections shown in figs. 22,23.

in this particular $\mathcal{G}$ there are two disjoint backprojection regions, one from each component of G. Furthermore, recursively-computed backprojections can *never* cover—or even intersect—any slice of $\mathcal{G}$ in which the goal vanishes.

The trick here was to view the motion planning problem with n degrees of motion freedom and k degrees of model error freedom as a planning problem in an $(n + k)$-dimensional generalized configuration space, endowed with the special physics described above. The physics is characterized precisely by axioms defining certain special sensing and control uncertainties in $\mathcal{G}$. The definitions and results for pre-images and backprojections [LMT,E] in configuration space generalize *mutatis mutandis* to $\mathcal{G}$ endowed with this physics; this is proved in an appendix(A.3). Thus our framework reduces the problem of constructing guaranteed motion strategies with model error to computing preimages in a somewhat more complicated. and higher-dimensional configuration space.

In this example, because the position of B varies linearly with α, the surfaces in $\mathcal{G}$ are planar and the generalized configuration space obstacles are polyhedral. Below, in sec. 6, we give polynomial-time algorithms for computing these backprojections. While they have been computed by hand here, note that this reduction gives us an efficient planning algorithm for an important special case.

3. Error Detection and Recovery

If we were exclusively interested in constructing guaranteed motion strategies in the presence of model error, we would be done defining the framework: having reduced the problem to computing preimages in $\mathcal{G}$, we could now turn to the important and difficult problems of computing and constructing $\mathcal{G}$, and further extend the work of [LMT,E] on computing preimages in general configuration spaces.

However, guaranteed strategies do not always exist. In example (1), (figs. 14–16) there is no guaranteed strategy for achieving the goal, since the goal may vanish for some values of α. Because tolerances may cause gross topological changes in configuration space, this problem is particularly prevalent in the presence of model error. In the peg-in-hole problem with model error (figs. 3-13) the goal may also vanish (the hole may close up) for certain regions in J. More generally, there may be values of α for which the goal may still exist, but it may not be reachable. For example, in a variant of the problem in fig. 3, an obstacle could block the channel to the goal. Then G is non-empty, but also not reachable. Finally, and most generally, there may be values of α for which the goal is reachable but not *recognizably* reachable. In this case we still cannot guarantee plans, since a planner cannot know when they have succeeded.

These problems may occur even in the absence of model error. However, without model error a guaranteed plan is often obtainable by back-chaining and adding more steps to the plan. In the presence of model error this technique frequently fails: in example (1), no chain of recursively-computed preimages can ever cover the start region $R \times J$. The failure is due to the peculiar sensing and control characteristics (1-4) in generalized configuration space .

In response, we will develop Error Detection and Recovery (EDR) strategies. These are characterized as follows:

- An EDR strategy should attain the goal when it is recognizably reachable, and signal failure when it is not.
- It should also permit serendipitous achievement of the goal.
- Furthermore, no motion guaranteed to terminate recognizably in the goal should ever be prematurely terminated as a failure.
- Finally, no motion should be terminated as a failure while there is any chance that it might serendipitously achieve the goal due to fortuitous sensing and control events.

These are called the "EDR Axioms", they will be our guiding principles. Can we construct such strategies? The answer is, basically, yes. Let us construct one for

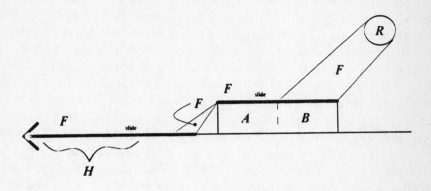

Fig. 24. A typical α-slice of the forward projection of the "bad" region. The forward projection is the region F. α is negative and almost zero. H is an EDR region in the forward projection.

a variant of example (1). We first restrict our attention to the environments where α lies in the interval $[d_1, d_0]$ where d_1 is small and negative.[1]

Call the start region $U = R \times J$. The strategy of example (1) commands velocity v_0^* (fig 15). It tries to terminate the motion in G by detecting sticking. Call this strategy θ. We will use θ as a starting point, and try to build an EDR strategy from it. Now, U is divided into a "good" region, from which θ is guaranteed, and a "bad" region, from which it is not. The goal vanishes for the bad region. We wish to *extend* θ to an EDR strategy from all of U.

Let us investigate the result of executing θ from the "bad" region. We employ the forward projection [Erdmann]. The *forward projection* of a set V under θ is all

---

[1]See fig. 15. Formally, if w is the width of A and B, and ϵ is the position sensing uncertainty, then $|d_1| < \min(w, \frac{\epsilon}{2})$. Otherwise, if α can be arbitrary, *no* strategy can always distinguish the right edge of A from the right edge of B!

configurations[2] which are possibly reachable from V under v_0^* (subject to control uncertainty). It is denoted $F_\theta(V)$. Forward projections only address reachability: the termination predicate is ignored and only the control uncertainty bound and commanded velocity v_0^* are needed to specify the forward projection.

Fig. 24 shows a typical α-slice of the forward projection of the "bad" region. The goal vanishes in this slice; the dashed line indicates where the goal would be in other slices. We can now define an EDR strategy as follows. Consider the region H in fig. 24. The termination predicate can distinguish between G and H based on position sensing, velocity sensing, or elapsed time.[3] Consider H as a two-dimensional region in $\mathcal{G}$; just a slice of it is shown in fig. 24. Note that in this example, H only exists in the slices in which G vanishes. Thus the motion is guaranteed to terminate recognizably in G iff the motion originated in the "good" region of U. Otherwise the motion terminates recognizably in H. In the first case, the termination predicate signals success, in the latter, failure.

Clearly this EDR strategy satisfies the "EDR axioms" above. The problem of constructing EDR strategies may be attacked as follows: We take a strategy θ as data. Next, an *EDR region H* is found. H is introduced as a "bad goal", and a strategy is found which achieves either G or H (subject to the EDR axioms). Finally, we must not only recognize that G or H has been attained, but also know *which* goal has been reached.

Now, think of θ as indexing the "angular direction" of the commanded velocity. By quantifying over all θ, we can in principle define "non-directional" EDR strategies. This problem is similar to constructing non-directional preimages. For now, we restrict our attention to one-step plans. Later, we consider n-step plans.

3.1. Generalizing the Construction

We now present an informal account of how the construction of EDR regions and strategies may be generalized. Do not be alarmed if some of our examples are without model error. Since we have reduced the planning problem with model error to planning in a (different) configuration space, it suffices to consider general configuration spaces in this discussion.

So far the preimages we have considered are *strong* preimages, in that *all* possible motions are guaranteed to terminate recognizably in the goal. The *weak* preimage [LMT] (with respect to a commanded velocity) is the set of points which could *possibly* enter the goal recognizably, given fortuitous sensing and control events. See fig. 25. We will use the weak preimage to capture the notion of serendipity in the

---

[2] Actually, forward projections are in phase-space, so this is the position component of the forward projection.

[3] Given the sensing uncertainties of example (1).

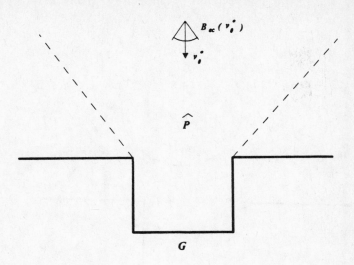

Fig. 25. The *weak* preimage of the goal G under v_θ^*. Compare fig. 20.

EDR axioms. The idea is that a motion may be terminated in failure as soon as egress from the weak preimage is recognized.

Now consider fig. 26. Assume sliding occurs on the vertical edges, and sticking on the horizontal ones. The (strong) preimage of the goal G is denoted P. A motion strategy θ with commanded velocity v_θ^* is guaranteed for the region R', but the starting region is the larger[4] R. The weak preimage of G is denoted $\hat{P}$. The forward projection of the "bad" region $R - R'$ is $F_\theta(R - R')$. In fig. 26, it is in fact equal to $F_\theta(R)$. Using θ as data, how can we construct an EDR strategy that is applicable for all of R? Let us first try taking the EDR region $H = H_0$, where H_0 is the set difference of the forward projection of the "bad" region and the weak preimage:

$$H_0 = F_\theta(R - R') - \hat{P}. \tag{1}$$

[4]Note that in general, R and R' need not be cylinders, but can be arbitrary subsets of $\mathcal{G}$.

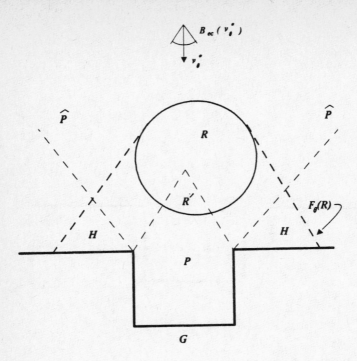

Fig. 26. R is the start region. P is the strong preimage of G. R' is the region in R from which the strategy is guaranteed to reach G recognizably. $\hat{P}$ is the weak preimage. H is the forward projection of R outside the weak preimage. It is the EDR region.

If we can distinguish between G and H, then H is a good EDR region, and we have constructed an EDR strategy.

Taking $H = H_0$ as above is not sufficiently general. Consider fig. 27. It is possible for a motion from R to stick forever in the region H_s, which is within the weak preimage. However, a motion through H_s is not guaranteed to stick in H_s: it may eventually slide into the goal. We want sliding motions to pass through H_s unmolested, while the termination predicate should halt sticking motions in H_s.

The EDR region H region should include H_0. But it should also include H_s, when sticking occurs. In other words, H should include H_0 for *all* velocities, but should only include H_s for *sticking* velocities (that is, zero velocities). To handle this idea we introduce simple velocity goals, as well as position goals. The position and velocity goals are regions in phase space.

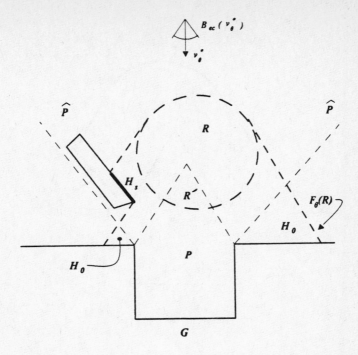

Fig. 27. H_0 in eq. (1) is not the entire EDR region. Sticking may occur within the weak preimage in H_s. The EDR region must include H_0 for all possible velocities, and H_s for "sticking velocities."

A goal in phase space is a region in Position-space × Velocity-space. A phase space goal is attained when the actual position and velocity can be guaranteed to lie in the region. Let us construct the phase-space EDR region $\tilde{H}$. If x is in H_0, then for any velocity v at x, (x, v) must be in $\tilde{H}$. Let $\pi^{-1}(H_0)$ denote all such (x, v) in phase-space.

Now, H_s is the set of all points x in the weak but not strong preimage, such that sticking can occur at x.[5] We wish to distinguish the sticking velocities in H_s. Under generalized damper dynamics, these are essentially the zero velocities. Let $Z(H_s)$ denote the zero velocities over H_s, that is, the set of pairs $(x, 0)$ for x in H_s. This set is in phase space. Then we see that $Z(H_s)$ is also in the phase space EDR region $\tilde{H}$. Thus $\tilde{H}$ is the union of the sticking velocities over H_s, and all velocities over the forward projection outside the weak preimage:

---

[5] [Erdmann] shows how to decide whether $x \in H_s$ using configuration space friction cones.

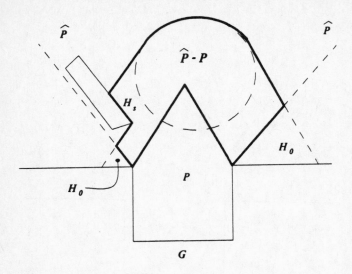

Fig. 28. The weak but not strong preimage $\hat{P} - P$, from fig. 27. Can a motion from R remain in $\hat{P} - P$ forever? One way this may happen is by sticking in H_s. In general, however, there are other ways.

$$\tilde{H} = Z(H_s) \cup \pi^{-1}(H_0). \tag{2}$$

To use $\tilde{H}$ as an EDR region, we must now ensure that $\tilde{H}$ and the cylinder over G are distinguishable goals. In an appendix, we show that if the strong preimage is known, the definition of (phase space) EDR regions is *constructive up to reachability*. By this we mean that when backprojections, set intersections and differences, and friction cones can be computed, then so can $\tilde{H}$. With $\tilde{H}$ in hand, we add the recognizability constraint to obtain an EDR strategy.

The structure of the "weak but not strong preimage," $\hat{P} - P$ suggests a number of implementation issues. Consider figs. 27,28 once more. Suppose we have a trajectory originating in R, subject to the control uncertainty shown. We do not wish to terminate the motion while it remains in the weak preimage, since fortuitous sensing and control events could still force recognizable termination in G. However, we can terminate the motion as soon as we recognize egress from the weak preimage. This is why the forward projection outside the weak preimage is contained in the EDR region.

As we have seen, however, it is possible for a trajectory to remain within the weak but not strong preimage forever. For example, it can stick in H_s forever. To handle this case, we introduced phase space EDR goals.

There are other conditions under which a trajectory could stay in $\hat{P} - P$ forever: (a) if the environment is infinite, or $\hat{P} - P$ is unbounded. (b) The trajectory "loops" in $\hat{P} - P$ forever. (a) and (b) are qualitatively different from the case of sticking forever in H_s, because they require motion for infinitely long. In practice this may be handled by terminating the motion in $\hat{P} - P$ after a certain elapsed time. We can model this case by constructing termination predicates which "time-out." In fact, this "solution" works for sticking in H_s also.

An alternative is to extend our earlier zero-velocity analysis to all of $\hat{P} - P$. That is, we terminate the motion in the weak but not strong preimage when the actual velocity is (close to) zero. It seems that time-out termination predicates and/or velocity thresholding must be used to solve the looping problem. Both solutions seem inelegant; the issue is subtle and is addressed further in a later section.

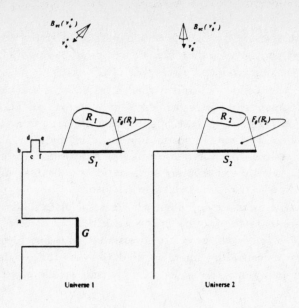

Fig. 29. There are two possible universes; the goal G exists in the first but not the second. The start region is $R_1 \cup R_2$. Motion θ is guaranteed to move from R_1 into S_1. Motion ψ is guaranteed to move from S_1 into f. There is an 8-step plan achieving G from R_1. The forward projections of R_1 and R_2 are indistinguishable. There exists no one-step EDR strategy from the motion θ.

4. Generalization to n-Step EDR Strategies

4.1. The "Twin Universe" Example

Example (3). So far we have only considered one-step EDR strategies. We now generalize the construction to n-step strategies. Consider fig. 29. Here there are two possible universes, both in the plane, so J is the two element discrete set, $\{1, 2\}$. The start region is the union of R_1 in universe 1, and R_2 in universe 2. The goal exists in universe 1 but not in universe 2. There is no one-step EDR strategy which, from the start region, can guarantee to achieve G or recognize that we are in universe 2. In particular, there is no one-step EDR strategy which can be derived from the motion v_θ^*.

There is an 8-step plan in universe 1 which recognizably achieves G from start region R_1. It is obtained by back-chaining preimages in universe 1. The plan moves from R_1 to the region S_1 under v_θ^*. Then it slides along the top surface to vertex f, and then to the successive vertex subgoals e through a, and finally into G. We can construct a 2-step EDR strategy, from this plan. First, we execute motion θ from the union of R_1 and R_2. This achieves a motion into S_1 in universe 1, or into S_2 in universe 2. The termination predicate cannot distinguish which has been attained. Suppose the second motion in the 8-step plan is v_ψ^* (see fig. 29), and is guaranteed to achieve the vertex subgoal f from start region S_1. We will try to construct an EDR strategy out of this second motion. Take as data: the subgoal f, the start region $S_1 \cup S_2$, the "southwest" motion ψ, and the preimage of f under ψ. The EDR region for these data is the forward projection of S_2 under ψ (see fig. 30). Presumably this EDR region is distinguishable from f, and so we have constructed an EDR strategy at the second step. After executing the second step, we either terminate the plan as a failure, or proceed to vertex e, and eventually to the goal.

There is a subtle issue of where to terminate the motion within the forward projection of $R_1 \cup R_2$; this "where" is $S_1 \cup S_2$ here, and is called the *push-forward*. Since they address termination, push-forwards are to forward projections as preimages are to backprojections. In chapter III and an appendix, they are defined formally and the n-step EDR construction is given in detail.

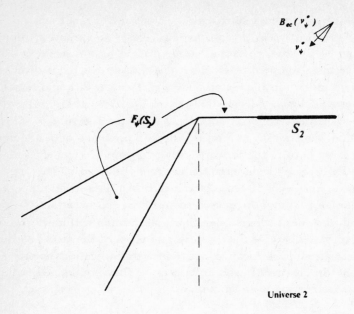

Fig. 30. The forward projection under ψ of S_2.

5. What is "Recovery"?

So far, we have taken a "radical" view with respect to "Recovery." We assume that in planning for error and recovery, one essentially specifies the maximum length plan one is willing to contemplate. The EDR planner considers the class of n-step strategies and tries to formulate a plan that will achieve the goal given the sensing, control, and model uncertainty.[1] Perhaps such a plan can be guaranteed. If not, then termination in an EDR region would signal failure. This means that there was no guaranteed n-step plan. (A third possibility is that G and H are never distinguishable at any of the n steps. This means that there is no EDR plan). If there is no guaranteed n-step plan, and some EDR region H is recognizably achieved, the recovery action might then be "give up," or "try again, using up the remaining

---

[1] Of course, one could in principle search for strategies of increasing length by quantifying over n. At any one time, however, one would reduce to the case described here and iterate.

number of steps in the plan," if we are serious in refusing to contemplate plans longer than n steps. As a corollary, the only "Error," then, is "being in the wrong universe," or more accurately, "being in the wrong start region." This viewpoint is a consequence of trying to address EDR and completeness simultaneously. More concretely, suppose we consider some sensory-control-geometric event to be an "error," make a plan to detect it, and a recovery plan in case it is detected. If the plan can be guaranteed, then it can be found using [LMT]. In this case the "error" is no longer an error, but simply an "event" which triggers a conditional branch of the plan.[2] If the plan cannot be guaranteed, then we have proposed the EDR framework, which allows us to try it anyway. If it fails, however, the only obvious recovery action entails the recursive construction of EDR sub-plans (see below). It is not clear what other kinds of recovery could be attempted without exploiting additional knowledge: the recovery branches have already been tried. The issue is subtle, and deserves further attention.

We give one example which highlights the complexity of the recovery problem. Suppose that we consider the class of 4-step plans. Given a 4-step plan as data, suppose we construct a multi-step EDR strategy which pushes forward on the first motion, and executes an EDR strategy on the the second. After executing the second motion, we have recognizably either achieved the second subgoal, or some EDR region H. If H is achieved, what is the correct recovery action? We could do nothing, and signal failure. Alternatively, we could try to construct a plan (of length less than or equal to two) to achieve the goal. Now, if such a plan exists and can be guaranteed, then the entire EDR analysis was unnecessary, since the [LMT] framework can (formally) find such plans. However, there might exist a 2-step EDR strategy to (try to) achieve the goal from H. While such a plan could not be guaranteed, it might be worth a try. This suggests that the failure recovery action in an n-step EDR strategy should be to recursively construct *another* EDR strategy to achieve the goal from the EDR region, using no more than the remaining number of steps. If n is 1, the planner should simply signal failure and stop.

EDR is ripe for probabilistic analysis. In our plans, the recovery action is often, "in case of failure, try it again." Probabilistic analysis would permit one to address the likelihood of success for such a plan. In particular, notice that after a failure, it is frequently the case that the run-time executive has learned something about the structure of the environment. This knowledge is embodied in the subset of J known to contain the world state. Even after achieving an EDR region and signalling failure, it is generally the case that the position in J is more precisely known than at the start of the plan execution. Hence we can quite precisely define our view of "Error Diagnosis"—it is simply the position in generalized configuration space, and, in particular, the position in J.

---

[2]Unless, of course, the error recovery action is not a motion.

One can envision different sorts of recovery actions. One type of recovery would be to set up to do the task with different parts. Extending EDR to the kind of cyclic activity found in certain applications would be very useful. While in principle it would be modeled within our framework, in practice, the dimensionality of the generalized configuration space would be prohibitive.

6. Implementation and Experiments: One-Step EDR Strategies

In this section we describe experiments with a implemented EDR planner, called LIMITED which is based on [LMT,E,D]. The discussion here focuses on how to use the EDR theory in a planner to generate one-step EDR strategies. Later in the thesis we discuss the implementation of multi-step EDR strategies generation.

6.1. Experiment: Computing EDR Regions

In order to synthesize EDR strategies, we must be able to compute EDR regions. To compute EDR regions, we must have tools for computing forward-projections and preimages in generalized configuration space. We now discuss these tools and experiments using them.

We approximate preimages using backprojections (see [Erdmann]). At present, the implementation can compute slice approximations to EDR regions for one-step plans where the generalized configuration space is three-dimensional. The particular generalized configuration space we consider is that of the gear example described in section 1.1. (See fig. 2). In this case, C is the cartesian plane, representing translations of gear A, and J is the 2D rotation group (i.e., a circle), representing orientations of the gear B. The implementation uses slices: by a *slice* we mean an α-slice of generalized configuration space for some α in J. α is the model error parameter, and represents the orientation of B. We have implemented an algorithm which computes slices of the three dimensional EDR regions for both variants of the gear example. In the first, B cannot rotate, so no motion across J is possible. In the second, B can rotate when pushed, so motion across J is possible. In the latter case, backprojections and forward projections must be computed across J, since it is possible to achieve the goal by moving across J (rotating B by pushing and possibly sliding on its surface).

Given a 2D slice of generalized configuration space, LIMITED employs a plane-sweep algorithm for computing unions, intersections, and projections. (By *projections* we mean forward projections, backprojections, and weak-backprojections in that slice). The algorithm uses exact (rational) arithmetic, and computes unions in $O((n + c) \log n)$ time, and projections in $O(n \log n)$ time.[1] The design and implementation of the 2D plane-sweep module is joint work with John Canny; the algorithm is based on [Neivergelt and Preparata] (who give a union algorithm) and related to [Erdmann] (who implemented an $O(n^2)$ backprojection algorithm, and suggested an improved $O(n \log n)$ version).

---

[1] Where n is the number of vertices in the slice, and c is the number of intersections.

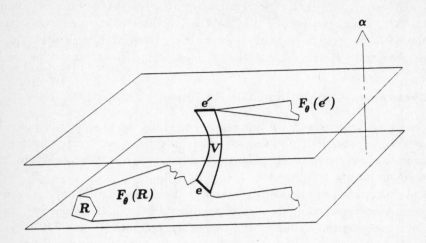

Fig. 31. Illustration of how forward projections are propagated across slices. In slice α, the forward projection of R, $F_\theta(R)$ is computed. e is an obstacle edge in $F_\theta(R)$. Configurations on e correspond to contact configurations between the gears. Quasi-static analysis indicates that commanding velocity v_θ^* from e can result in motion in the $+\alpha$ direction. As α varies in this direction, e rotates, sweeping out an algebraic surface V. V is followed into a nearby slice, α', and the intersection of V and this slice is e'. In slice α', the forward projection $F_\theta(e')$ is computed. This is the propagated forward projection.

To compute projections in the 3D generalized configuration space, LIMITED propagates projections across slices. For example, given a forward projection in a slice, the algorithm finds all obstacle edges and vertices from which it is possible to exert a positive torque on the obstacle (which is gear B in the figures). See fig. 40. Thus by pushing on these edges it is possible to move across slices in the $+\alpha$ direction. Each such edge is a slice of an algebraic ruled surface in generalized configuration space. The vertices are slices of algebraic (partial) helicoids. Sliding along the surface of B while causing B to rotate corresponds to following the surface (or helicoid). The surface is traced into the next α-slice, and taken as a start region from which to forward-project in that slice. For example, see figs. 41–42. The propagated forward projection must then be unioned with propagated forward projections from other slices, and with the forward projection of any start regions in that slice. See fig. 45. Weak backprojections are computed analogously.

In order to compute weak backprojections and forward projections, we assume that there can be stiction at the rotation center of B. Thus the ratio of sliding to turning is indeterminate. In general, the computation of strong backprojections under rotation due to pushing will be a second order problem, since it depends on the derivatives of this ratio. We employ a conservative approximation to the strong backprojection (namely, the backprojection in free space alone) to construct the EDR regions. This suffices, since EDR strategies require only the weak backprojection and forward projection (which depend only on the possibility, and not the velocity, of sliding and turning). Thus there is a deep sense in which EDR strategies with model error seem easier to compute than guaranteed strategies, because EDR strategies are "first order." This is consistent with the intuition that weak backprojections should be easier to compute than strong backprojections.

Figs. 32–39 show the EDR regions for the gear example (sec. 1.1) when no rotation of B is permitted. Only one slice of $\mathcal{G}$ is shown. In all the figures, the commanded velocity is "towards the center of B", up and to the right. The magnitude of the control error can be seen from the "fan-out" in the forward projection (fig. 35).

Next, we allow B to rotate. Figs. 43–48 show the EDR regions at four α-slices of the 3D generalized configuration space. In this case motion across J is possible by pushing B, when B rotates. The projections have been propagated across slices and unioned. The results are slices of the 3D EDR regions across J.

6.2. Experiment: Planning One-Step EDR

The computation of the EDR regions is at the heart of EDR planning. To generate one step EDR strategies LIMITED performs a search by discretizing the space of possible commanded velocities. The discretization generates a set of commanded velocities to try. The following loop is executed to search for an EDR strategy. Below, we use the phrase *"the strategy recognizably terminates in G or H"* to mean that the run-time executor can always distinguish which of G or H has been achieved, when the motion terminates.

Algorithm 1EDR

1. *Generate a commanded velocity v_θ^*.*
2. *Compute the EDR region H for v_θ^*,*

3.   *Determine whether the EDR region H and the goal G are distinguishable using sensors. If so, then v_θ^* yields a one-step EDR strategy which recognizably terminates in G or H by monitoring position and force sensors.*

4.   *Let ∂G and ∂H denote the set of obstacle edges within G and H, resp. Determine whether the regions ∂H and ∂G are distinguishable using sensors. If so, then v_θ^* yields a one-step EDR strategy which recognizably terminates on an obstacle edge in G or H. The termination condition is contact with[2] or sticking on a surface in G or H.*

5.   *Let $\text{push}_\theta(G)$ and $\text{push}_\theta(H)$ denote the sticking push-forwards. They are the set of obstacle edges within G and H, resp., on which sticking can occur under v_θ^*. Determine whether these regions are distinguishable using sensors. If so, then v_θ^* yields a one-step EDR strategy which recognizably terminates when sticking is detected.*

Here is how LIMITED decides the question, "Are G and H distinguishable using sensors?"

H and G are distinguishable using position sensing alone if their convolutions (Minkowski sums) by the position sensing error ball B_{ep} do not intersect.

Each obstacle edge of H and G has an associated configuration space friction cone. Two edges are distinguishable using force sensing if the convolutions of their friction cones by the force sensing uncertainty B_{ev} have a trivial intersection.[3]

Similarly, the set of possible sensed reaction forces at an obstacle vertex w of G or H may be found by taking the direct sum of the friction cones of the edges cobounding w, and convolving by B_{ev}. Again, a vertex of H and a vertex (or edge) of G are distinguishable using force sensing if their associated cones of sensed reaction forces have a trivial intersection.

LIMITED decides that G and H are distinguishable using position sensing and force sensing if all edges and vertices of G and H are pairwise distinguishable using the position and force sensing criteria above. The procedure works equally well for determining the distinguishability of ∂G and ∂H, and on the push-forwards $\text{push}_\theta(\cdot)$.

Note that the procedure is correct for linear edges, where position and force-sensing are separable because the set of possible reaction forces is constant along an edge. In general, the sets which must be distinct are of the following form. Let $N(x)$ be the convolution of the friction cone at x with the velocity sensing uncertainty B_{ev}. Let $B_{ep}(x)$ denote the position sensing uncertainty ball translated to x. Then the set $I(G)$ of possible sensor interpretations from points in G is defined to be

---

[2] However, see section 7 for a technical point on recognizing whether the contact is within $G \cup H$.

[3] An intersection containing only the zero-vector.

$$I(G) = \bigcup_{x \in G} N(x) \times B_{ep}(x).$$

For general goals and EDR regions, we must have that $I(G)$ and $I(H)$ are distinct.

A final comment is required with regard to sticking as a termination condition. EDR plans generated with this termination predicate only make sense if sticking is possible in the goal. That is, if sticking is impossible in the goal, then *all* motions will terminate in H. It is better still if sticking is in fact *necessary* in the goal. If this is the case, then all motions entering the goal will terminate in the goal, whereas all motions entering H will terminate there. For example, recall the peg-in-hole strategy in figs. 3–13, chapter I. In this example, sticking is necessary in the goal under both the first and the second motions. For a motion θ, the formal criterion that necessary sticking satisfies is

$$F_\theta(G) = G.$$

That is, if we view θ as a "mapping" then G is a fixed point. Of course, it is a simple matter to verify this criterion given our plane-sweep algorithms for forward projection. Note also that there are other termination conditions that satisfy the fixed-point equation—one example is the "stationary subgoals" in the tray-tilting planner of [Erdmann and Mason].

Further details of the one-step planning algorithms in LIMITED can be found in section 7. At this point, however, we digress to discuss the complexity of EDR planning.

6.3. Complexity Bounds

We now give some complexity bounds for subproblems in EDR planning. All our bounds are upper bounds. The first question is, what is the complexity of EDR planning in one slice?

Suppose we are given a motion direction v_θ^*, and a planar polygonal environment containing n edges. The environment represents the configuration space obstacles in a planar slice. The configuration space obstacle polygons may be nonconvex, but may not intersect. The start region and goal are polygons of constant size. Suppose that the termination condition to be employed is sticking. What is the complexity of verifying that θ yields an EDR strategy in this slice?

Theorem: *There exists an $O(n^3)$ algorithm for deciding the validity of a one-step EDR strategy with sticking termination in a planar slice.*

Proof: Unions and set-differences can be computed in time $O((n + c) \log n)$, where c is the number of intersections. c is between 1 and n^2 [Neivergelt and Preparata].

Forward projections, backprojections, and weak backprojections can be computed in time $O(n \log n)$. All projections have size $O(n)$. Determining the sticking edges and vertices of a polygon is $O(n)$. Hence computing the EDR region H requires time $O((n + c) \log n)$ and the output has size $O(n + c)$.

While the goal G has constant size, the algorithm only needs to distinguish H from *the closure of the free-space goal*. The free-space goal is the set difference of G and the configuration space obstacles, CO. $G - CO$ has size $O(n)$.

Determining whether H and $G - CO$ are distinguishable can require a pairwise test of their edges and vertices. This takes time $O((n + c)n)$. $\square$

Now, in LIMITED, the input is given as a set of convex, possibly overlapping real-space polygons. Suppose the input is given as real space polygonal obstacles of size $O(m)$. That is, the total number of edges is m. The configuration space obstacles must first be computed. This can take time $O(m^2)$, since the input could consist of two sets of $\frac{m}{6}$ convex (in fact, triangular) polygons which must be pairwise convolved. The output—a set of overlapping convex configuration space obstacle polygons—has size $O(m)$. The union of the configuration space obstacles must be computed. This requires time $O((m + c') \log n)$ and the output has size $O(c')$. c', the number of intersections, is between 1 and m^2. Taking n to be c', we find that the complexity of EDR verification in a planar slice is $\leq \left((\frac{m}{6})^2 \right)^3$, or $O(m^6)$, when measured in the size of the real space input.

These bounds are not for an idealized form of the one-step EDR algorithm, but rather for a full, exact-arithmetic implementation. In practice—by which we mean for the experiments in this thesis—we found that while c', the complexity of the configuration space obstacles, can indeed approach m^2, the complexity of the EDR regions is roughly linear in n, (and therefore merely quadratic in m). This is probably due to the structure of the projection regions. Each projection region contains *free-space* edges and *obstacle* edges. Because the free-space edges of any projection region are in at most two orientations, it is difficult to get n^2 crossings of edges in free-space. This difficulty is exacerbated by the fact that the obstacle edges in two intersecting projection regions will be identical. Thus the only source of quadratic intersection complexity can be free-space crossings of projection edges. While superlinear intersection complexity seems unlikely for projection regions, it remains open to prove a linear bound.

6.4. Critical Slices: An Introduction

While upper bounds for the complexity of planning in a single slice are established, the complexity of planning with many EDR slices is less well understood. Two questions remain:

- How many slices are necessary for EDR planning?
- What is the complexity of propagating the projection regions across slices?

The key to answering the first question may be addressed using *critical slices*. The idea is as follows. Consider the gear experiment, where gear A can translate and B has unknown orientation. *Initially, assume that the orientation of B is fixed, so it cannot rotate when pushed by A.* Let α denote the orientation of B. Then consider the three-dimensional backprojection of G in $\mathcal{G}$. By taking x-y slices of the backprojection at different values of α, it is clear that generically, as α varies, the topology of the backprojection remains unchanged. Similarly for the forward projection or weak backprojection: The topology of two backprojection slices are the same if no edges or vertices appear or disappear at α values between them. At singular values of α, however, a small change in α will result in a change in the topology of the backprojection slice. Such a change is called a "catastrophe." These singular values are called *critical α*, and the generic values of α are called non-critical. Two critical values are called *adjacent* if there is no critical value between them.

The idea is that the planning algorithm can compute a backprojection slice at each critical value of α. In addition, between each adjacent pair of critical values, the algorithm computes a slice at a non-critical α. This slice of the backprojection at that value is representative of a continuum of intermediate non-critical slices. Between critical slices, in addition, it is clear how the surfaces of the backprojection change. The obstacle vertices of the backprojection, for example, move along curved edges that are algebraic helicoids. The obstacle edges are developable algebraic surfaces. The equations of the surfaces are found in [Brooks and Lozano-Pérez]. The equations of the edges, as parameterized by orientation, are found in [D1]. No additional vertices may be introduced except at critical values. The free-space edges of the backprojection remain fixed across α between critical values. What we obtain is a complete combinatorial characterization of the 3D backprojection in $\mathcal{G}$. It can be used to derive precise, combinatorial algorithms for decision problems about the backprojection.

For example, suppose we wish to decide whether a start region R is contained in the 3D backprojection. (That is, to decide whether the goal is guaranteed reachable from the start region). This problem has the following application. By deciding the containment question, guaranteed strategies can be planned. This is because backprojections approximate preimages. Thus by deriving upper bounds on the containment problem in the backprojection, we obtain bounds for the planning of guaranteed strategies. In turn, by obtaining bounds on the guaranteed planning problem, we can gain insight into the complexity of EDR planning.

Suppose R has the form $U \times J$ for U a polygon in the plane. Then U must be tested for containment in each critical and non-critical slice as defined above. In addition, we must ensure that U lies inside the backprojection as the boundaries of the backprojection move with α. Since the equations of these surfaces are algebraically defined, we simply test them for intersection with the boundary edges of U.

The next question is: how many critical values of α are there? In the following lemma, when we speak of edges of the backprojection, or convex configuration space obstacle (CO) vertices, we mean edges of the backprojection in a slice, or a vertex which is convex in a slice. Of course these edges and vertices sweep out surfaces and curves (resp.) as α changes.

Lemma: *Let C be $\Re^2$, J be the circle S^1. Suppose m is size of the input in real-space edges so that $n = O(m^2)$ is the number of generalized configuration space constraints. Let G have constant size, and $B_\theta(G)$ be the backprojection of G in $C \times J$ as above. Then there are $O(n^3)$ critical values of $\alpha \in J$ for $B_\theta(G)$.*

Proof: We enumerate the various types of critical values:

A. First, an α value is (potentially) critical when a new edge or vertex is introduced into, or disappears from, the union of the configuration space obstacles. This can introduce a topological change in the obstacle boundary of the backprojection. If A and B are convex, then as α varies, there are potentially m^2 topological changes in the configuration space obstacles. These generate $O(m^2)$ critical values of α, which we call *obstacle*-critical. However, when A and B are non-convex, there can be $O(m^6)$ obstacle-critical values. This bound arises as the number of critical values for an arrangement of m^2 surfaces in dimension $d = 3$.

B. In addition, an α value can be critical if the determination of sliding vs. sticking on an edge can change there. A change in sliding can result in the introduction or deletion of a free-space constraint, and hence change the free-space boundary of the backprojection. This occurs when an edge of the friction cone on some edge becomes parallel to an edge of the velocity cone of control uncertainty. Now, as a configuration space edge rotates with α, its friction cone rotates with it. Thus as α changes, a friction cone edge can be parallel to a velocity cone edge at most 4 times. Hence there can be at most $4n$ values of α at which the sliding determination changes. These values are called *sliding*-critical.

C. Next, the topology of a slice of $B_\theta(G)$ can change when a convex vertex of a rotating configuration space obstacle edge touches a free-space edge of the backprojection. These α-values are called *vertex*-critical. Now, each free-space edge of a backprojection slice is anchored at a convex configuration-space obstacle (CO) vertex. Vertex-criticality occurs when a free-space edge of a backprojection slice joins two CO vertices in that slice. The edge then lies in the visibility graph of the generalized configuration space obstacles in that slice. Now, we can obtain a bound of $O(m^6)$ on the number of vertex-critical values as follows. Introduce an additional $O(m^2)$ constraints, each anchored at a convex CO vertex and parallel to the left or right edge of the velocity cone. These, together with the $O(m^2)$ obstacle surface constraints form an arrangement of $O(m^2)$ surfaces in 3 dimensions, yielding a total of $O(m^6)$ critical values. This bound may be improved to $O(m^4)$, by observing that each vertex-critical value is generated by a pair of convex CO vertices, and that there exist $O(m^2)$ such vertices.

D.   Finally, an *edge*-critical value occurs when a configuration space edge, rotating with α, touches a free-space backprojection vertex. Free-space backprojection vertices are formed by the intersection of two free-space edges of the backprojection. Each free-space edge of the backprojection is anchored at a convex CO vertex. The number of edge-critical values is $O(m^6)$, because each is generated by a CO edge, and two convex CO vertices (one per free-space backprojection edge).

Finally, we observe that these bounds are additive, and that n is $O(m^2)$. $\square$

Comments: We conjecture that the bounds on edge-critical values (D) can be improved to $O(m^4)$. One approach to proving the improved bound is to identify each free-space vertex v of the backprojection, with the right generating CO vertex. Follow the locus of v as α varies. It remains to show that the locus is piecewise-smooth, and touches each CO edge at most a fixed number of times.

We can now address the complexity of deciding containment in the backprojection. In this discussion we address only the combinatorial complexity, and not the algebraic complexity, of the decision procedure. Here is what this means. We have obtained a combinatorial upper bound on the number of critical values of α. Once rotations are algebraically parameterized, these critical values are, in fact, all algebraic; that is, in general, a critical value of α will be an algebraic, but not necessarily rational number. However, the plane sweep algorithm (which is discussed in more detail in chap. VI) operates on rational numbers. Hence to obtain a decision procedure one must first approximate α by a "nearby" rational number q. By "nearby", we mean that the approximation must be known to be sufficiently close so that the decision procedure will give the correct answer for containment. As the approximation gets closer, the rational numbers will become more "larger" (i.e., as a quotient of two integers, the integers will become larger), and the plane sweep algorithm will run correspondingly slower. To choose q algorithmically, one might make use of a "gap" theorem, such as in [Canny].

Theorem: *Let U be a polygon of constant size, C be $\Re^2$, J be S^1, $B_\theta(G)$ be the backprojection of G in $C \times J$ as above. Suppose G is of constant size. Then there exists an algorithm deciding the containment of $R = U \times J$ in $B_\theta(G)$ in time*

$$O(n^4 \log n).$$

Proof: $O(n^3)$ slices of the backprojection can be computed in time $O(n^4 \log n)$. Now, to test for containment of U in the 3D backprojection region between two adjacent critical slices will take time $O(n)$, since the backprojection has size $O(n)$. The cost of deciding the containment of U between successive adjacent pairs of n^3 slices, each of size n, is $O(n^4)$. Since the time for computation of the slices dominates, this yields total complexity $O(n^4 \log n)$. $\square$

Some comments are in order. First, our algorithm is naive, in that each back-projection slice is recomputed from scratch. In fact, this extra work is unnecessary. At a critical value of α, very few aspects of the topology of the backprojection will change. That is, typically, only one or two edges will be introduced or disappear at any critical value. We can make this notion precise as follows. If α is a generic singularity, then exactly one edge or vertex will appear or disappear there. Hence, for example, we can ensure that all critical values are generic singularities with probability one by subjecting the input to small rational perturbations.

Suppose that a backprojection has been computed in a critical slice at α. Then to compute a backprojection in a nearby non-critical slice at $\alpha + \epsilon$, we merely need to update the portion of the backprojection boundary that was critical at α. This requires only constant work: only one edge or vertex must be changed to derive a backprojection in the new slice! It seems reasonable to conjecture that this technique would yield an algorithm of complexity $O(n^3 \log n)$ for deciding containment in a backprojection.

Finally, it appears that there are many problems in which the number of critical values fails to achieve the theoretically possible n^3 bound. This is because characteristically, there are orientation restrictions; typically, even with model error, B is not allowed to rotate freely. In other cases, there are symmetries. For example, in the gear case, even though B is allowed to rotate freely, it is unnecessary to consider n^3 slices since due to symmetry the configuration spaces "repeat" periodically.

6.4.1 Comparison with Lower Bounds

From a theoretical point of view, this result has the following interest. Consider the one-step compliant motion planning problem in 3D amidst precisely known polyhedral obstacles. This problem may be addressed via 3D backprojections in $\Re^3$. [CR] have shown that deciding containment in such a 3D backprojection is NP-hard.

In particular, such backprojections can have an exponential number of faces. However, in the previous theorem we demonstrated a special class of 3D backprojections that have only $O(n^4)$ faces, along with an efficient algorithm for deciding containment. This special class of backprojections arises in the presence of model error. Specifically, they arise when C is $\Re^2$, J is one-dimensional, and no motion is permitted across J. In this case, the non-holonomic constraints that keep the robot within one slice essentially disallow the kind of fanning out and branching that [CR] discovered in $\Re^3$. Thus, our polynomial-time algorithm identifies a tractable subclass of the 3D motion planning problem with uncertainty. This subclass is also interesting in that it arises naturally in planning with model uncertainty.

6.4.2 Issues in the Critical Slice Method

The critical slice method represents a theoretical algorithm. It has not been implemented in LIMITED. It was described here to give some characterization for bounds on planning with model error. In particular, it gives a precise, combinatorial description for the 3D backprojection in $\Re^2 \times S^1$, and an exact algorithm for deciding containment. The containment algorithm directly addresses the question of planning guaranteed strategies, since a backchaining preimage planner can be constructed by approximating preimages using backprojections. The termination condition for such a planner is when the start region is contained within a backprojection.

Most important, the critical slice method attempts to put the slice techniques used in LIMITED on a firm mathematical footing.[4] It provides a principled way—a specific method—for choosing which slices to consider, a bound on how many slices are required, and a conservative algorithm for deciding containment.

Much work remains however:

- We have only addressed deciding the containment problem in a precise combinatorial fashion. Generalize to computing set-differences and to deciding their distinguishability—that is, deciding G vs. H distinguishability—using the critical slice approach.

- J is one dimensional in our discussion. Generalize the critical slice method to multi-dimensional model error.

- This analysis addresses the complexity of verifying an EDR strategy, but does not speak to the complexity of the search. What is the complexity of finding a strategy or determining that none exists? This issue will be attacked in a later section, by developing a combinatorial description of the non-directional backprojection.

---

[4]Note that slice methods have been studied in other domains. See, for example, [Lozano-Pérez, Schwartz and Yap, Erdmann].

- Derive bounds on deciding containment after relaxing the no-pushing restriction and allowing motion across J.

Let us say a few words about the last point. Suppose now that B can rotate passively when pushed. Hence motion across J is possible, and projection regions must be propagated across slices. For example, a forward projection can begin in free-space in one slice, contact an obstacle edge generated by B, rotate across J into another slice, and fly off the edge into free-space in that slice. Hence forward projections must be propagated across slices. This process was described above in sec. 6.1. The obvious question is: What is the complexity of propagating the projection regions across slices? The complexity of one step of the propagation is not difficult to derive. For example, consider the forward projection. There are $O(n)$ obstacle edges in the forward projection in a planar slice. For each edge, a constant time quasi-static analysis is performed to determine whether pushing against that edge can cause rotation of B, that is, motion across J. See fig. 38. If so the forward projection must be propagated along that algebraic surface into an adjacent slice. This can result in a *propagated start region* of size $O(n)$ in the adjacent slice. This start region is used to compute a new forward projection in that planar slice. See figs. 39 and 40. This propagated forward projection must then be unioned with any other forward projections within that slice. See fig. 43, which is a detail of fig. 42. When does the propagation process terminate? A correct termination condition is: Terminate propagation when any propagated start region lies within an existing forward projection.

Now while the complexity of each of these steps is known, it is not clear how long it takes for the propagation process to terminate. In particular, results of [CR] suggest that 3D forward projections may even have exponential size.[5] Experimental evidence—the backprojector of [Erdmann]—concurs. Furthermore, when propagation is permitted, more slices may be required. For example, it is conceivable that a path within the forward projection may break contact and fly off into a slice which is between the chosen critical values. In other words, propagation may increase the number of critical values. The additional critical values can occur as follows. The plane sweep algorithm is only correct when the velocity cone is smaller than the friction cone on any edge (see chapter VI). Hence we will assume it is convex. Then contact can be broken when the inner product of an extremal vector in the velocity cone by an outward-facing edge normal is positive. Hence the zero-crossings of this dot-product are potentially critical values; there are $O(n)$ such values. While this is a start, the complexity of computing projections when pushing can cause motion across J requires further study.

---

[5][CR] provide an exponential lower bound for the size of the forward projection in $\Re^3$ amidst polyhedral obstacles. It remains to determine the applicability of their proof in the non-holonomic (model error) case.

*   *   *

This completes the informal discussion of the one-step EDR planner in LIMITED. Later in the thesis we will discuss the details of the plane-sweep algorithm and how LIMITED implements the EDR theory to compute multi-step strategies. In the next section, we will discuss a number of theoretical and practical issues relating to the construction and implementation of the one-step EDR planning algorithms in LIMITED.

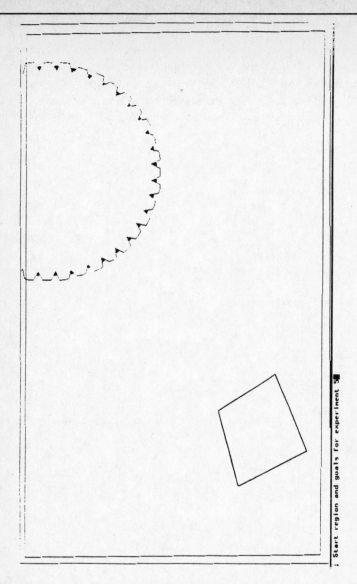

Fig. 32. The configuration space for the gear example (fig. 2) at one α-slice ($\alpha = 0$) of $\mathcal{G}$. The goal region is the "valleys" of the cspace obstacle. The start region is the diamond to the lower left. For figs. 32–39, B is not allowed to rotate, so no motion across J is possible.

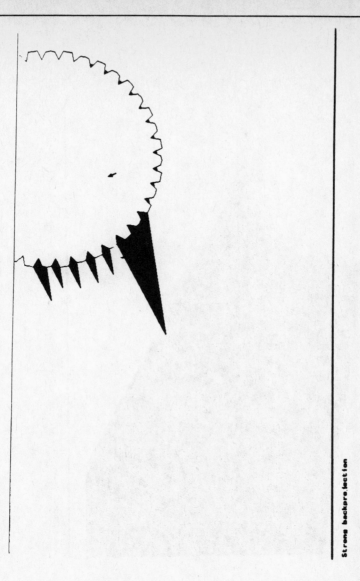

Fig. 33. The strong backprojection in slice $\alpha = 0$ of the goals in fig. 32, assuming that B cannot rotate. In all these experiments, the coefficient of friction is taken to be .25.

Fig. 34. The weak backprojection of the goals in slice $\alpha = 0$.

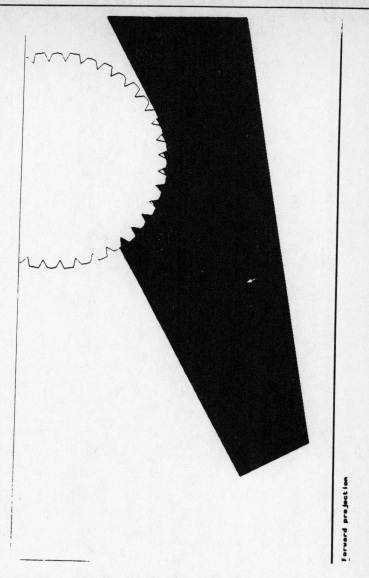

Fig. 35. The forward projection of the start region in slice $\alpha = 0$.

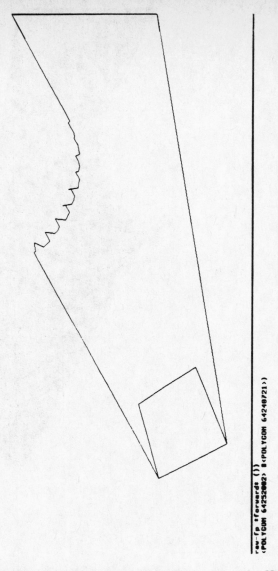

Fig. 36. The forward projection of the start region in slice $\alpha = 0$. Note the degenerate edges due to sliding.

Fig. 37. The weak minus the strong backprojection.

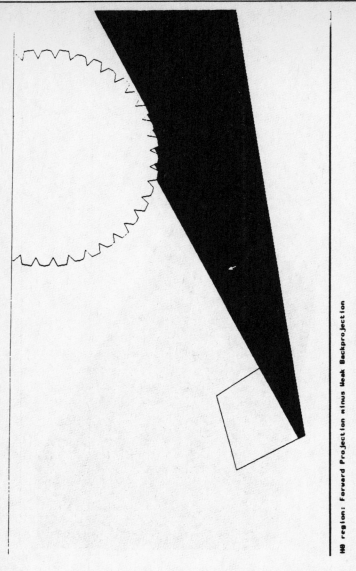

H0 region: Forward Projection minus Weak Backprojection

Fig. 38. The H_0 region (the forward projection minus the weak backprojection).

(Experiment 5) Sticking edges and vertices in Weak minus Strong backprojection

SHEEP: iyi

Lisp Machine Jim Hendri

0420+2/86 19:54:07 8:4F 10MPH 1 Brd

Fig. 39. The H_s region (sticking within the weak but not strong backprojection).

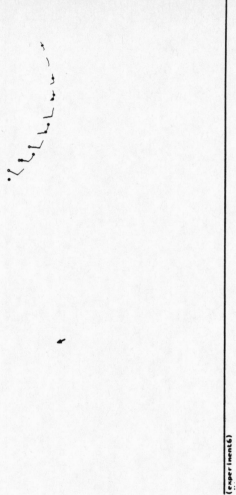

Fig. 40. Now assume that B can rotate when pushed (for figs. 40–48). Here we show the region within the forward projection (fig. 35) from which it it possible to exert positive torque on B. This region is called the *differential forward projection across J in the +α direction*.

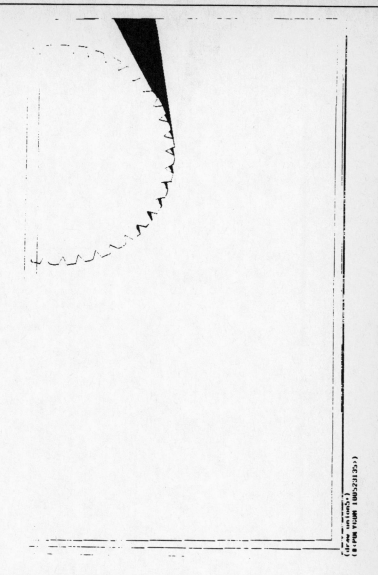

Fig. 41. The differential forward projection is propagated to the next slice in the $+\alpha$ direction. Here we take its forward projection in the next slice.

Fig. 42. Another view of fig. 41.

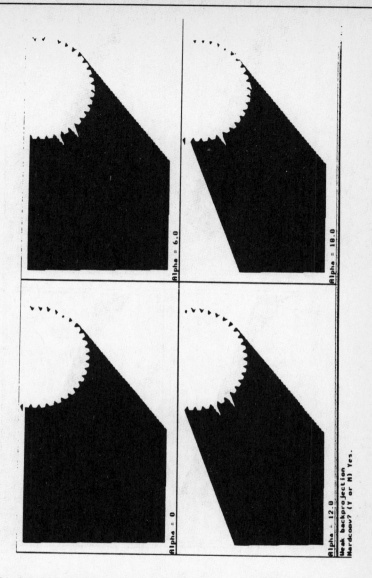

Fig. 43. In the next figures, B is permitted to rotate when pushed. The projection regions are computed across J by the propagation and union algorithm. We show four slices of generalized configuration space, at $\alpha = 0°, 6°, 12°$, and $18°$. The projections take into account possible rotation of B under pushing. Here the weak backprojections across slices are shown. The "spikes" represent regions from which jamming of the gears must occur.

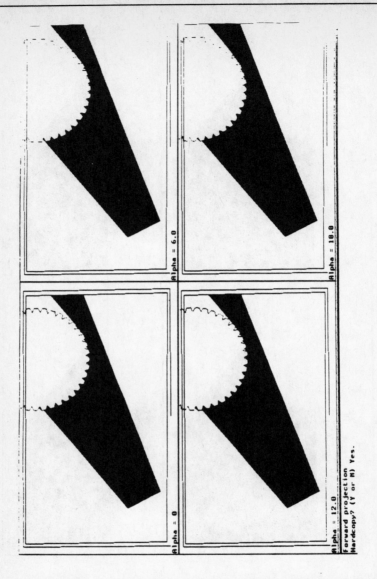

Fig. 44. The forward projections of the start region, propagated and unioned across slices.

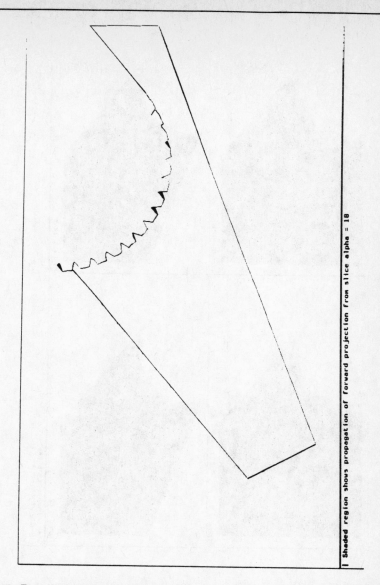

Fig. 45. Detail of the forward projection for $\alpha = 12°$. Note the effect of propagation in the clockwise-most region of the forward projection. This region can only
be reached when rotated to from neighboring slice. The shaded region shows the
portion of the forward projection which has been propagated by pushing from
slice $\alpha = 18°$.

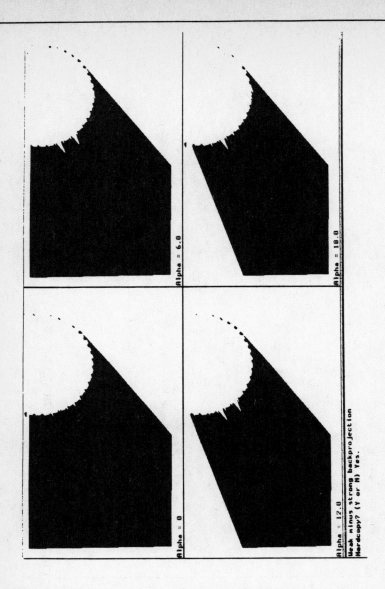

Fig. 46. The weak minus strong backprojections, propagated and unioned across slices.

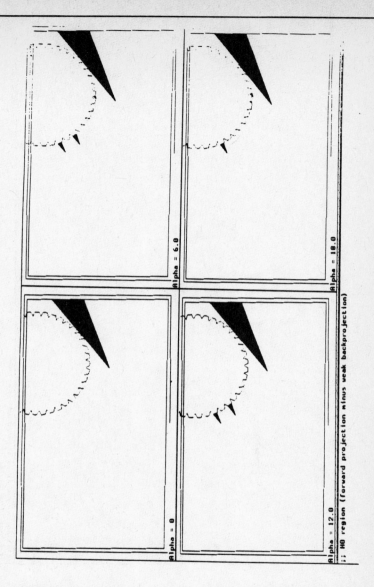

Fig. 47. The H_0 region (forward projection minus weak backprojection) across slices.

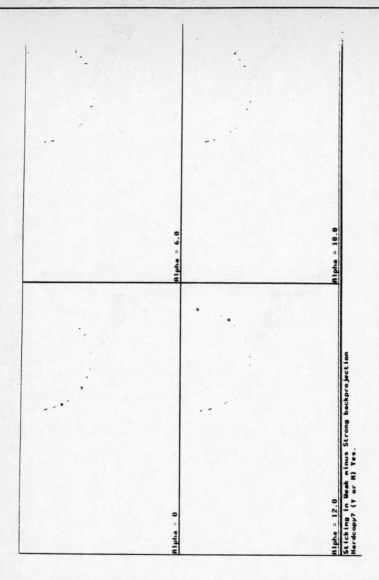

Fig. 48. The H_s region (sticking regions within the weak but not strong back-projection) across slices.

7. Implementing One-Step EDR Planning in LIMITED

In this section, we discuss a number of theoretical and practical issues relating to the construction and implementation of the one-step EDR planning algorithms in LIMITED. This discussion is the sequel to the informal description of one-step EDR planning in section 6. While these issues arise in implementing an EDR planner, they illustrate several interesting theoretical and practical points. They also introduce a series of more advanced concepts that are required to make the EDR theory rigorous.

7.1. The Search for a Strategy

Some comments are in order about the search for a commanded motion in LIMITED. First of all, the commanded motion generator is obviously trivial. The initial commanded motion LIMITED tries is obtained by subtracting the centroids of the start and goal regions. LIMITED then searches outwards on either side of this direction. Obviously, such a search strategy is not complete. Later, we will discuss precise, combinatorial algorithms for a complete search strategy using critical slices of the non-directional backprojection.

Second, since the search is relatively blind, it may take a while to converge. A better technique for generating commanded motions to try might involve using a path-planner with no uncertainty to suggest an initial path. However, the focus of this research is not on optimizing the search algorithm in the planner, but rather on testing the geometric characterization of EDR.

It is often possible to generate planning strategies that satisfy the EDR axioms trivially by *always* failing. For example, consider a strategy that moves directly away from the goal. While such a motion may be useful in multi-step EDR strategies (see below), we wish to disallow them for one-step EDR. This is done as follows: on one-step planning LIMITED discards all strategies whose forward projection does not intersect the goal. This heuristic ensures that the strategy has at least some chance of succeeding.

A better approach might be to consider the *size* of the intersection of the goal and the forward projection. Such a technique might be used to generate probabilistically optimal strategies. In particular, it would give a criterion for choosing between two EDR strategies. For example, it might be possible to place some probability distribution over the forward projection. Then the intersection could be integrated with respect to this distribution to determine the probability of reaching the goal. In addition, different sized velocity cones could be employed to generate forward projections of varying likelihood. To be more than a mathematical abstraction, such a technique requires a better understanding of the probabilistic characteristics of generalized damper control than are currently available; it is a promising direction for future research.

7.2. Termination using Contact and the Role of Time

In polyhedral environments with a bounding box, sticking termination is sufficient to ensure that all pure translations eventually terminate [Buckley]. Let us assume the sufficiency of sticking termination for the discussion below.

Recall step (4) of algorithm *1EDR* in sec. 6.2:

4. *Let ∂G and ∂H denote the set of obstacle edges within G and H, resp. Determine whether the regions ∂H and ∂G are distinguishable using sensors. If so, then v_θ^* yields one-step EDR strategy which recognizably terminates on an obstacle edge in G or H. The termination condition is contact with or sticking on a surface in G or H.*

If the termination condition can be "contact" as computed in step 4 then unless $G \cup H$ can be recognized using position and force sensing alone, a termination predicate with time-out must be employed. This is because it is insufficient to terminate on first contact; we must first know that the contact lies within $G \cup H$. Ensuring that this will be the case requires indexing the forward projection by time. (See [Erdmann] for a discussion of time-indexed forward projections). However if the contact regions of G and H are distinguishable, then so are the possible sticking regions, since these are contained in the contact regions. So if ∂G and ∂H are distinguishable using sensors, then so are $\mathrm{push}_\theta(G)$ and $\mathrm{push}_\theta(H)$. Hence v_θ^* yields a one-step EDR strategy which recognizably terminates by sticking in $\mathrm{push}_\theta(G)$ or $\mathrm{push}_\theta(H)$.

Thus if the distinguishability condition in step (4) is met, then the motion can be terminated either based on contact, once enough time has elapsed to ensure that $G \cup H$ has been entered, or using sticking, if the run-time executor does not have a clock. In fact, this is something of a relief, because time-indexed forward-projections appear hard to compute.

If sticking is not sufficient to terminate all motions, then termination predicates with time-out can be employed to ensure that all motions terminate somewhere. This is discussed further in sec. 8.3.

7.3. Employing History in EDR Planning

The forward projection was introduced by [Erdmann] to formalize the role of *history* in [LMT] guaranteed plans. He formalized the notion that by knowing where a motion began, a planner can obtain constraint on where the motion can terminate. This constraint can be very useful both in planning guaranteed and EDR strategies. We now describe two techniques where LIMITED uses history to constrain planning and aid distinguishability.

Throughout the rest of section 7, the goal G, the EDR region $H = H_0 \cup H_s$, and the forward projection $F_\theta(R)$ are all taken to lie in phase space. That is, they are position and velocity sets.

7.3.1 The Role of History in Constructing H_s

In general, LIMITED approximates preimages using backprojections. There are a few interesting points about computing this approximation. Recall that H_s denotes sticking regions within the weak minus strong preimage. To see that H_s is contained within $F_\theta(R)$, we must use the fact that preimages in fact depend on the start region R (see [LMT]), and that weak and strong preimages are contained within $F_\theta(R)$ [Erdmann]. We postpone further discussion of this point until sec. 8.1.

Now let K_s denote sticking regions within the weak minus strong *backprojection*. Now we ask: can H_s intersect the strong backprojection of G, $B_\theta(G)$? The answer is no. If x is in H_s, then sticking is possible there. Hence x cannot be in $B_\theta(G)$, since motions from x can stick there instead of reaching G. Thus, in particular, H_s does not intersect the set difference formed by the strong backprojection minus the strong preimage. Thus $H_s \subset K_s$ since backprojections are "upper bounds" on preimages.[6] Thus K_s is a conservative approximation to H_s. (By *conservative*, we mean that while the approximation may be larger than H_s, an algorithm approximating H_s by K_s will generate correct plans). However, we also have the inclusion

$$H_s \subset F_\theta(R) \cap K_s,$$

where R denotes the start region. This inclusion derives from the fact that, given that the motion must start in R, a strong preimage of G is contained within the intersection of the forward projection $F_\theta(R)$ and the strong backprojection $B_\theta(G)$. A similar containment holds for the weak preimage with respect to the forward projection and the weak backprojection $W_\theta(G)$. Hence, to construct an upper bound on H_s, we are simply required to compute all sticking regions within

$$F_\theta(R) \cap (W_\theta(G) - B_\theta(G)).$$

The advantage of using this tighter approximation is that H_s must be distinguishable from G in order for θ to yield an EDR strategy. Tighter approxima-

---

[6]By "upper bound" we mean that the backprojection (under θ) contains the preimage (under θ), for any goal.

tions heuristically result in a greater likelihood of distinguishability. Furthermore, the approximation is fully algorithmic, since projections and set differences can be computed by the exact plane-sweep algorithm described in sec. 6 .

The dependence of the preimage on R was noted first in [LMT] and later developed by [Erdmann], who also determined the inclusion of the preimage within the intersection of the forward and backprojections. This dependence is discussed in some detail in chapter III.

7.3.2 The Role of History in Distinguishing H from G

There is another case where intersection with the forward projection yields an advantage in distinguishability. In the development of EDR theory, we found that in an EDR strategy, it was necessary that H and G be distinguishable. This condition is supplanted by a tighter one in LIMITED, requiring only that H and

$$F_\theta(R) \cap G$$

be distinguishable. The justification is that it is unnecessary to be able to distinguish between *arbitrary* points of G and H. Instead, it suffices merely to distinguish between the *reachable* points. Again, this technique shrinks the size of the goal regions that must be distinguishable from H, which heuristically makes it easier for a strategy to meet the EDR criteria. Note that H does not need to be shrunk further, because it already lies within the forward projection.

7.4. *A Priori* Push-Forwards Based on Sticking

The push-forward operator $push_\theta(\cdot)$ is a restricted implementation of the general push-forward described in sections 4 and 10. It is called the *a priori push-forward based on sticking*. The difference is as follows. The theoretical *general* push-forward "decides" where the motion should terminate so that the motion strategy will terminate recognizably, the *a priori* push-forward computes where the motion will terminate given that *a priori* the termination condition is *sticking*.

7.5. Sticking as a Robust Subtheory of EDR

In the abstract EDR theory, one envisions the run-time termination predicate performing whatever computations are necessary to terminate a motion recognizably in G or H. That is, in principle, the planner decides what termination conditions are appropriate for a successful EDR strategy, and encodes them into the motion strategy. Of course, it is also the responsibility of the planner to verify that this encoding will always result in a distinguishable termination. In short, the abstract EDR theory can employ the full power of the [LMT] preimage framework to generate motion strategies.

However, LIMITED employs only certain restricted termination conditions, as we saw above. In particular, sticking is used in most experiments. This restricts the class of strategies LIMITED can generate. The restriction requires some justification, and that is the purpose of this section.

First, recall that in polyhedral environments with a bounding box, sticking termination is sufficient to ensure that all pure translations eventually terminate [Buckley]. In general, in this thesis we have made the heuristic assumption that motions can eventually be terminated via sticking. Failing this, we also entertain the weaker assumption that if sticking is insufficient, then time can be employed to wait until $G \cup H$ has been achieved before termination; see sec. 8.3.

To analyze the structure of sticking termination, let us introduce the following notation. If the robot recognizably achieves $G \cup H$, this means that the run-time executor can determine that G or H has been achieved, but cannot necessarily tell which of G or H has been entered. If the robot recognizably achieves $\{G, H\}$, then it can further distinguish which of G or H it has reached. $G \cup H$ is called the *union* while the set notation is called the *distinguishable union*.

Throughout this section we assume without loss of generality that the goal G is contained within the forward projection (see sec. 7.3 for justification). If this is not the case, then intersect them to obtain a new goal.

LIMITED tries to decompose this problem—of ensuring that all trajectories terminate recognizably in $\{G, H\}$—into two subproblems. The first is to ensure that the motion in fact terminates in $G \cup H$. That is, the problem is to determine that *at least* one of G or H has been achieved, although the robot may not know which. The second problem is to distinguish between G and H, once $G \cup H$ has been achieved.

Note that the first problem requires distinguishing between $G \cup H$ and its complement. Here is the key point:

- The construction of H guarantees tautologously that with sticking termination, $G \cup H$ will be recognizably achieved when the motion terminates. That is, with sticking termination, no motion can terminate outside of $G \cup H$.

This resolves the first subproblem. Thus

- *With sticking termination, all candidate one-step EDR strategies eventually terminate recognizably in $G \cup H$ (but not necessarily in $\{G, H\}$). Of these, all valid EDR strategies can distinguish between G and H after termination, and hence recognizably terminate in $\{G, H\}$.*

The second subproblem is how to distinguish between G and H once $G \cup H$ has been achieved. In developing the [LMT] framework for planning guaranteed strategies, [Erdmann] developed an elegant formalization of the question, "Using sensors and history, when can the termination predicate decide that a motion has recognizably entered a goal G_β?" The answer was as follows. Let R be the start region. The forward projection, $F_\theta(R)$ captures the notion of history: it is all positions and velocities that can be reached given that the motion started in R. At a particular instant t in time, let $B_{ep}(t)$ and $B_{ev}(t)$ be the sets of possible positions and velocities. These are the sensing uncertainty balls about a sensed position and velocity in phase space at time t. Thus sensing provides the information that the actual position and velocity must lie within the set $B_{ep}(t) \times B_{ev}(t)$. The forward projection further constrains the actual position and velocity to lie within $F_\theta(R)$. Thus the termination predicate can terminate the motion as having recognizably reached G when

$$F_\theta(R) \cap (B_{ep}(t) \times B_{ev}(t)) \subset G_\beta. \qquad (*)$$

Now, when is it the case that the termination predicate can distinguish which of G or H has been reached? Exactly when $(*)$ is true for G_β in $\{G, H\}$. However, in our case, sticking termination guarantees that the actual position and velocity lie within $G \cup H$. Furthermore, $G \cup H$ is a subset of the forward projection, and G and H are disjoint by construction. The forward projection provided no further constraint in distinguishing between G and H. Thus history plays no role in the run-time distinguishing actions of the robot executive; history has been pre-encoded into the structure of H. Hence, we can predict that the run-time executor can distinguish which of G or H has been achieved when the planner can predict that G and H are distinguishable using sensors alone. A procedure—albeit not completely general—for deciding this question was described in sec. 6.2.

7.5.1 Generalizations

There are several possible generalizations of these termination techniques. First, it may be possible for the run-time executor to use time to ensure that the motion terminates in $G \cup H$. That is, forward projections may, in principle, be indexed by time. Hence in $(*)$, $F_\theta(R)$ is replaced by $F_\theta(R, t)$, which is typically much smaller. $F_\theta(R, t)$ denotes the set of positions and velocities that are possibly achievable at elapsed time t, under motion θ, given that the motion started in R. The termination predicate in this case monitors a clock, in addition to position and velocity sensors. However, in this case, history (by which we mean $F_\theta(R, t)$) could be employed to distinguish G from H, even though the motion had terminated recognizably in $G \cup H$. The reason for this is that the time-indexed forward projection has not been pre-encoded into the structure of H. That is, H was constructed using the *timeless* forward projection, which the union of all time-indexed forward projections. Hence, we can summarize these observations as follows:

- *If a termination predicate without time uses sticking to terminate the motion, then distinguishing G from H is a history-free decision. However, for a termination predicate with a sense of time, the decision is not history-free.*

Thus sticking subtheory does not preclude more general termination techniques based on position, force, and time sensing. However, two computational issues become more difficult. First, sticking termination is a robust method for ensuring termination in $G \cup H$. With time termination, or more general position/force termination criteria, it is more difficult to ensure termination in $G \cup H$—although admittedly these criteria are more powerful. Second, after sticking termination, deciding between G and H is history-free. With more general termination predicates, history can provide extra constraint in distinguishing between G and H.

Finally, note that [Buckley] recognized the value of sticking termination when implementing an [LMT] planner for guaranteed strategies in $\Re^3$. His planner used sticking termination. In particular, he provided certain criteria for guaranteeing that a strategy eventually terminates in sticking. Buckley's criteria amount to ensuring that the environment is finite polyhedral, within a bounding polyhedral box.

7.5.2 Forward vs. Backward Chaining

One obvious disadvantage of sticking termination is that it is not complete. For example, a planner employing sticking termination exclusively will not be able to find strategies that require "stopping in mid-air", even when such strategies would be feasible given the position sensing accuracy of the robot. Sticking termination requires all strategies to "run aground", that is, to be in contact (and in fact, sticking) at termination time.

With more general position/force/time termination criteria, the requirement that motions must terminate in contact is relaxed. However, a forward-chaining planner (such as LIMITED) is still left with the problem of deciding where a motion should terminate in a multi-step strategy. That is, the decision problem involves existential quantification not only over the commanded directions, but also over all subsets of the forward projection corresponding to possible push-forwards. Put simply, a forward-chaining planner must not only guess the direction to command a motion, but must also guess where it terminates, before chaining ahead to the next motion. While the space of commanded motions may be realistically quantized and searched, the space of push-forwards may not be searched in this manner.

While LIMITED is a forward-chaining planner, the problem of existential quantification over the push-forward is finessed by restricting LIMITED to a few very simple termination conditions (there are only three; see sec. 6.2), one of which is sticking. Given these termination types, it is possible to generate the corresponding *a priori* push-forwards, and test them to see whether they yield an EDR strategy. For example, the push-forward for contact termination is simply the obstacle edges in the forward projection. The push-forward for sticking termination is the *a priori* push-forward based on sticking, which was discussed above.

More generally, it may be possible to define a parameterized family of termination predicates, each with an associated *a priori* push-forward. Each push-forward could then be tested for distinguishability. For example, consider the class of termination conditions

$$\{ \text{ "Terminate after } t \text{ seconds." } \mid t \geq 0 \}$$

An associated family of push-forwards might be the time-indexed forward projections

$$\{ F_\theta(R, t) \mid t \geq 0 \}.$$

However, the existential quantification over the push-forward in the decision problem for EDR planning is, in fact, an artifact of forward-chaining. We can see this by comparing and contrasting backchaining vs. forward-chaining in preimage planners for *guaranteed* strategies. In a backward-chaining planner, this extra computation is eliminated. The difference is as follows. Consider how a guaranteed-strategy preimage planner would construct a motion strategy $\theta_1, \ldots, \theta_n$ to achieve a goal G. θ_1 is the first motion in the plan, θ_n is the last. Consider the difference in how a forward-chaining planner and a backchaining planner would compute steps θ_i and θ_{i+1}:

- A forward-chaining planner must calculate where motion θ_i will terminate, since this termination region is the start region for the next motion, θ_{i+1}. Since this calculation involves some choice, it amounts to a formulation of the decision problem with existential quantification over the push-forward of motion θ_i. In a back-chaining planner, where the motion θ_i must terminate has already been computed: it is the next preimage with respect to θ_{i+1}, namely $P_{\theta_{i+1}}(P_{\theta_{i+2}}(\cdots (P_{\theta_n}(G))\cdots))$.

Thus we have seen why a back-chaining planner can (in principle) be complete for guaranteed strategies, while a forward-chaining planner cannot, unless it guesses push-forwards.

This suggests the following approach to EDR planning:

- Use a back-chaining planner to find a guaranteed strategy for *part* of the start region. Then extend it to an EDR strategy using forward-chaining verification.

This appears to be a reasonable heuristic approach. However, for EDR planning, it is still merely a halfway measure. While it removes from the EDR planner's responsibility the decision of where to terminate a motion within a subgoal, the problem remains of deciding where within the EDR region H a motion should terminate. This is one of the key theoretical questions in EDR; it is addressed at some length later. The computational solution seems to involve quantifying over push-forwards even when a combination backward- and forward-chaining planner is envisioned. LIMITED uses only forward-chaining for this reason. However, the combination back- and forward-chaining approach deserves more exploration. In particular, the backchaining first stage could be used to suggest and guide the search for good candidate EDR strategies. Randy Brost has reported[7] a backchaining planning algorithm which can generate multi-step plans in which each motion is a one-step EDR strategy.

---

[7][Personal Communication]. See also Brost's forthcoming Ph.D. thesis.

8. The Preimage Structure of EDR Regions

Our characterization of the EDR regions—and of EDR strategies in general—has been somewhat informal up to now. This is because we have not employed the full power of the preimage framework [LMT] in developing the model. In particular, we have not yet tied together the role of history and the definition of the EDR region H. This section remedies this deficiency. Recall our characterization of H as $H_0 \cup H_s$. Our definition of phase-space, and of the sticking region H_s must be be made more precise. That is the second goal of this section: to link the preimage concepts for representing strategies, with the phase-space concepts for representing error detection in generalized configuration space.

First, we briefly introduce some preimage notation. A formal review of [LMT,E] preimages can be found in an appendix. A key notion deals with recognizable termination in a collection of goals. We can illustrate this notion using a familiar example: for a goal G and an EDR region H, $\{G, H\}$ is a natural collection of goals to consider. We know that an EDR strategy recognizably terminates in some member of the collection. Below, we give a formal notation for this concept. However, the question of distinguishable collections of goals also arises in planning guaranteed strategies, as we shall see.

8.1. On the Recognizability of EDR regions

In section 7, we elaborated on the role of history, time, position-sensing, and force-sensing in motion termination and in distinguishing G from H. The role of history must be formalized further using the preimage framework. To this end, we now formalize the distinguishability requirements for G and H using preimages.

In section 2.1 it was observed that if the termination predicate can distinguish between the goal G and the EDR region H, then H is a good EDR region and an EDR strategy was in hand. Formally, we write this recognizability constraint as[8]

$$P_{\theta,R}(\{G, H\}) = R. \tag{3}$$

We say that the preimage (3) is taken *with respect to* R. (3) means that the (strong) preimage of the set of goals $\{G, H\}$, with respect to commanded velocity v_θ^*, is all of R. When we have a *set* of goals, the termination predicate must return *which* goal (G or H) has been achieved. This is different from $P_{\theta,R}(G \cup H)$, which means the termination predicate will halt saying "we've terminated in G or H, but I don't know which." The region R appears on both sides of (3) because the preimage depends on knowing where the motion started. This is a subtle point, see [LMT,E].

---

[8] We view $P_{\theta,R}$ as a map. In the informal development we denoted the image of this preimage map by P.

Thus solving preimage equations like (3) for R is like finding the fixed point of a recursive equation. Here, however, we know R, H, and G, so (3) is a constraint which must be true, rather than an equation to solve. Presumably (3) is easier to check than to solve for R; see [LMT,E].

With this understood, we can now characterize P and R' precisely (see fig. 26). This requires specifying the start regions :

$$R' = P_{\theta,R'}(G) \tag{4}$$
$$P = P_{\theta,F_\theta(R)}(G). \tag{5}$$

$\hat{P}$ is analogously defined by adding "hats" to the P's in (5).

8.1.1 The Most General Preimage Equation

We now introduce the most general form of the preimage equation. Suppose $\{\, G_\beta \,\}$ denotes a collection of goals, and $\{\, R_\alpha \,\}$ is a collection of start regions. Recall θ denotes the direction of the commanded motion. Most generally, the preimage equation is

$$P_{\theta,\{\, R_\alpha \,\}}(\{\, G_\beta \,\}) = \{\, R_\alpha \,\}.$$

This says that if the run-time executor knows that the robot is in some particular but arbitrary start region R in the collection $\{\, R_\alpha \,\}$, then if velocity v_θ^* is commanded, then the termination predicate is guaranteed to achieve some goal G in $\{\, G_\beta \,\}$, and, furthermore, it can recognize which goal has been achieved.

In chapter III, a detailed example using preimages is worked out. There, we solve a particular motion planning problem—grasp centering— with model error by solving the preimage equations. This example provides an illustration of planning using preimages. Both guaranteed and EDR strategies for this problem are developed.

8.2. The Structure of Goals in Phase Space

In this section, we examine the structure of phase space goals in some detail, using the general form of the preimage equations described above.

A goal in phase space is a region in Position-space $\times$ Velocity-space. A phase space goal is attained when the actual position and velocity can be guaranteed to lie in the region. We have actually been using phase space goals all along, since the

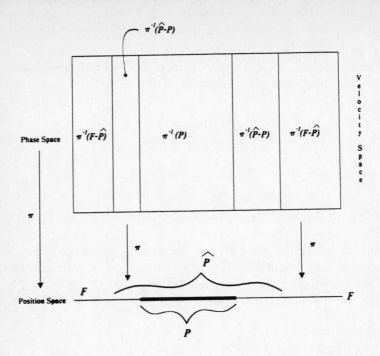

Fig. 49. Position-space is one dimensional. Therefore phase space, which is Position-space × Velocity-space, is 2-dimensional. The velocity "axis" is shown vertically. π projects a position and velocity to the position. We lift the strong preimage P to a cylinder $\pi^{-1}(P)$. We also obtain the cylinders over the weak but not strong preimage $\hat{P} - P$, and over the forward projection outside the weak preimage, $F - \hat{P}$.

velocity sensors are used to recognize goals. The introduction of arbitrary phase-space goals is problematic, see [Erdmann]. Here the goals are sufficiently simple that these dangers are avoided.

We begin with the simpler example. In fig. 26 we proposed a partition of the forward projection F of R into three regions:

Strong preimage, P

Weak but not strong preimage, $\hat{P} - P$

Forward projection outside the weak preimage, $F - \hat{P}$.

Here, the partition was "good" for the purposes of EDR for all velocities, and we could let H be the forward projection outside the weak preimage. We can extend this partition into phase space as shown in fig. 49. There is a natural projection π of Position-space × Velocity-space onto Position-space which sends a pair $(x, \text{velocity-at-}x)$ to its position x. Given a region U in position space, we can lift it to phase space to obtain $\pi^{-1}(U)$, the *cylinder* of all velocities over U. A point in $\pi^{-1}(U)$ is (x, v) where x is in U, and v is any velocity at x.[9]

We lift the partition by applying the inverse projection map to obtain a partition of phase space:

$$\text{Cylinder over strong preimage, } \pi^{-1}(P)$$
$$\text{Cylinder over weak but not strong preimage, } \pi^{-1}(\hat{P} - P)$$
$$\text{Cylinder over forward projection outside the weak preimage, } \pi^{-1}(F - \hat{P}).$$

See fig. 49. Now, the cylinder over G and the cylinder over $F - \hat{P}$ are the new goals in phase space. The latter cylinder is the *phase space EDR region* for fig. 26. Both are simply cylinders: all velocities are legal. [10]

Now we must deal with the tricky sticking region H_s in fig. 27. We begin by lifting the partition to phase space again (see fig. 50). Next, we "mark off" regions in the lifted partition to form a phase space EDR region, which we denote $\tilde{H}$. The entire cylinder over $F - \hat{P}$ is clearly in $\tilde{H}$, since its projection (under π) is outside the weak preimage. But the cylinder over H_s is not entirely within $\tilde{H}$: only sticking velocities over H_s are.

Formally, H_s is the set of all points x in the weak but not strong preimage, such that sticking can occur at x. We wish to distinguish the sticking velocities in H_s. Under generalized damper dynamics, these are essentially the zero velocities. Let $Z(H_s)$ denote the zero velocities over H_s, that is, the set of pairs $(x, 0)$ for x in H_s. This set is in phase space.[11] Then we see that $Z(H_s)$ is also in the phase space EDR region $\tilde{H}$. Thus $\tilde{H}$ is the union of the sticking velocities over H_s, and all velocities over the forward projection outside the weak preimage:

$$\tilde{H} = Z(H_s) \cup \pi^{-1}(F - \hat{P}). \tag{6}$$

---

[9] The cylinders may then be intersected with the forward projection of R (in phase space) to obtain more constraint. This may be done by first restricting the domain of π to the forward projection.

[10] The weak and strong preimage, and the forward projection are drawn Venn-diagrammatically in one-dimension.

[11] We could also let $Z(H_s)$ be the set of velocities over H_s which are smaller than some threshold.

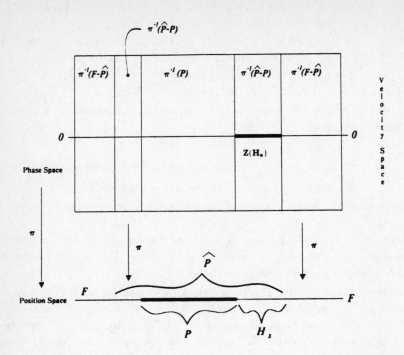

Fig. 50. Compare fig. 49. We have indicated the sticking region H_s in the weak preimage. The zero-velocities $Z(H_s)$ over H_s are in the cylinder over H_s. The EDR region $\tilde{H}$ is the union of $Z(H_s)$ and the shaded cylinders over the forward projection outside the weak preimage $F - \hat{P}$.

To use $\tilde{H}$ as an EDR region, we must now ensure that $\tilde{H}$ and the cylinder over G are distinguishable goals. This amounts to allowing goals in phase space—that is, allowing the preimage operator to take simple phase space goals as arguments, and rewriting (3) as

$$P_{\theta,R}(\{ \pi^{-1}(G), \tilde{H} \}) = R. \tag{3a}$$

The impact of (3a) is discussed in more detail in an appendix. One point is worthy of comment. If the strong preimage is known, the definition of (phase space) EDR regions is *constructive up to reachability*. By this we mean that when backprojections, set intersections and differences, and friction cones can be computed, then so can $\tilde{H}$. With $\tilde{H}$ is hand, we add the recognizability constraint (3a) to obtain an EDR strategy.

8.3. More on Weak Preimages

Armed both with the general form of the preimage equation, and with our new grasp of the structure of phase-space goals, we now examine the structure of the "weak but not strong preimage," $\hat{P} - P$ in more detail. It suggests a number of implementation issues. Consider figs. 27,28 once more. Suppose we have a trajectory originating in R, subject to the control uncertainty shown. We do not wish to terminate the motion while it remains in the weak preimage, since fortuitous sensing and control events could still force recognizable termination in G. However, we can terminate the motion as soon as we recognize egress from the weak preimage. This is why the forward projection outside the weak preimage is contained in the EDR region.

As we have seen, however, it is possible for a trajectory to remain within the weak but not strong preimage forever. For example, it can stick in H_s forever. To handle this case, we introduced phase space EDR goals.

There are other conditions under which a trajectory could stay in $\hat{P} - P$ forever: (a) if the environment is infinite, or $\hat{P} - P$ is unbounded. (b) The trajectory "loops" in $\hat{P} - P$ forever. (a) and (b) are qualitatively different from the case of sticking forever in H_s, because they require motion for infinitely long. In practice this may be handled by terminating the motion in $\hat{P} - P$ after a certain elapsed time. This is called "constructing termination predicates which time-out." In fact, this "solution" works for sticking in H_s also.

An alternative is to extend our earlier zero-velocity analysis to all of $\hat{P} - P$. That is, we terminate the motion in the weak but not strong preimage when the actual velocity is (close to) zero. Formally this rewrites (6) as

$$\tilde{H} = Z(\hat{P} - P) \cup \pi^{-1}(F - \hat{P}). \qquad (6a)$$

Both this and our formal handling of phase space goals for H_s (6) are subject to the "Rolles theorem bug." That is, a trajectory which "reverses direction" will have zero velocity at some point. Hence by (6, 6a) it will be judged to have stuck. This is undesirable. In practice this can be fixed by again requiring the trajectory to stick for some elapsed time. Time-out termination predicates have the following practical justification. We imagine some low-level control mechanism which detects sticking, and after a certain time interval freezes the robot at that configuration and signals termination. Presumably such a mechanism is designed to avoid damage to the robot from burning out its joint motors. It also avoids plans with long delays while the planner waits for the motion to slide again.

The role of time in constructing EDR regions can be formalized by explicitly introducing time into the goal specification. Thus, goals become regions in phase space-time; points in goals have the form (x, v, t), where x is a position, v a velocity, and t a time. Suppose given a goal G in generalized configuration space, we form a phase space-time goal which is the product of $\pi^{-1}(G)$ with a compact time interval. It seems that the EDR axioms are satisfiable by EDR regions which have the form of a product of (6) with a compact time interval. More study is required.

One also can conceive of alternative models for sticking behavior. H_s is all points in the weak but not strong preimage such that sticking *might* occur there. Note that we cannot guarantee that sticking will occur, since then the point would not be in the weak preimage. We could assume a probabilistic distribution of control velocities in B_{ec}. In this case we could infer that eventually, given an unbounded amount of time, a motion will be commanded which will cause sliding away from any point in H_s at which a trajectory originating in R sticks. In this case, the trajectory cannot stick forever in H_s. I don't think robot controllers reliably enforce probabilistic distributions of commanded velocities, even if "dithering" control strategies are employed. Even if they could, this model of sticking makes life easier, since it essentially eliminates the possibility of sticking forever in $\hat{P} - P$. We will not make this assumption here. It does not address with the problem of "looping forever" within $\hat{P} - P$ in finite environments. It seems that time-out termination predicates and/or velocity thresholding must be used to solve the looping problem. Both solutions seem inelegant; the issue is subtle and should be addressed further in future research (see chapter VI).

8.3.1 Summary

When the goal is specified in phase space-time as the product of a cylinder over a generalized configuration space goal with a compact time interval, our geometrical characterization of EDR satisfies the EDR axioms. Without time, or with goals of the form $\pi^{-1}(G) \times [t, \infty)$, the definition of $\tilde{H}$ does not completely fulfill the EDR axioms. This is because it is possible for motions sticking in H_s to eventually slide into the goal, violating the principle that no motion should be terminated as a failure while serendipitous goal achievement is still possible.

III. Multi-Step Strategies

In this chapter we explore multi-step strategy construction. Now, in principle, having reduced both model error and EDR to essentially "preimage-theoretic" equations, multi-step strategies could be synthesized by solving these preimage equations. While this is proved or at least implicit in previous work [LMT,Mason,E,D], it is far from obvious; furthermore, there are almost no published examples of such strategies. For this reason we begin by presenting a worked-out example of a motion plan using preimages. The motion problem is grasp-centering for a robot gripper in the presence of model error. Both guaranteed and EDR strategies are found by solving the preimage equations.

Preimages are a key underlying tool for the geometric EDR theory, and the [LMT] framework is in some sense a "universal" method for synthesizing multi-step strategies. However, the technique of solving the preimage equations is not computational. For this reason, we introduce a construction called the *push-forward*. Roughly speaking, the push-forward is that subset of the forward projection where the motion can terminate. Since push-forwards address termination whereas forward projections do not, we may regard them as "dual" to preimages. That is, push-forwards are to forward projections as preimages are to backprojections. Second, the push-forward permits us to develop rather simple algorithms for planning multi-step strategies. These algorithms have been implemented in LIMITED. While the push-forward method for multi-step strategy synthesis is algorithmic, it is less general than the full preimage method (solving the preimage equations). We characterize the loss of power in push-forward algorithms.

In chapter I we presented two EDR plans generated by LIMITED. These were the peg-in-hole insertion strategy with model error, and the gear-meshing plan. Both were two-step plans. We will go into more detail in describing how these plans were generated. The peg-in-hole plan used push-forward techniques. The gear plan used a seemingly unrelated technique called *failure mode analysis*. We describe failure mode analysis and algorithms for computing it.

Next, we will present a view of multi-step strategies which essentially unifies all these techniques. This is called the "weak" EDR theory. The motivation behind this theory is that when a motion terminates ambiguously, a subsequent motion may be synthesized which disambiguates the success or failure of the first. Oddly enough, it is not necessary for either motion individually to satisfy the EDR axioms. However, when taken together, the two-motion plan can often be considered "equivalent" to a one-step EDR strategy.

The weak EDR theory effectively defines some laws of "composition" that permit two single-step plans to be concatenated into a two-step plan satisfying the

EDR axioms. Hence it is often possible to construct multi-step plans that are EDR plans "globally" although not "locally". That is, considered as entire plans, they satisfy the EDR axioms; this is the "global" condition. However, "locally" they are not EDR plans, in that no single step is an EDR strategy. The key to pasting together non-EDR plans to make a global EDR strategy lies in defining certain local "niceness" conditions for how plans must mesh. These are called the *linking conditions*.

When we cross-reference figures in another chapter, we denote this by II.29 for figure 29 in chapter II, for example.

We remind the reader that starred sections may be skipped if desired.

9. Planning using Preimages: A Detailed Example

In this section we show how the [LMT] framework can be used to synthesize multi-step strategies. Here are the key points of this section:

- In principle, multi-step plans may be found by solving a family of preimage equations.
- While this was proved by [LMT,Mason,E], it is not obvious how to effect the solution. This example intends to elucidate the process.
- The technique is general enough to plan EDR strategies under model error, once we have cast both the problem of planning with model error and the EDR problem in an essentially "preimage-theoretic" form, as in [D] and chapter II.
- However, the technique of solving the preimage equations is not algorithmic.

Furthermore, preimages are a key underlying tool for the geometric EDR theory. It is necessary to make further acquaintance with preimages in order to continue our development of the EDR framework. To that end, this section presents a worked-out example of a motion plan using preimages. The motion problem is grasp-centering for a robot gripper in the presence of model error. The example illustrates the use of the preimage framework to derive a multi-step motion strategy in the presence of model error. The strategy employs time-sensing and force-sensing. This discussion is designed both as a tutorial in solving preimage equations for a motion plan, and as an introduction to the planning of multi-step strategies.

9.1. Example: Planning Grasp-Centering using Preimages

The remainder of this thesis builds on the preimage framework to develop the EDR theory. To make the framework more accessible, we provide here a fairly detailed description of a motion planning problem using preimages.[1]

We are now ready to work an example. We solve a particular motion planning problem with model error by solving the preimage equations. This example provides an illustration of planning using preimages. For simplicity, we initially address only the problem of finding a guaranteed strategy. Finding EDR strategies in this domain is discussed afterwards.

Consider the grasp-centering problem shown in fig. 1. The task is to center the robot gripper over the block D. The gripper can translate but not rotate in the plane. In its start position, the gripper is somewhere over D, such that the bottom

---

[1]This problem arose in discussions with Tomás Lozano-Pérez, John Canny, and Mike Erdmann.

of the fingers FA and FB are below the top of D. The width of D is unknown, but must be less than the distance between FA and FB. We assume D is fixed (it cannot be accidentally pushed).

Hence we can regard this as a planning problem with model error. C is taken to be the cartesian plane, and J is a bounded interval of the positive reals. Our first question is, what does the generalized configuration space look like? This is easily answered by considering the motion planning problem in fig. 2. The problem is to find a motion strategy for a point robot so that it can achieve a goal exactly halfway between the blocks A and B. The distance α between A and B is unknown and positive. The point robot is known to start between A and B. Again, the point can translate in the plane. The distance α is the model error parameter. It is easy to see that the problems in figs. 1 and 2 are equivalent.

However, we already know what the generalized configuration space for fig. 2 looks like. It was discussed at length in chapter II, and is shown in fig. II.14. Hence our example is a planning problem in a familiar generalized configuration space.

Next, we assume that the robot has perfect control, perfect velocity sensing, and a perfectly accurate sense of time. However, it has infinite position sensing error. [2]

Now, since the gripper starts over D with the bottom of the fingers below the top of D, and since the robot has perfect control, it suffices to consider the x axis of C. Since the y axis can be ignored, we develop our example in the plane, that is, in the generalized configuration space where C and J are both one-dimensional. This 2D generalized configuration space is shown in fig. 3, which is essentially an x-J cross-section of fig. II.16, holding y constant with α constrained to be positive. In fig. 3, L and R are left and right obstacle edge boundaries generated by A and B. The goal is the line in free-space bisecting L and R. The start region T is the triangular region in free-space between L and R. (T is the convex hull of L and R).

Now, since motion across J is not permitted, all motions are parallel to the x axis, that is to say, horizontal in fig. 3. There are only two kinds of motions the planner can command. Let $+$ denote a motion to the right, and $-$ a motion to the left. We assume the robot has perfect control over the magnitude as well as the direction of the commanded velocity.

See fig. 3. Now, if α is a point on the J axis, let E_α be the point on the left obstacle edge L with J coordinate α. We will denote the collection of all such points on L by $\{E_\alpha\}$. Let S_α denote the maximal line segment within T containing E_α and parallel to G. Formally, if E_α has coordinates (x, α), then S_α is the line segment extending from E_α to (x, d) where d is an upper bound on the distance between A and B. We denote the collection of all lines S_α by $\{S_\alpha\}$.

---

[2] This example is easily generalized to non-zero control, time-sensing, and force-sensing error, and finite position-sensing error. This requires giving the goal non-empty interior, however.

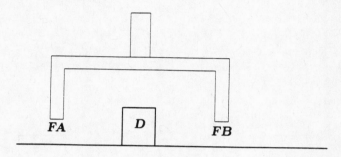

Fig. 1. The grasp centering problem. The width of the block D on the table, and the position of the gripper are only known approximately.

At this point we are prepared to derive a motion strategy for centering the grasp, that is, for attaining G from T. The strategy has three steps. The termination conditions for the motions involve time- and force-sensing. Here is the motion strategy in qualitative terms:

Strategy Guarantee-Center

1. *Command a motion to the right. Terminate on the right edge R based on force sensing.*
2. *Command a velocity of known magnitude to the left. Terminate when in contact with the left edge L, using force sensing. Measure the elapsed time of the motion. Compute the distance traversed. This gives exact knowledge of where the motion terminated on L. The effect of this step is to measure the distance α between the blocks.*
3. *Move distance $\frac{\alpha}{2}$ to the right, terminating in G based on time sensing.*

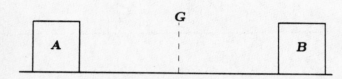

Fig. 2. An equivalent problem. A point robot must be navigated halfway between the blocks A and B. The distance between A and B is not known. The robot has force sensing, and a clock. However, it has poor position sensing. We regard C as $\Re^2$ and J as the bounded interval $(0, d]$ for d positive. The generalized configuration space for this problem is the same as in fig. II.16, for the positive values in J.

We now derive this strategy by solving the preimage equations for the motion planning problem.

First, note that if the run-time executive knows that the robot is inside a *particular* S_α, then G can be reliably achieved by commanding a motion to the right. Since the robot has perfect control and time sensing, the motion can be terminated after moving distance $\frac{\alpha}{2}$, that is, exactly when the line G is achieved. Using the preimage notation, we write this as

$$P_{+,\{S_\alpha\}}(G) = \{S_\alpha\}. \tag{1}$$

Next, we take the collection $\{S_\alpha\}$ as a set of subgoals, and try to find a motion that can recognizably attain this collection, and, furthermore, can distinguish which

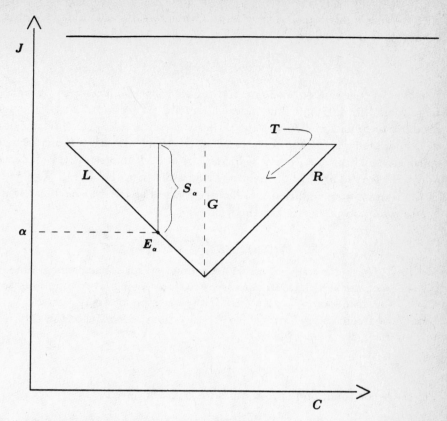

Fig. 3. Assuming that the gripper fingers are initially lower than the top of the block D, the y dimension can effectively be ignored. This allows us to examine a cross-section of fig. II.16. We treat C as the x axis of motion freedom, yielding a 2D $C \times J$ planning space. L and R are obstacle boundaries in generalized configuration space . The goal is the bisector G between L and R in free-space. The start region T is the triangular region between L and R. E_α is a point on L. S_α is a line in T parallel to G and containing S_α.

S_α the motion achieves. Consider a leftward motion starting from anywhere on the right edge R. The robot does not know where on R the motion starts, however. To recognizably achieve some S_α, such a motion should move leftward, and terminate when force-sensing indicates that L has been reached. If the termination predicate measures the elapsed time of the motion, and knows the magnitude of the commanded velocity, then it can recognize which point E_α has been reached, and hence which subgoal S_α has been achieved. Writing this down in preimage equations,

$$P_{-,R}(\{\, S_\alpha \,\}) = P_{-,R}(\{\, E_\alpha \,\}) = R. \qquad (2)$$

Finally, the right edge R may be achieved from anywhere within the start region

T by moving rightward, and terminating when force sensing indicates contact. This is simply

$$P_{+,T}(R) = T. \tag{3}$$

It is instructive to examine the termination conditions for motions (1)–(3). In motion (1), only the time-indexed forward projection $F_+(S_\alpha, t)$ is relevant to deciding termination. The motion terminates when $F_+(S_\alpha, t) \subset G$. Motion (3) can be terminated using pure force sensing. It could also be terminated using time, since there exists some t for which $F_+(T, t) = R$. In motion (2), both force sensing and time are required to terminate within a distinguishable E_α. The general form of the termination condition for all three cases is as follows. Recall that in general, the termination predicate has the form

$$F_\theta(U, t) \cap \big(B_{ep}(t) \times B_{ev}(t)\big) \subset G_\beta$$

for a goal G_β and a start region U. (Assume that all subgoals have been lifted into phase space; see sec. 8.2). In our case, position sensing error is infinite, so $B_{ep}(t)$ is $C \times J$. Let us denote $(C \times J) \times B_{ev}(t)$ by the simpler expression $B_v(t)$. Then the termination conditions for motions (1)–(3) are as follows. For the first motion (3), to terminate, we must have

$$F_+(T, t) \cap B_v(t) \subset R. \tag{4}$$

For the second motion (2) to terminate, we must have

$$F_-(R, t) \cap B_v(t) \subset S_\alpha \tag{5}$$

for some S_α. We think of the termination predicate as "returning" this S_α. Finally, for termination of the last motion (1), we must have

$$F_+(S_\alpha) \cap B_v(t) \subset G, \tag{6}$$

where the S_α in (6) is the same as the one returned by the termination predicate after the second motion as the satisfying assignment for (5).

Finally, note that time is the source of some complexity in this example. This complexity might be removed by employing a distance sensor instead. The output of such a sensor could be modeled as position sensing in J. The sensing action in J would entail measuring the distance between A and B. This relaxes the assumption of no position sensing in the J dimensions, but such modification to the generalized configuration space framework is trivial. With this modification, B_{ep} is simply regarded as a product of a position sensing ball in C and a position sensing set in J.

This concludes the example. We have shown how to derive a multi-step guaranteed motion strategy in the presence of model error. The strategy was derived by solving the preimage equations in generalized configuration space for the motion plan. These preimage equations made the role of time- and force-sensing explicit in deriving conditions for distinguishable termination in a collection of subgoals. With this example in mind, the reader should be well-equipped to wade into the remainder of this thesis.

9.1.1 An EDR Strategy for Grasp-Centering

We now generalize the grasp-center example and show how to develop an EDR strategy for this problem.

Assume that the radius of position sensing uncertainty is larger than the diameter of T, but not infinite.[3] Furthermore, assume that α, the distance between A and B, can be zero (but not negative) in the above example. That is, D can be too big to grasp. Hence the hole between A and B can close up, as in fig. II.16. Assume that the gripper starts above the height of the block D, in the circular region R in fig. II.15. Generalize the discussion of preimages above to describe an EDR strategy using preimages. We will need to consider the y dimension of motion freedom as well, in the 3D generalized configuration space shown in fig. II.16, but only the non-negative α in J. Note that EDR is "required" here, since if α can be zero, there exists no guaranteed strategy.

Let us rename the circular start region in fig. II.15 to be U, and continue to use R for the right edge in fig. 3. Assume that the x-J slice of generalized configuration space in fig. 3 is taken at $y = 0$, i.e., at the level of the table, and that under the commanded motion v_θ^*, shown in fig. II.15, sliding occurs on all horizontal and vertical surfaces. However, clearly sticking will occur under v_θ^* on the concave left edge L between A and the table.

Now, let H be as in fig. II.24. Here is the EDR strategy in qualitative terms:

Strategy EDR-Center

E1. *From U, command the motion v_θ^*. Terminate on the left edge L based on sticking, or in H based on time.*

E2. *If H is attained, signal failure. Otherwise, go to step (1) of strategy* Guarantee-Center.

---

[3] This assumption is not necessary, but it simplifies our discussion somewhat.

Now, since $H_s = \emptyset$, the preimage equation[4] (II.3a) for step (E1) simply reduces to

$$P_{\theta,U}(\{L, H\}) = U. \tag{7}$$

At this point, the remainder of the strategy may be developed in the x-J slice shown in fig. 3. To finish the preimage characterization of the EDR strategy, we must replace eq. (3), which characterizes the first step (1) of strategy *Guarantee-Center*, by

$$P_{+,L}(R) = L. \tag{8}$$

Note that (8) is actually a logical consequence of (3), since L is a subset of T. Analogously, (4) must be changed by replacing T by L. The remainder of the preimage equations (1)–(2) and (5)–(6) remain unchanged.

9.2. Solving the Preimage Equations is General but Not Computational

This example shows how multi-step EDR strategies under model error can be generated by solving a family of preimage equations. However, the technique is not an algorithm. We do not claim that such an algorithm could not be developed, but merely that as described above and in [LMT,Mason,E], the method is not (yet) computationally effective.[5] The first reason it is non-computational is that the number of subgoals $\{E_\alpha\}$ and $\{S_\alpha\}$ is infinite. The second, and more important reason is that solving the preimage equation is, as stated, a decision problem in second-order set theory. Even if the sets are, say, algebraic, this theory is undecidable. However, there may exist a reformulation of the problem rendering it decidable. Below we describe one such reformulation, using push-forwards, which can be used in effect to solve certain "simple" preimage equations and hence to generate a restricted class of EDR plans.

---

[4] See sec. 8.2.

[5] However, note that Erdmann's techniques of approximating preimages by backprojections may lead toward a fully-algorithmic method.

10. Push-Forwards: A Simple Generalization to n-Step EDR Strategies

The generalized preimage framework [LMT,Mason,E,D] gives a kind of "universal" method for generating multi-step EDR strategies. However, the technique of solving the preimage equations is not algorithmic—it is more like doing a proof by hand. For this reason, we introduce the *push-forward* technique for synthesizing multi-step strategies. While considerably less general than solving the full preimage equations, it leads to rather simple multi-step strategy-generation algorithms, which were implemented in LIMITED. The push-forward technique is powerful enough to generate an EDR plan for the peg-in-hole insertion strategy with model error described in chapter I. However, it is not general enough to solve all steps of the grasp-centering example discussed above. This gives us a measure of the relative power of push-forward vs. preimage equation techniques.

This section first discusses the push-forward technique for synthesizing n-step EDR strategies in some detail. When we cross-reference figures in another chapter, we denote this by II.29 for figure 29 in chapter II, for example.

We first review the "Twin Universe" example (3) (figs. II.29,II.30), highlighting a subtle recognizability issue not emphasized in the prelude. However, this review may be skipped at first reading if you already have example (3) firmly in mind.

A Review of the "Twin Universe" Example (3)

Consider fig. II.29. Here there are two possible universes, both in the plane, so J is the two element discrete set, $\{1,2\}$. The start region is the union of R_1 in universe 1, and R_2 in universe 2. The goal exists in universe 1 but not in universe 2. There is no one-step EDR strategy which, from the start region, can guarantee to achieve G or recognize that we are in universe 2. In particular, there is no one-step EDR strategy which can be derived from the motion v_θ^*.

However, there clearly exist multi-step EDR strategies. We will construct one as follows. Recall that to construct one-step EDR strategies, we took as data a goal, a start region R, a commanded motion θ, and the preimage of the goal under θ. Given this data we constructed an EDR region. From the EDR region, we attempted to construct an EDR strategy that achieved the distinguishable union of the goal *or* the EDR region. Now, why does this fail in fig. II.29? To answer this question, let us consider what the motion θ was supposed to achieve in universe 1. There is an 8-step plan in universe 1 which recognizably achieves G from start region R_1. It is obtained by back-chaining preimages in universe 1. The plan moves from R_1 to the region S_1 under v_θ^*. Then it slides along the top surface to vertex

f. Next it slides to vertex e. It slides to the successive vertex subgoals d through a, and then a horizontal sliding motion achieves the goal G.

The strategy θ is guaranteed to achieve the surface S_1 from start region R_1. Suppose we try to extend it to an EDR strategy with start region the union of R_1 and R_2. The EDR region is then simply the (cylinder over the) forward projection of the "bad" region, $F_\theta(R_2)$. (See fig. II.29). There is no way that the termination predicate can distinguish between the forward projection of R_1 and the forward projection of R_2, hence no EDR strategy from θ exists.

We can easily construct a 2-step EDR strategy, however. First, we execute motion θ from the union of R_1 and R_2. This achieves a motion into S_1 in universe 1, or into S_2 in universe 2. The termination predicate cannot distinguish which has been attained. Suppose the second motion in the 8-step plan is v_ψ^* (see fig. II.29), and is guaranteed to achieve the vertex subgoal f from start region S_1. We will try to construct an EDR strategy out of this second motion. Take as data: the subgoal f, the start region $S_1 \cup S_2$, the "southwest" motion ψ, and the preimage of f under ψ.[1] The EDR region for these data is the forward projection of S_2 under ψ (see fig. II.30). Presumably this EDR region is (eventually) distinguishable from f, and so we have constructed an EDR strategy at the second step. After executing the second step, we either terminate the motion as a failure, or proceed to vertex e, and eventually to the goal.

10.1. Generalization: Push-Forwards

Now, let us attempt to capture the salient aspects of the n-step EDR strategy construction. We take as data an n-step plan, with start region R_1. The actual start region is some larger region, say, R. Above, we had R as the union of R_1 and R_2. The first motion in the plan is guaranteed to achieve some subgoal S_1 from R_1. Using this first motion from start region R, we try to construct an EDR region H_1, and a one-step EDR strategy that either achieves S_1 or signals failure by achieving H_1. If this succeeds, we are, of course, done.

Suppose we cannot distinguish between H_1 and S_1. In this case, we want to execute the first motion "anyway," and terminate "somewhere" in the union of S_1 and H_1. The termination predicate cannot be guaranteed to distinguish which goal has been entered.

This "somewhere" is called the *push-forward* of the first motion from R. The push-forward is a function of the commanded motion θ, the actual start region

---

[1] While S_1 is the preimage of f under ψ with respect to start region S_1, the preimage with respect to the entire forward projection of $S_1 \cup S_2$ includes the top edge between S_1 and f. See sec. 8.

R, the region R_1 from which θ is guaranteed, and the subgoal S_1.[2] A particular type of push-forward is defined formally in an appendix; we describe it informally below. In example (3), the push-forward (under θ) of R_2 is S_2. The push-forward of $R_1 \cup R_2$ is $S_1 \cup S_2$. The push-forward is similar to a forward projection, except that it addresses the issue of termination. In example (3), informally speaking, the push-forward from the region R (under some commanded motion θ) is the result of executing θ from R and seeing what happens. It is defined even when the strategy θ is only guaranteed from some subset (R_1) of R.

Having terminated in the push-forward of R (the union of S_1 and S_2 above), we next try to construct a one-step EDR strategy at the second motion of the n-step plan. The data are: the next subgoal T_1 after S_1 in the plan, the actual start region $S_1 \cup S_2$, the second commanded motion in the plan, and the preimage of T_1 under this motion.[3] This defines a formal procedure for constructing n-step EDR strategies. At each stage we attempt to construct a one-step EDR strategy; if this fails, we push-forward and try again.

Actually, this description of the procedure is not quite complete. At each step we construct the EDR region as described. However, the one-step strategy we seek must achieve the distinguishable union of the EDR region and *all unattained subgoals* in the plan. That is, the EDR motion must distinguishably terminate in the EDR region, or the next subgoal, or *any* subsequent subgoal. This allows serendipitous skipping of steps in the plan.

By considering different data, that is, quantifying over all motions at each branch point of the n-step strategy, we can in principle consider all n-step strategies and define non-directional EDR strategies. This is at least as difficult as computing n-step non-directional preimages. If we wish to consider plans of different lengths, we must also quantify over all n. Needless to say, the branching factor in the back-chaining search would be quite large.

10.2. More on the Push-Forward

The problem of defining the push-forward may be stated informally as follows: "Where should the motion be terminated so that later, after some additional number of push-forwards, a one-step EDR strategy may be executed."

Many different push-forwards can be defined. Using the notation above, note the motion is not even guaranteed to terminate when executed from R: it is only guaranteed from R_1. This means that velocity-thresholding and time may be necessary in the termination predicate. There are other difficulties: for example, *a priori*

---

[2] Of course, it also depends on the termination predicate, sensing and control characteristics, etc.

[3] The preimage is with respect to the forward projection of the actual start region $S_1 \cup S_2$.

it is not even necessary that entry into the union of the subgoal S_1 and the EDR region H_1 be recognizable. Thus defining the push-forward is equivalent to defining where in $S_1 \cup H_1$ the motion can and should be terminated. (However, see note (1) in the appendix).

Depending on that push-forward is employed, we may or may not obtain an n-step EDR strategy. It is possible to define constraints on the push-forward that must be satisfied to ensure that a strategy will be found if one exists. These constraints are given in an appendix. While in the appendix we can give equations that the push-forward must satisfy, at this time a constructive definition is not known. This situation is similar to, and possibly harder than the problem of solving the general pre-image equation.

10.3. An Approximation to the Push-Forward

We may have to approximate the desired push-forward. We give such an approximation here. In general, it does not satisfy the constraints given in the appendix. We provide it to show what the push-forwards alluded to above are like. Such approximate push-forwards may prove useful in approximating the desired push-forward. The issue deserves more study. Since this approximate push-forward is incomplete, the reader should consider its description here as illustrative of the research problem, and not as an endorsement.

The push-forward employed in example (3) was formed by "executing the strategy anyway, and seeing where it terminated." How do we formalize this idea? Consider the termination predicate as a function of the starting region, the initial sensed position, the commanded velocity, the goal(s), and the sensor values. The sensor values are changing; the predicate monitors them to determine when the goal has been reached. Now, if the termination predicate "knew" that in example (3) the start region was the union of R_1 and R_2, then the first motion strategy θ could never be terminated: the predicate could never ensure that the subgoal S_1 had been reached. This is simply because S_1 and S_2 are indistinguishable. But if we "lie" to the termination predicate and tell it that the motion really started in R_1, then the predicate will happily terminate the motion in $S_1 \cup S_2$, thinking that S_1 has been achieved. Viewing the termination predicate as a function, this reduces to calling it with the "wrong" arguments, that is, applying it to R_1 instead of $R_1 \cup R_2$. The push-forward we obtain is "where the termination predicate will halt the motion from all of $R_1 \cup R_2$, thinking that the motion originated in R_1." S_2 is obtained as the set of places outside of S_1 where the lied-to termination predicate can halt.

Even formalizing the construction of this simple push-forward is subtle; details are given in an appendix. While this approximate push-forward is incomplete, it does suffice for a wide variety of EDR tasks. The approximate push-forward captures the intuitive notion of "trying the strategy anyway, even if we're not guaranteed to be in the right initial region." It is incomplete because it fails to exploit sufficiently the geometry of the forward projection of the "bad" region. Better push-forwards must be found; this one is merely illustrative of the problems.

10.4. Example: Multi-step EDR Plan for Peg-in-Hole with Model Error

The advantage of the push-forward technique is that it can be made computational. We now give LIMITED's algorithm for generating multi-step strategies using push-forwards, and describe an experiment which used this method.

Recall chapter I, figs. 6-16, which described a two-step EDR plan for a peg-in-hole plan with 3 DOF model error. Here is how this multi-step strategy was generated:

Algorithm Multi

1. *First, try to generate a one-step EDR strategy using the algorithm in sec. 6.3. Suppose this fails. Then:*
2. *Generate a commanded velocity v_θ^*, such that the forward projection of the start region intersects the goal in some slice.*
3. *Compute the EDR region H for v_θ^*.*
4. *Compute the sticking push-forward of the motion, $R_1 = \text{push}_\theta(G \cup H)$.*
5. *Using R_1 as the start region, generate a one-step EDR strategy using the algorithm in sec. 6.3.*

Of course, in LIMITED the computation is memoized so that the projection and EDR regions computed in step (1) are not recalculated in steps (2) and (3). Obviously, we can extend this algorithm to generate longer strategies which push-forward several times and finally terminate in a single-step EDR strategy.

Now, LIMITED is a multi-resolution planner. The algorithm outlined above generates a multi-step strategy at a single resolution. The *resolution* of planning is simply the set of α values in which slices are taken. A resolution S_1 is *finer* than S_2 if it contains more slices. The multi-resolution outer loop works like this:

M1. *At a coarse resolution, generate a multi-step EDR strategy $\theta_1, \ldots, \theta_n$ using the forward-chaining single-resolution algorithm above.*
M2. *Select a finer resolution. Use the directions $\theta_1, \ldots, \theta_n$ as a suggested strategy and attempt to verify that it is an EDR strategy at the finer resolution.*

M3. *If $\theta_1, \ldots, \theta_n$ is not an EDR strategy at the finer resolution, try to modify it so that it is, by using $\theta_1, \ldots, \theta_n$ as suggested directions, and searching nearby directions at all levels.*

The process terminates when the resolution is finer than some predetermined level.[4] The critical slice method described in chapter II may be one way to obtain such an *a priori* bound and know that it is sufficient. In LIMITED, however, the bound is a user input because otherwise the number of slices required would be prohibitive.

In the peg-in-hole example there were 3DOF of model error: the *width* of the hole, the *depth* of the chamfers, and the *orientation* of the hole. The resolutions used in planning the two-step strategy were as follows:

R1. Holding orientation fixed, 4 slices of the depth × width axes.

R2. Holding orientation fixed, 16 slices of the depth × width axes.

R3. Holding orientation fixed, 72 slices of the depth × width axes.

R4. 100 slices of the depth × width × orientation axes.

The figures show details of the slices and the plan.

10.5. The Loss of Power with Push-Forward Techniques

While push-forwards permit us to develop simple algorithms for generating multi-step strategies, clearly these algorithms are theoretically less powerful than solving the preimage equations in full generality. We now attempt to give an intuitive characterization of the loss of power. In particular, push-forwards are general enough for the peg-in-hole EDR strategy with model error. However, they are not general enough to generate the grasp-centering plan. We now discuss where in the grasp-centering example the push-forward techniques are inadequate. The key point is this: if each commanded motion and termination condition could be non-deterministically "guessed," and a push-forward for each motion and termination condition could be computed, then in the grasp-center example this would suffice to generate a strategy. However, the push-forward algorithms we have developed are not powerful enough to do this.

First, let us derive the push-forwards of each motion in strategies *EDR-Center* and *Guarantee-Center*. Recall that *E1* is the first step of the EDR plan, and motions 1, 2, and 3 are steps in the (subsequent) guaranteed plan. In the third column we note whether or not the push-forward technique is computationally effective for this motion.

---

[4] Or, when at some level, no EDR strategy can be found.

Motion	Push − Forward	Computational?
$E1$	$\{ L, H \}$	yes
1	R	yes
2	$\{ E_\alpha \}$	no
3	G	no

The push-forwards for motions $E1$ and 1 can be computed using the algorithms of sec. 6.2 and algorithm *Multi* above. In motion $E1$, L may be found using sticking termination. H may be found using time, or position and force sensing termination. In motion 1, R may be found using contact, or sticking termination. However, our algorithms cannot compute the push-forward $\{ E_\alpha \}$, which contains an infinite number of components. Furthermore, we have not developed algorithms for computing push-forwards based on time-termination (except for elapsed time termination, of the form "terminate anytime after t seconds"). Thus the push-forward G for the last motion cannot be computed by our algorithms either.

10.5.1 Discussion

Let us pause to review. We first described a fully-general, but non-computational technique for generating multi-step strategies. This method—solving the preimage equations—was applied to the grasp-centering example. Next the push-forward techniques were introduced as a computational, although less powerful approach to the synthesis of multi-step strategies. Push-forward algorithms were described, and we saw how LIMITED used these techniques to generate a two-step plan for the peg-in-hole problem with model error. Finally, we discussed the limitations of the push-forward techniques. We saw that they were not powerful enough to solve the grasp-center problem in its entirety. By describing an experiment where push-forwards suffice, and showing an example where they are insufficiently general, we have tried to give an intuitive but fairly precise characterization for the relative power of push-forwards.

124

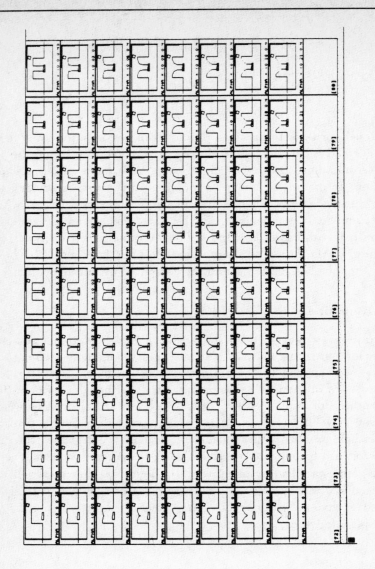

Fig. 4. Configuration space slices at resolution R3: holding orientation fixed, 72 slices of the depth × width axes.

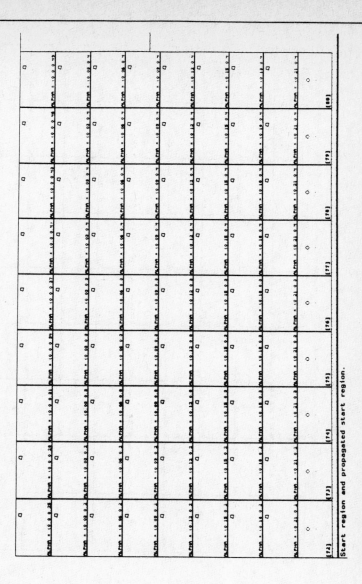

Fig. 5. Start region in each slice. (At resolution R3).

126

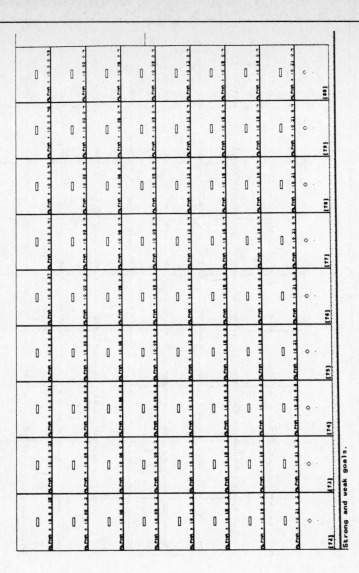

Fig. 6. Goal region in each slice. (At resolution R3).

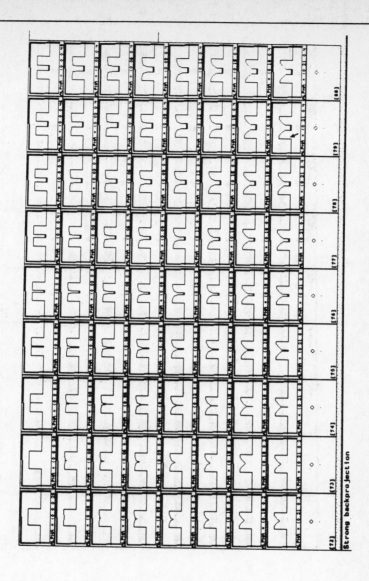

Fig. 7. Strong backprojection of goal under motion θ_1. (At resolution R3).

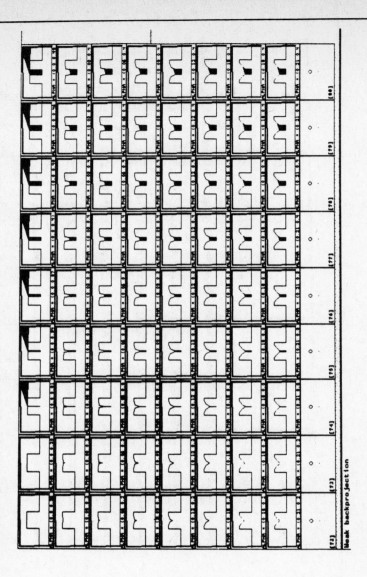

Fig. 8. Weak backprojection of the goal under motion θ_1. (At resolution R3).

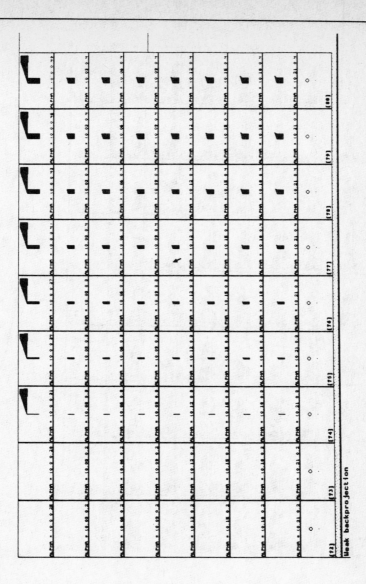

Fig. 9. Weak backprojection of the goal under motion θ_1. Obstacles not shown. (At resolution R3).

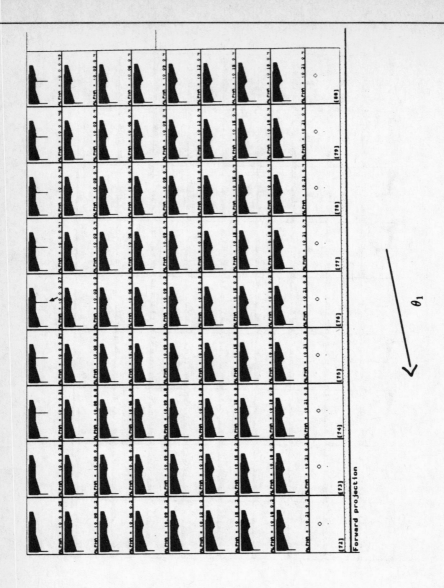

Fig. 10. Forward projection of start region under motion θ_1. Obstacles not shown. The arrow shows an edge of the forward projection that reached the goal. (At resolution R3).

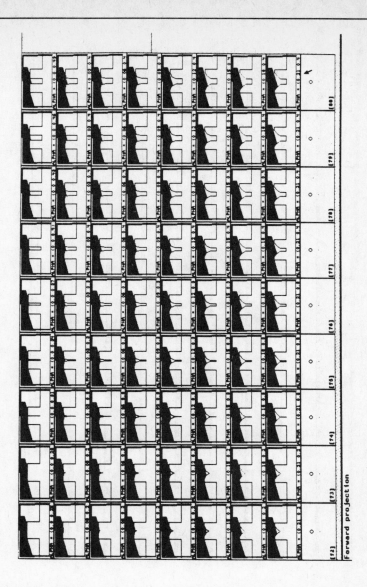

Fig. 11. Forward projection of the start region under motion θ_1. (At resolution R3).

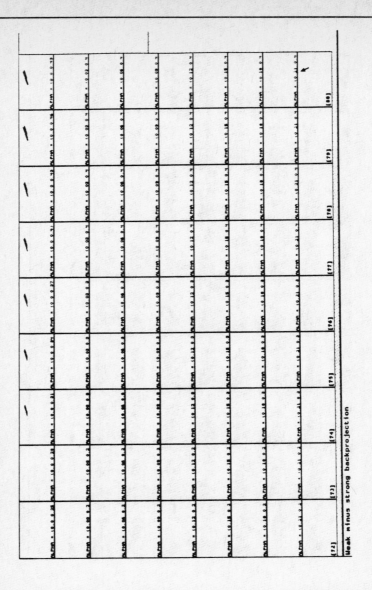

Fig. 12. Weak minus strong backprojection for θ_1. (At resolution R3).

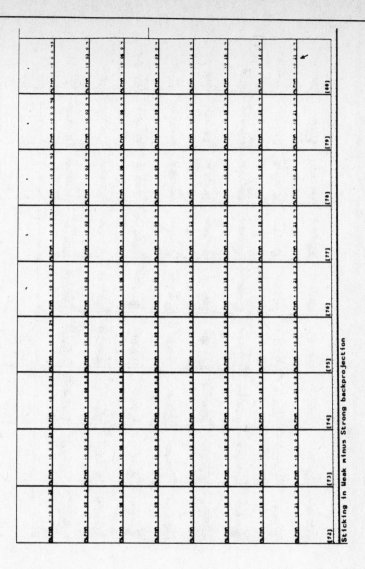

Fig. 13. Sticking in the weak minus strong backprojection for θ_1. (H_s region). (At resolution R3).

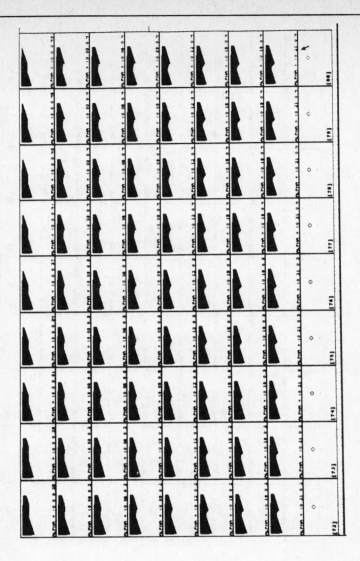

Fig. 14. H_0 EDR region for θ_1. (Forward projection minus weak backprojection). (At resolution R3).

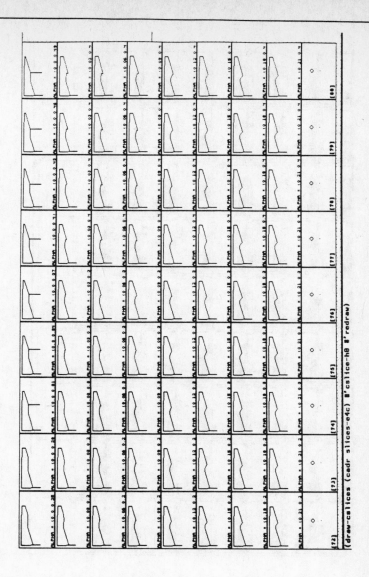

Fig. 15. H_0 EDR region for θ_1 (shown without fill to illustrate degenerate edges sliding into goal). (At resolution R3).

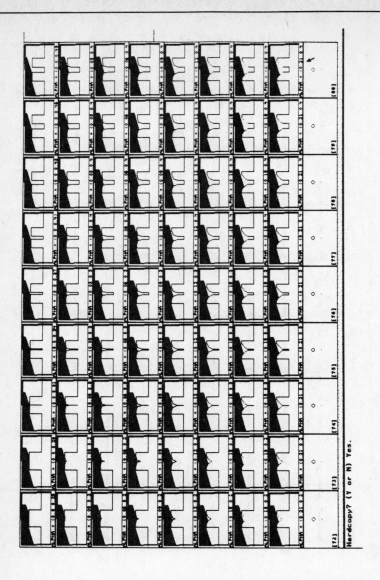

Fig. 16. H_0 EDR region for θ_1, shown amidst obstacles. (At resolution R3).

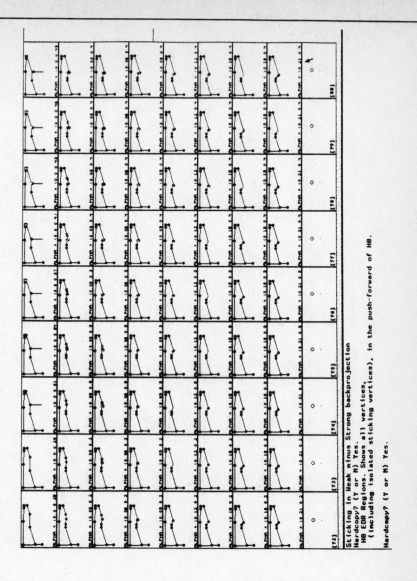

Fig. 17. All vertices of the H_0 EDR region. (At resolution R3).

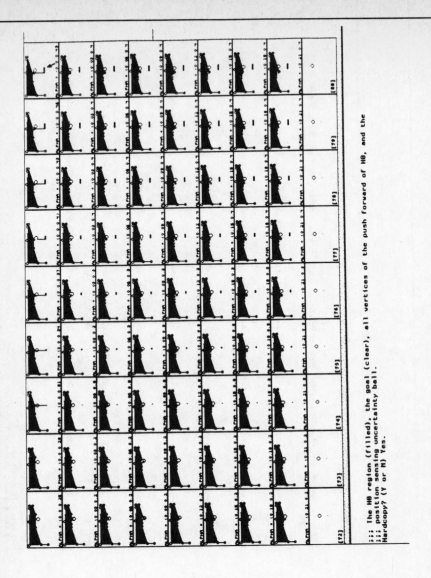

Fig. 18. The EDR region H is not distinguishable from the goal. (At resolution R3).

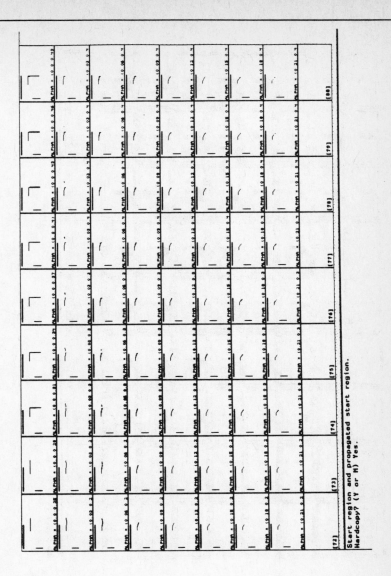

Fig. 19. The push-forward of θ_1 is the start region for θ_2. Here is the push-forward/start region in each slice. (At resolution R3).

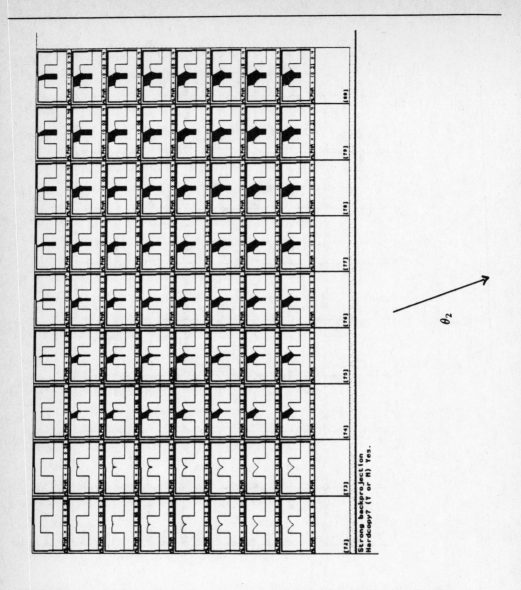

Fig. 20. Strong backprojection of goal under motion θ_2. (At resolution R3).

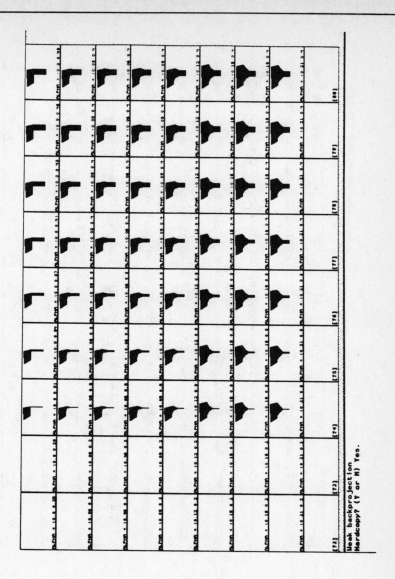

Fig. 21. **Weak** backprojection of goal under motion θ_2. Obstacles not shown. (At resolution R3).

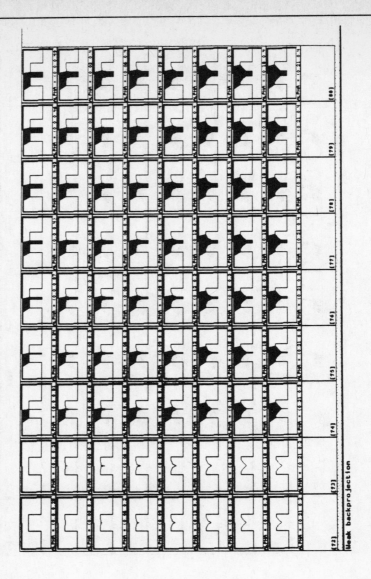

Fig. 22. Weak backprojection of the goal under motion θ_2. (At resolution R3).

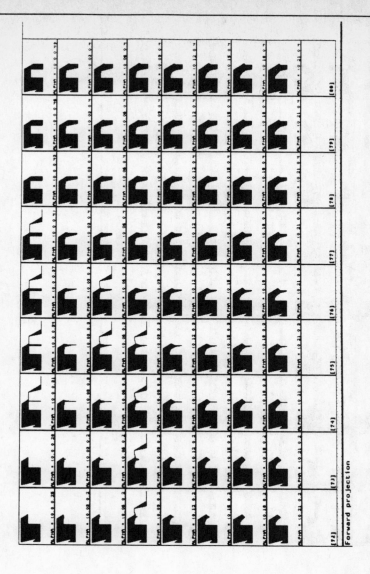

Fig. 23. Forward projection of start region under motion θ_2. Obstacles not shown. (At resolution R3).

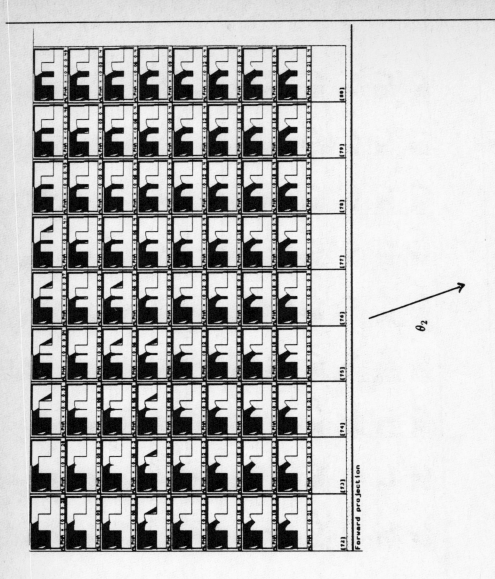

Fig. 24. Forward projection of the start region under motion θ_2. Obstacles are shown. (At resolution R3).

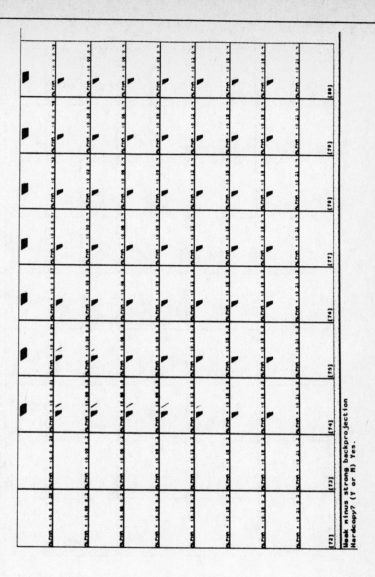

Fig. 25. Weak minus strong backprojection for θ_2. (At resolution R3).

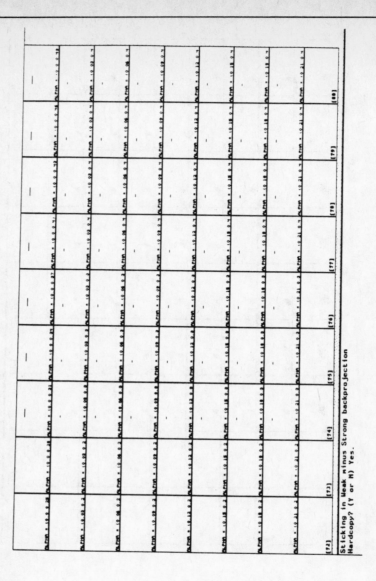

Fig. 26. Sticking in the weak minus strong backprojection for θ_2. (H_s region).
(At resolution R3).

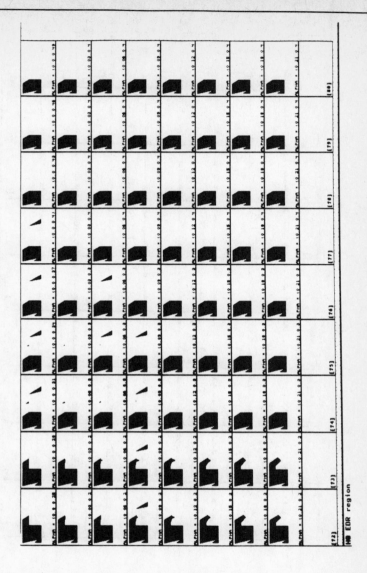

Fig. 27. H_0 EDR region for θ_2. (Forward projection minus weak backprojection). (At resolution R3).

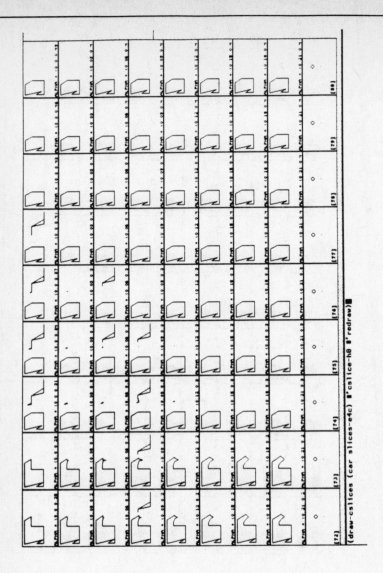

Fig. 28. H_0 EDR region for θ_2 (shown without fill to illustrate degenerate edges). (At resolution R3).

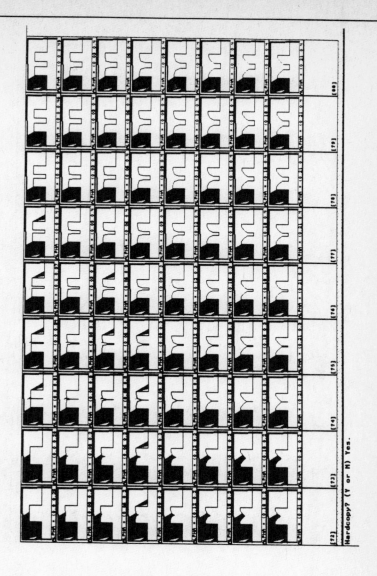

Fig. 29. H_0 EDR region for θ_2, shown amidst obstacles. (At resolution R3).

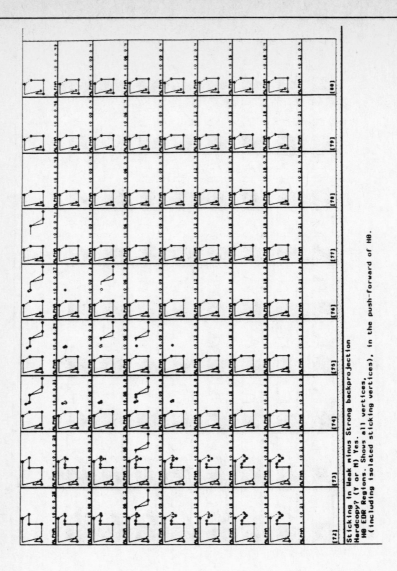

Fig. 30. All vertices of the H_0 EDR region. (At resolution R3).

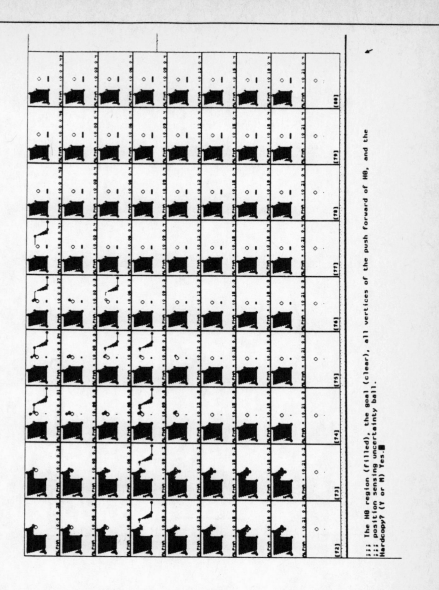

Fig. 31. The EDR region $H = H_0 \cup H_s$ for θ_2 is distinguishable from the goal. (At resolution R3).

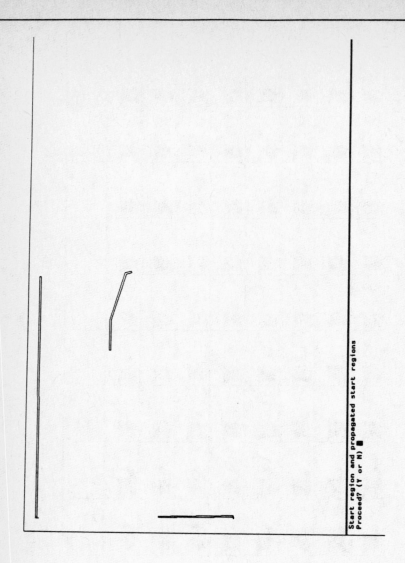

Fig. 32. In figs. 32–40 we examine the commanded motion θ_2 in detail for one slice. The slice occurs at resolution R3, for $\alpha \approx (.9, .34)$. Fig. 32 shows the start region in this slice, which is the push-forward of motion θ_1. (Actually, this start region should include the entire left edge of the bounding box. A portion of the edge was not found due to a numerical error).

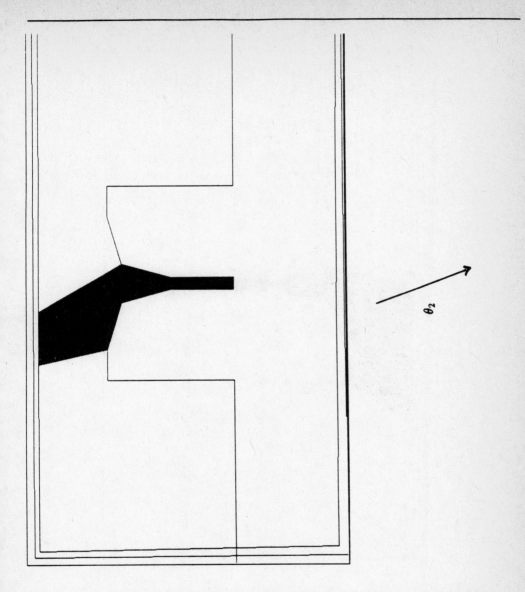

Fig. 33. Strong backprojection of the goal under θ_2. (Detail of motion θ_2 in slice $\alpha \approx (.9, .34)$).

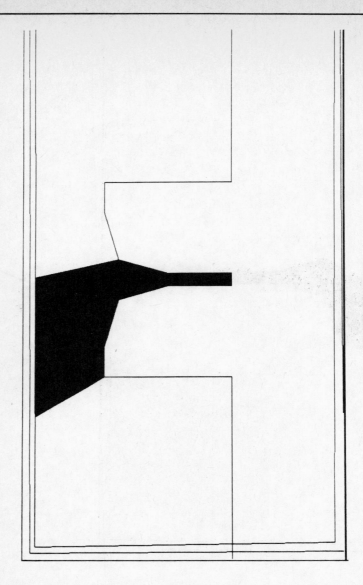

Fig. 34. **Weak backprojection of the goal under motion** θ_2. (Detail of motion θ_2 in slice $\alpha \approx (.9, .34)$).

Fig. 35. Forward projection under θ_2 of the push-forward of θ_1. (Detail of motion θ_2 in slice $\alpha \approx (.9, .34)$).

Fig. 36. Forward projection under θ_2 of the push-forward of θ_1. The obstacles are shown as well. (Detail of motion θ_2 in slice $\alpha \approx (.9, .34)$).

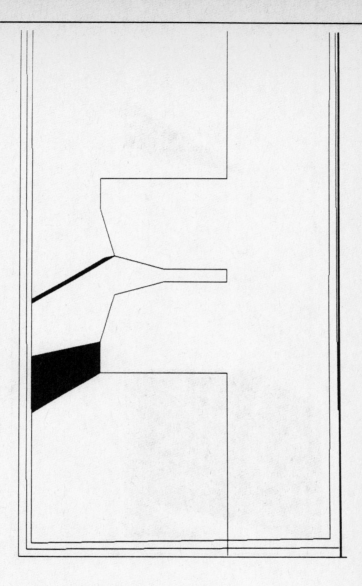

Fig. 37. Weak minus strong backprojection under θ_2. (Detail of motion θ_2 in slice $\alpha \approx (.9, .34)$).

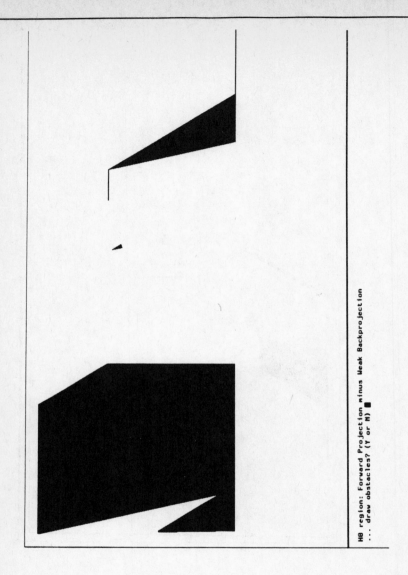

Fig. 38. H_0 region for motion θ_2. (Forward projection minus the weak backprojection). (Detail of motion θ_2 in slice $\alpha \approx (.9, .34)$).

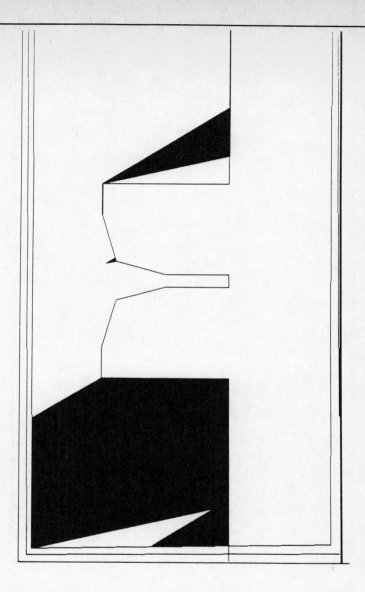

Fig. 39. H_0 region for motion θ_2. Shown amidst obstacles. (Detail of motion θ_2 in slice $\alpha \approx (.9, .34)$).

Fig. 40. Sticking region in the weak minus strong backprojection, shown by arrow. (H_s region). (Detail of motion θ_2 in slice $\alpha \approx (.9, .34)$).

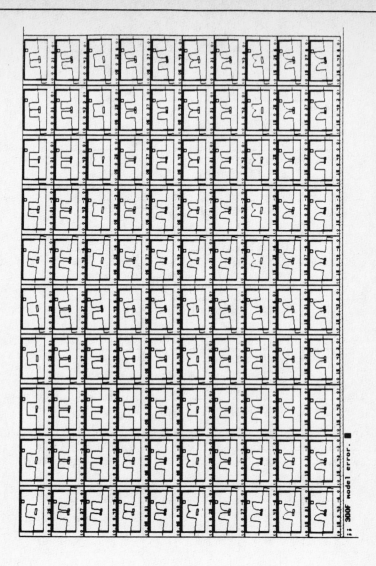

Fig. 41. Configuration space slices at resolution R4: 100 slices of the depth ×
width × orientation axes. After finding an EDR strategy that succeeds at resolutions R1-R3, and using it as a suggested strategy at resolution R4, LIMITED
found this two-step EDR plan at resolution R4 in 888 minutes.

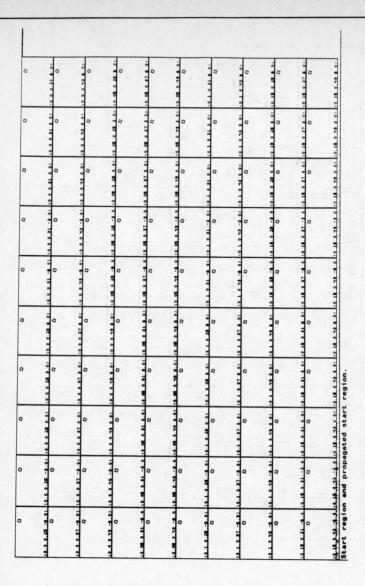

Fig. 42. Start region in each slice. (At resolution R4).

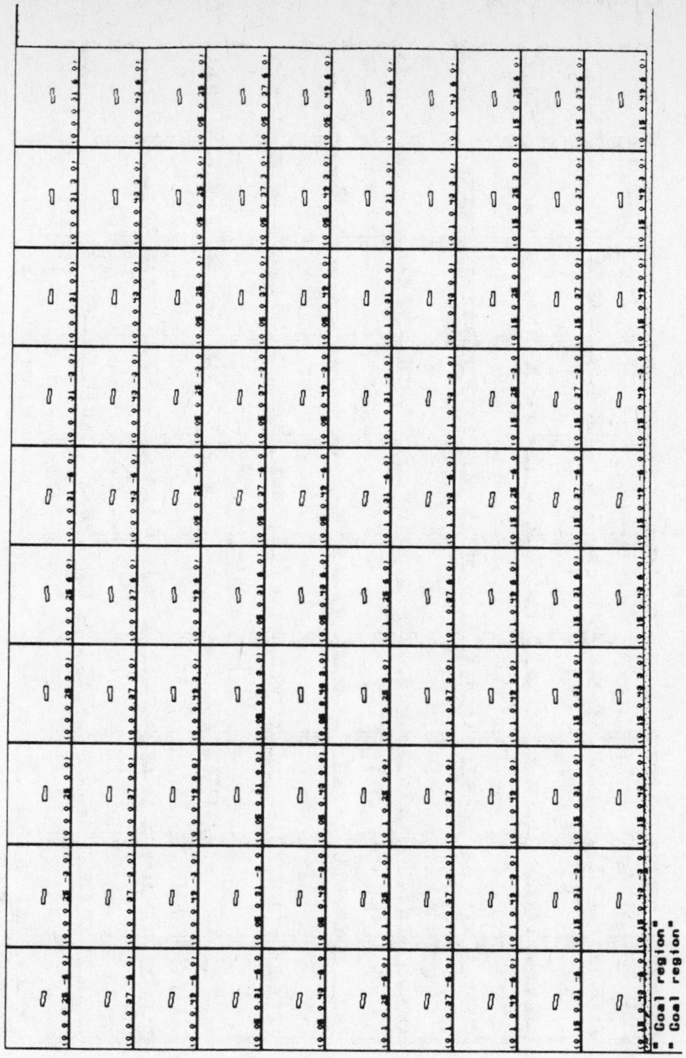

163

Fig. 43. Goal region in each slice. (At resolution R4).

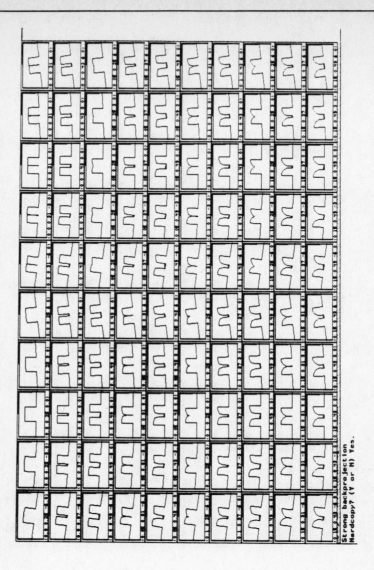

Fig. 44. Strong backprojection of goal under motion θ_1. (At resolution R4).

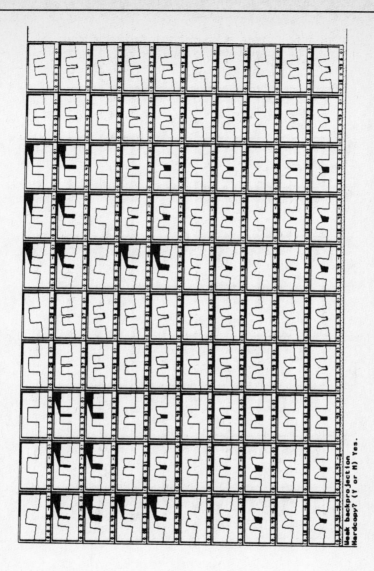

Fig. 45. Weak backprojection of the goal under motion θ_1. (At resolution R4).

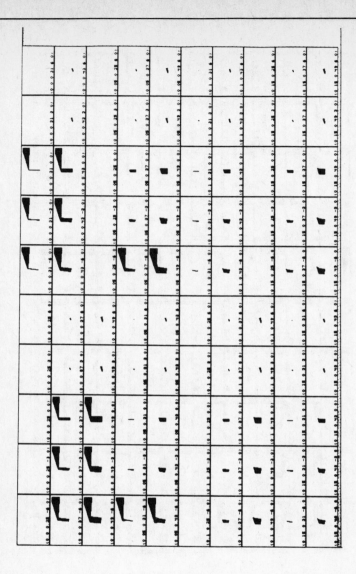

Fig. 46. Weak backprojection of the goal under motion θ_1. Obstacles not shown. (At resolution R4).

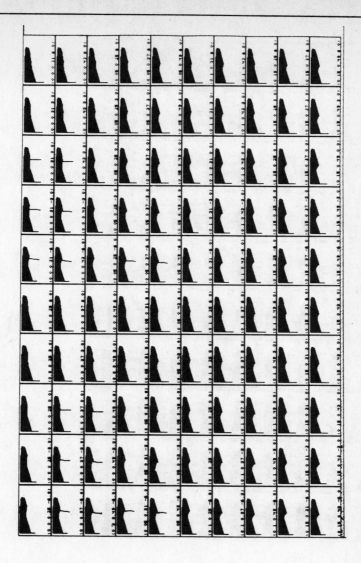

Fig. 47. Forward projection of start region under motion θ_1. Obstacles not shown. (At resolution R4).

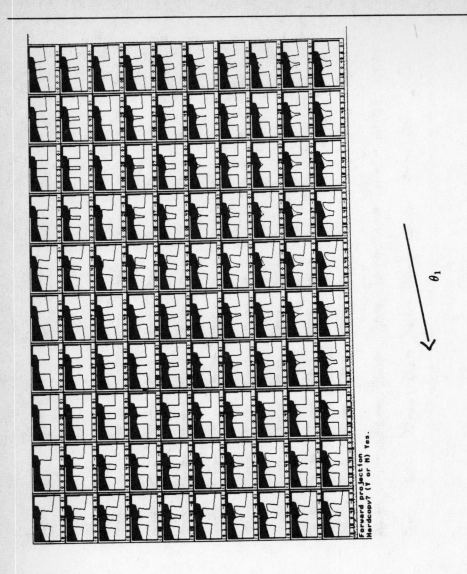

Fig. 48. Forward projection of the start region under motion θ_1. (At resolution R4).

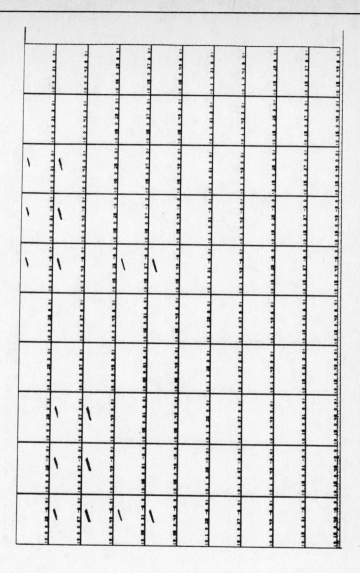

Fig. 49. Weak minus strong backprojection for θ_1. (At resolution R4).

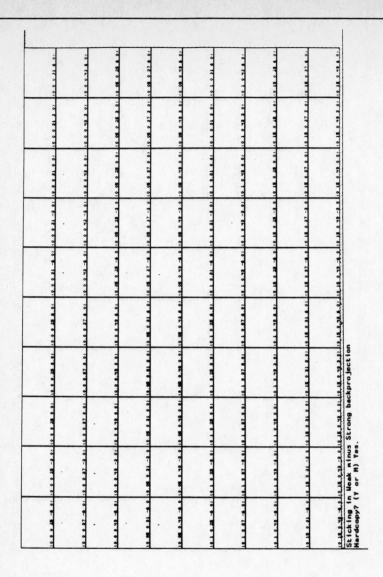

Fig. 50. Sticking in the weak minus strong backprojection for θ_1. (H_s region). (At resolution R4).

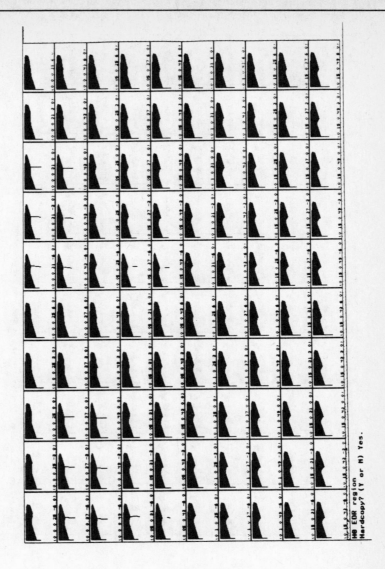

Fig. 51. H_0 EDR region for θ_1. (Forward projection minus weak backprojection). (At resolution R4).

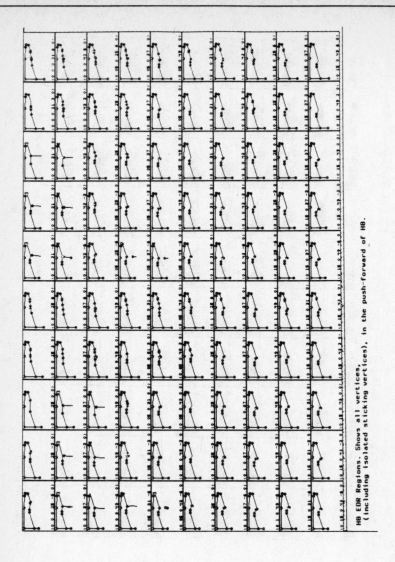

Fig. 52. All vertices of the H_0 EDR region. (At resolution R4).

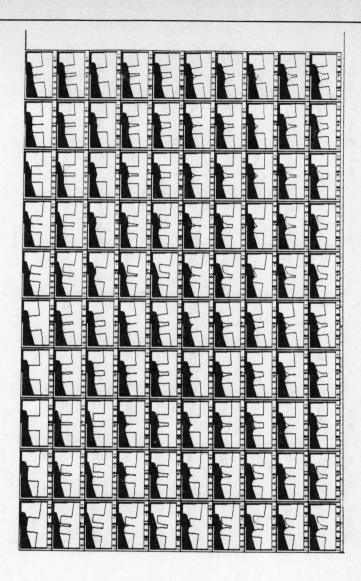

Fig. 53. H_0 EDR region for θ_1, shown amidst obstacles. (At resolution R4).

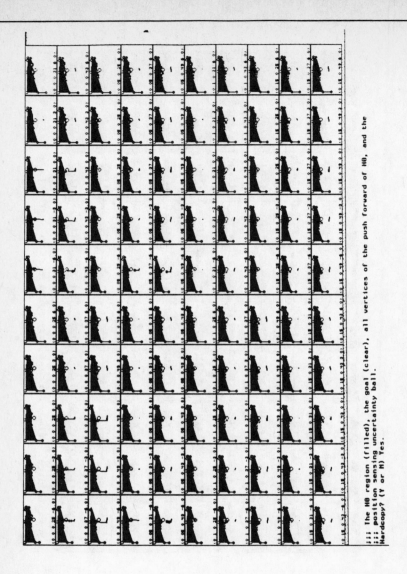

Fig. 54. The EDR region H is not distinguishable from the goal. (At resolution R4).

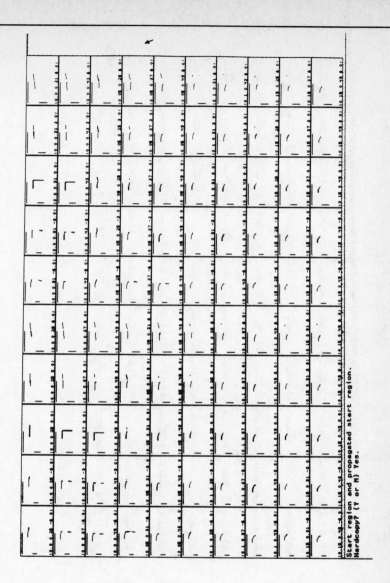

Fig. 55. The push-forward of θ_1 is the start region for θ_2. Here is the push-forward/start region in each slice. (At resolution R4).

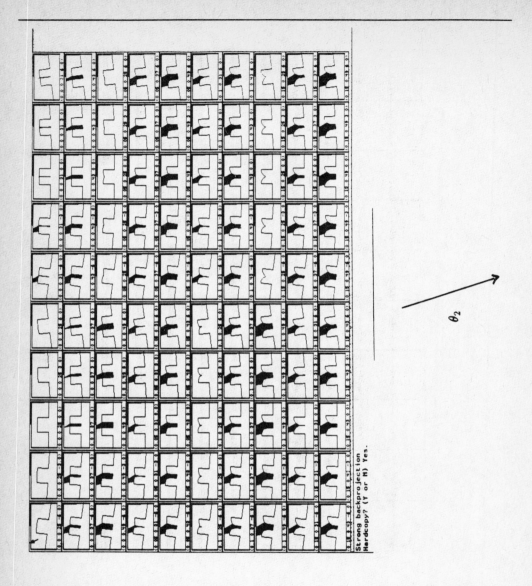

Fig. 56. Strong backprojection of goal under motion θ_2. (At resolution R4).

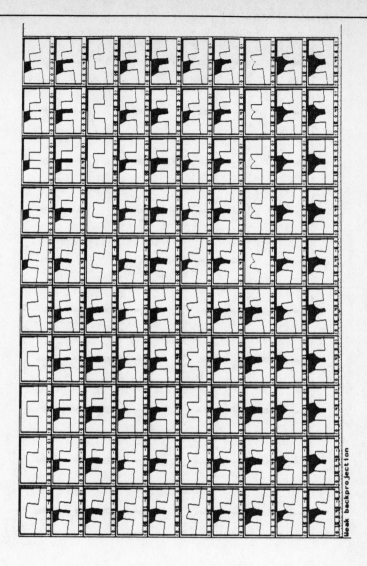

Fig. 57. Weak backprojection of the goal under motion θ_2. (At resolution R4).

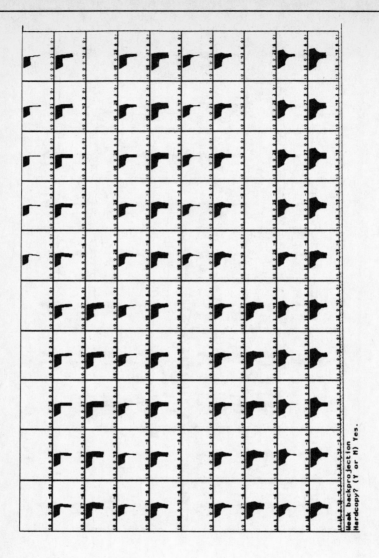

Fig. 58. **Weak** backprojection of goal under motion θ_2. Obstacles not shown. (At resolution R4).

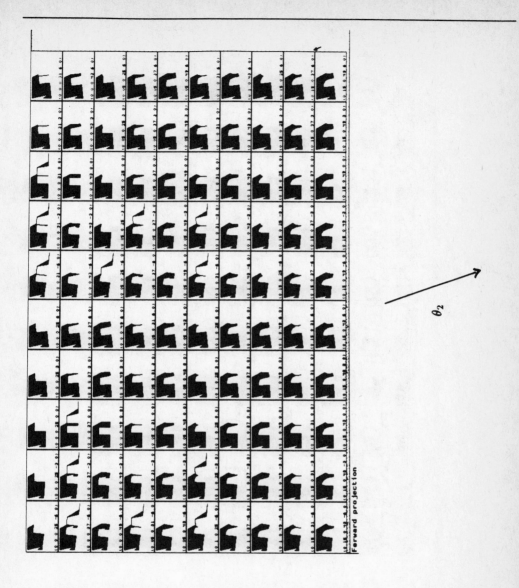

Fig. 59. Forward projection of start region under motion θ_2. Obstacles not shown. (At resolution R4).

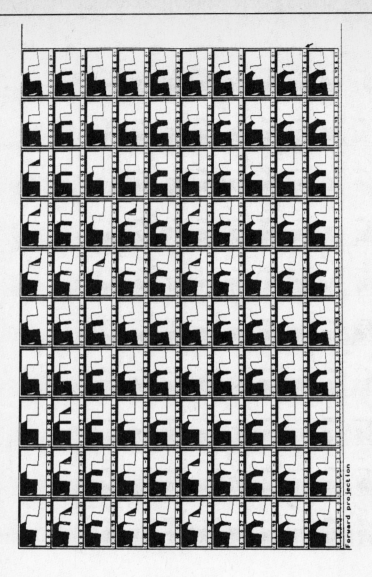

Fig. 60. Forward projection of the start region under motion θ_2. Obstacles are shown. (At resolution R4).

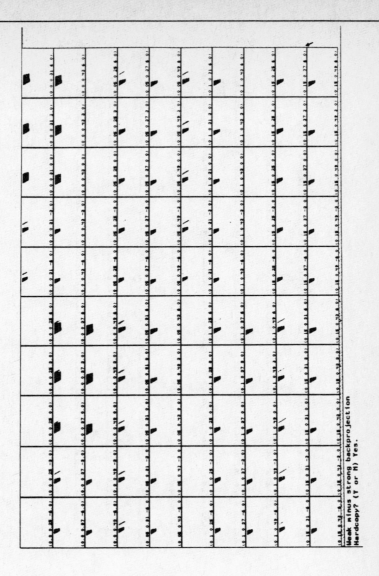

Fig. 61. Weak minus strong backprojection for θ_2. (At resolution R4).

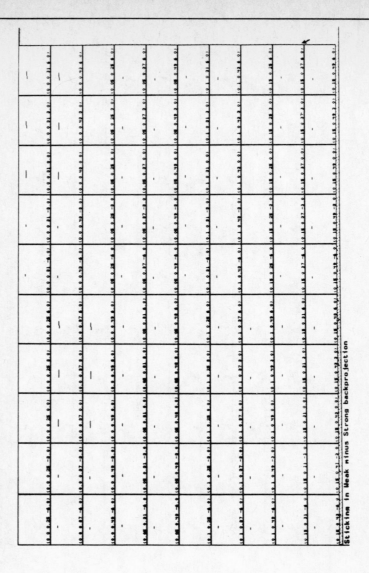

Fig. 62. Sticking in the weak minus strong backprojection for θ_2. (H_s region). (At resolution R4).

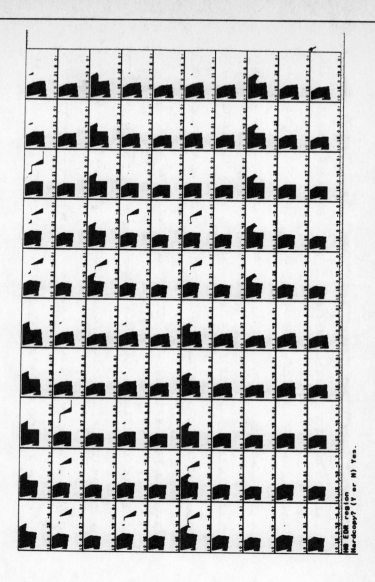

Fig. 63. H_0 EDR region for θ_2. (Forward projection minus weak backprojection). (At resolution R4).

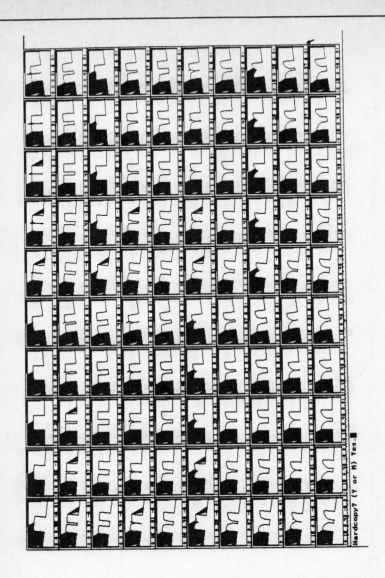

Fig. 64. H_0 EDR region for θ_2, shown amidst obstacles. (At resolution R4).

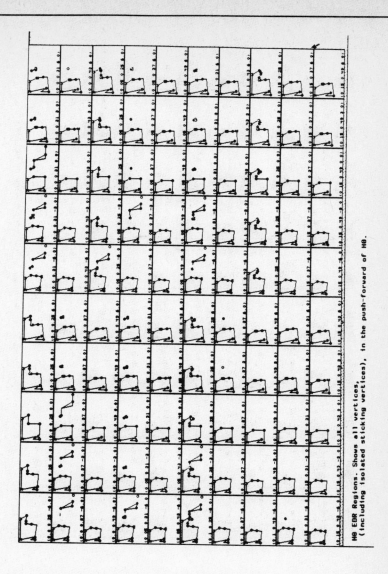

Fig. 65. All vertices of the H_0 EDR region. (At resolution R4).

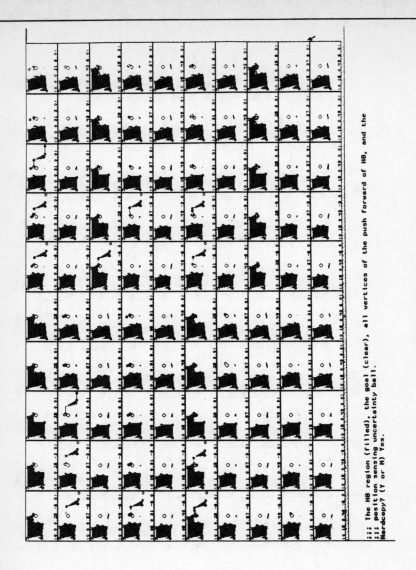

Fig. 66. The EDR region $H = H_0 \cup H_s$ for θ_2 is distinguishable from the goal. (At resolution R4).

11. Failure Mode Analysis

Push-forward techniques require a precise geometrical characterization of the forward-projection, and algorithms for computing it. The gear-meshing example of chapter I is a problem in a four-dimensional generalized configuration space with pushing. Two of the dimensions are rotational: one of these can be commanded, and the other cannot, but the position along this dimension may be changed via pushing. It is difficult to develop good forward projection algorithms in this generalized configuration space, although our critical-slice methods are a start. For this reason, a different technique was developed for planning multi-step strategies in this domain. It is applicable for any generalized configuration space with the same degrees of freedom and pushing characteristics (that is, any polygonal shapes in place of the gears). The new technique is called *failure mode analysis*; we describe it in this section.

Failure-mode analysis is a method for synthesizing multi-step strategies using a kind of "approximate" or *"a priori"* forward projection. At first glance, it may appear unrelated to push-forward or preimage techniques. However, in the next section, on the weak EDR theory, we present a viewpoint which essentially "unifies" the three approaches.

11.1. Example: Multi-Step Strategy for Gear Meshing

Recall the gear-meshing plan LIMITED generated in chapter I, fig. 4. Consider the problem of meshing two planar gears, under uncertainty as in chapters I and II. Suppose that gear B can rotate passively but has unknown initial orientation, as above. Suppose that A has been gripped by a robot. The initial position of A is uncertain. The robot can impart either pure forces (translations), or pure torques (rotations) to A. The planner can choose the direction of translation or rotation. Can a multi-step strategy of commanded translations and rotations be found to mesh the gears?

LIMITED was able to generate an EDR strategy for this problem. The characteristics of the experiment are:

1. There are three degrees of motion freedom (two translational and one rotational) for A.
2. There is one degree of rotational model error freedom (the orientation of B).
3. Pushing is possible to change the orientation of B.
4. There is sensing and control uncertainty.
5. The geometry of the gears is complicated.

6. Quasi-static analysis is used to model the physics of interaction between the gears.

7. We suppose that vision is poor, or that the gears are accessible to the robot gripper, but not to the camera. This means that position sensing will be very inaccurate, and hence may be of no use to determine whether the gears are successfully meshed. This will often be the case in practice. In this case, force sensing must be used to disambiguate the success of the first motion (meshing) from failure (jamming in an unmeshed state).

8. Hence, a multi-step strategy is required.

Thus we have a kind of four-degree of freedom planning problem with uncertainty and pushing. To generate multi-step EDR strategies under pushing, LIMITED uses the EDR theory together with *failure mode analysis*. Here is the plan LIMITED generates:

θ_1. *Command a pure translation of A into B.*[1]
Terminate the motion based on force-sensing when sticking occurs (when there is no motion).

θ_2. *Command a pure rotation of A.*
If breaking contact or sticking occurs, signal failure. Otherwise, signal success.

In this plan, motion θ_1 does not terminate distinguishably in success (meshed) or failure (jammed). That is, after motion θ_1 terminates, the plan executive cannot necessarily recognize whether or not the gears are meshed. LIMITED predicts this, and generates motion θ_2, which disambiguates the result of motion θ_1. The generation of the second, disambiguating motion involves the use of *failure mode analysis*. *Breaking contact* and *sticking* are examples of failure modes. The second motion is generated so that from any unmeshed state resulting from motion θ_1, all possible paths will terminate distinguishably in a failure mode. Failure mode analysis is a robust subtheory of EDR by which LIMITED generates multi-step strategies under pushing.

11.2. Introduction to Failure Mode Analysis

In the gear-meshing plan, motion θ_2 is used to disambiguate the result of motion θ_1. The technique used is *failure mode analysis*. LIMITED is given a repertory of qualitative failure modes, which comprise sticking and breaking contact. Motion θ_1 can end in a "good" region (meshed) or a "bad" region (jam). LIMITED tried to generate a disambiguating motion as a second step. This motion is required to terminate in a failure mode from all "bad" regions.

---

[1] LIMITED generates the actual force vector $v_{\theta_1}^*$.

Here is how LIMITED generates motion θ_2. Let H be the EDR region for motion θ_1. The planner determines all configurations where motion θ_1 can terminate outside of G. Call this region $\text{push}_{\theta_1}(H)$. $\text{push}_{\theta_1}(H)$ then forms the start region for motion θ_2. LIMITED then uses quasi-static analysis to "prove" that when A is at any configuration in $\text{push}_{\theta_1}(H)$, and a pure rotation of A is commanded, that all possible motions of A result in sticking or breaking contact. Sticking and breaking contact are called *failure modes*; there is a class of EDR plans which can be terminated in failure when sticking or breaking contact are detected. EDR planning with failure modes constitutes a robust subtheory of EDR. It is a subtheory because assuming this kind of failure mode is a restrictive assumption to make planning tractable. It is robust because sticking and breaking contact are easy to recognize, relatively speaking, as failure modes by a run-time robot executor.

From the preimage point of view, failure modes are implemented simply as different classes of termination predicates.

11.3. Specifying the Goal: Functional Descriptions

Recall our discussion of sticking as a termination condition in chapter II. Sticking had the advantage of ensuring "good" behavior in the EDR region H. In particular, it could be guaranteed that all motions would eventually terminate in $G \cup H$, rendering the distinguishability of G vs. H a history-free decision. However, in order for a sticking termination predicate to generate good EDR plans, it was in fact necessary to ensure that the motion strategy has "good" behavior at the goal as well. In particular, the commanded motion should stick at the goal.

In failure mode analysis, we have a similar situation. The purpose of motion θ_2 is to force all motions starting from $\text{push}_{\theta_1}(H)$ to terminate in sticking or breaking contact. Clearly this is only useful if *no motion* from $\text{push}_{\theta_1}(G)$ can *even possibly* terminate in sticking or breaking contact. This is the required "good" behavior at the goal. Thus, in an EDR plan generated by failure mode analysis,

F1. *Under motion θ_2, all motions starting from $\text{push}_{\theta_1}(H)$ must terminate in a failure mode.*

F2. *No motion from $\text{push}_{\theta_1}(G)$ can possibly terminate in a failure mode.*

F3. *The goal is a fixed-point under motion θ_2.*

LIMITED decides whether or not (F1) is true. However, (F2) is given as input to LIMITED. We will now discuss how (F2) is specified. In the next section we will describe algorithms for computing (F1). (F3) may be decided using forward projections; the actual condition we require is

$$F_{\theta_2}(\text{push}_{\theta_1}(G)) \subset G,$$

which is implied by the fixed-point equation

$$F_{\theta_2}(G) = G, \tag{F3}$$

since of course $\text{push}_{\theta_1}(G)$ is contained in G.

The goal state for gear meshing may be viewed purely geometrically. That is, it may be viewed as a set in generalized configuration space. This view is useful for computing the EDR regions. Alternatively, the goal may be specified through a functional description. For example, we might specify the goal as a difference equation (DE). The intuition behind this difference equation formulation of the goal is, *"In the goal, any finite rotation of A results in an equal and opposite rotation of B."* More precisely, the difference equation specifies:

DE. *Command any non-zero finite rotation* $\Delta\alpha_1$ *to A. In the goal, this results in a finite rotation of A by* $\Delta\alpha_1$ *and of B by* $-\Delta\alpha_1$.[2]

This difference equation captures the functional aspects of the gears in their meshed state. Now, it is clear that this equation may be "differentialized." That is, we consider it to be true for all non-zero displacements, no matter how small. If this is the case, then it is clear that breaking contact is in direct contradiction to the truth of the difference equation (DE). This is because if contact is broken, then there exists some finite rotation of A that will not affect the orientation of B. Similarly, sticking contradicts the truth of the difference equation, for if the gears stick, then they are not properly meshed, i.e., we do not obtain equal and opposite rotations.

In LIMITED failure mode analysis, we view the goal state as a combined geometrical and functional specification. Here are the three ways of specifying the functional aspects of the goal. The last, which decides questions about goal predicates via the theory of real closed fields, is only of theoretical interest. The second is a heuristic approximation to such an inference engine. The first is a more robust solution with an engineering flavor. It places on the user the burden of ensuring well-behaved qualitative behavior at the goal.

11.3.1 Specifying the Functional Aspects of the Goal

Method 1. User input. In this method, it is the responsibility of the user to ensure that (F2) is true. That is, the user must guarantee that failure modes cannot occur at the goal. This, of course, is the easiest method. If the user guarantees that (F2) holds, then it remains only for LIMITED to show (F1).

---

[2] A and B are the same size. Clearly, this may be generalized to different pitch gears.

*11.3.2 Computational Methods for Functional Goal Specification

Method 2. Inference. If the user cannot guarantee that (F2) holds, it is possible for LIMITED to make certain kinds of deductions to infer that (F2) is true.

How can such an inference mechanism work? We can view the difference equation as a kind of predicate on paths. This is similar to the termination predicate with continuous history studied by [Mason]. In this model, when the predicate is true, the path has been recognized as a member of a particular class—say, the goal class, or the failure class. Similarly, sticking and breaking contact can be represented as path predicates. If p is a path in generalized configuration space, we wish to prove that if the difference equation predicate (DE) is true of p, then

$$stick(p) \vee break(p)$$

is false. It is possible to write a semi-decision procedure for this question using resolution refutation. I wrote a front-end to LIMITED which can decide this question in special cases. *goal*, *stick* and *break* can be defined as predicates on paths. To do this, we must view paths as lying in phase space, that is,

$$p : [0, \infty). \rightarrow T\mathcal{G}.$$

hence $p(t)$ is a pair representing the actual position of the robot and the actual net force on (equivalently, velocity of) the robot at time t. $stick(p)$ is defined to be true if sticking occurs along p. $break(p)$ is true if p ever breaks contact.

The inference system tries to find a contradiction among the set of formulas

$$\{ goal(p), stick(p) \vee break(p) \}.$$

If a contradiction is found, the system assumes that sticking or breaking contact cannot occur in the goal, and (F2) has been established.

The quantified difference equation inference mechanism was implemented to explore the feasibility of the approach. It is *ad hoc*, special-case, and incomplete. It should not be viewed as a focus of this research, but more as an heuristic experiment on the interaction of geometrical and functional goal specifications. While it is possible to write a more complete inference engine, that is not the point of this work. From a practical standpoint, the user input method for ensuring the validity of (F2) is probably preferable.

Method 3. Second Order Theory of Real Closed Fields. Method 2 described a heuristic implementation of a mechanism for inferring (F2) from a goal predicate. We must now mention a complete, albeit strictly theoretical mechanism for this inference. In particular, we describe a semi-decision procedure for deriving (F2) from a goal predicate on semi-algebraic paths. First, we define an extension to the theory of real closed fields. Next, we show it is semi-decidable. Finally, we note that the specification of the goal predicate, above, may be encoded in this language.

Definition. A *semi-algebraic (s.a.) function* is a univariate piecewise-polynomial function.

Definition. The *Second Order Theory of Real Closed Fields (2RCF)* is the first order language with the following augmentations:

quantification over s.a. functions,

s.a. function application,

differentiation of s.a. functions.

While the first order theory can quantify only over variables, sentences in 2RCF can universally and existentially quantify over functions, such as s.a. paths.

Definition. The *Existential Second Order Theory of Real Closed Fields (X2RCF)* consists of all 2RCF sentences of the form $(\exists p_1, \ldots, p_k \in \Re[t])F(p)$ where $F(\cdot)$ is a 2RCF predicate containing no quantified functions.

Theorem. *X2RCF is recursively enumerable.*

Proof. Given a formula $(\exists p F(p))$ where $p \in \Re[x_1, \ldots, x_n]$, enumerate s.a. multinomials p by degree. Test whether $F(p)$ is true using the first order theory. $\Box$

Our paths lie in real d-space where d is the dimension of $T\mathcal{G}$.[3]

Now, the questions we wish to decide are

$$(\forall p \in (\Re[t])^d)goal(p) \Rightarrow \text{im } \pi \circ p \subset \partial CO$$

or

$$(\forall p \in (\Re[t])^d)goal(p) \Rightarrow \neg stick(p).$$

The negations of both formulae are semi-decidable in X2RCF. If either negation is true, then failure mode analysis will not work for this goal predicate. This gives a theoretical means to decide when failure mode analysis is inapplicable. It is interesting only as an in-principle approach. It can be shown that X2RCF is at least non-elementary. It is probably undecidable.

Some of the greatest and most interesting unsolved problems in geometrical robotics lie in the interaction of functional and geometrical descriptions of goals. In particular, we would like to devise algorithms for computing a geometrical goal region given a functional description—for example, a quantified difference equation—for the desired behavior in the goal state. Conversely, we would like to be able to

---

[3] Actually, d is the dimension of a real space in which the manifold $T\mathcal{G}$ embeds.

infer a functional description of the goal from its geometrical aspects. The latter would be useful in automatically generating termination predicates to recognize the goal.

11.4. Approximate Algorithms for Failure Mode Analysis

We now describe algorithms for deciding whether

F1. *Under motion θ_2, all motions starting from $\text{push}_{\theta_1}(H)$ must terminate in a failure mode.*

Let us denote $\text{push}_{\theta_1}(H)$ by H_1. These algorithms use time-indexed forward projections to prove that under θ_2, all paths starting in H_1 eventually stick or break contact. The algorithms are approximate, although conservative. That is, if they terminate then (F1) is true. However, they may not terminate if (F1) is false, and they may miss cases where (F1) is true. The accuracy of the algorithm increases as the time steps for the time-indexed forward projections are taken to be finer. In the 4D generalized configuration space for the gears, which is $\Re^2 \times S^1 \times S^1$, these time-steps correspond to the fineness of the slice resolution across the rotational dimensions.

We will first describe a quite general algorithm for deciding (F1). It is applicable wherever we can obtain a computational characterization of time-indexed forward projections. Later, we will give a specialized algorithm in the generalized configuration space for the gears, and show that it is in fact a special case of the general algorithm.

11.4.1 A General Algorithm

The basic idea is to step along in time, simulating the motion, and determine whether or not it breaks contact or sticks. Of course, we must simulate all possible motions, using forward projections.

First we must develop some notation. Recall that for a planar set H_1, ∂H_1 denotes its obstacle edges. Here, we will use it to more generally to denote the obstacle surfaces (as opposed to the free-space surfaces) bounding a set H_1 in generalized configuration space. (In our case H_1, the input to the algorithm, is the push-forward of motion θ_1).

Let x be a point in generalized configuration space. Then $stick_\theta(x)$ is true if sticking is necessary at x under all control velocities $B_{ec}(v_\theta^*)$ consistent with the nominal commanded velocity v_θ^*. Let $stick_\theta(H_1)$ denote all points x in H_1 where $stick_\theta(x)$ holds.

Now, assume some positive minimum modulus bound on the commanded velocity. We use $F_{\theta,\Delta t}(\cdot)$ as the time-indexed forward projection operator (see [Erdmann]). So $F_{\theta,\Delta t}(H_1)$ denotes the set of possible positions the robot can be at at time Δt, having started in H_1 at time $t = 0$.

Now, we are ready to give the general algorithm for deciding (F1):

Algorithm Gen

1. *Let $F \leftarrow F_{\theta,\Delta t}(H_1)$.*
2. *Let $H_2 \leftarrow \partial F - stick_{\theta_2}(\partial F)$.*
3. *When $H_2 = \emptyset$, we have proven that all paths from H_1 must eventually stick or break contact. Halt.*
4. *Else, $H_1 \leftarrow H_2$. Goto (1).*

Note that H_1 is permitted to be in free-space, although given the sticking push-forward it will, in fact, always be on a generalized configuration space boundary. Note that *Gen* is a semi-decision procedure. Clearly, if the algorithm halts, then all paths originating in H_1 eventually break contact or stick. Fig. 67 illustrates the algorithm. Suppose the H_1 region is the edge e. Its forward projection after Δt is the region $U \cup g$. The obstacle edges of the forward projection are e', f, and g. Sticking must occur on f. Hence, H_2 is $e' \cup g$.

We now mention a basic property of forward projections that this algorithm exploits. It is the property that forward projection commutes with union. In particular, if we have

$$H_1 = \overbrace{H_B}^{\text{boundary}} + \overbrace{H_F}^{\text{free-space}} .$$

then

$$F_{\theta}(H_1) = F_{\theta}(H_B \cup H_F) = F_{\theta}(H_B) \cup F_{\theta}(H_F).$$

This key property permits the algorithm to decompose the failure mode analysis into essentially independent decision problems about the forward projections of the free-space, sliding, and sticking regions in the push-forward.

11.4.2 A Specialized Algorithm

For failure-mode analysis, LIMITED employs an algorithm that is a special case of the general algorithm above. The idea is that when commanding a pure rotation of A, the time-indexed forward projection across slices can be well approximated by

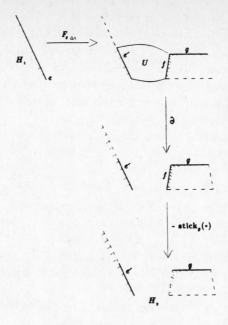

Fig. 67. Illustration of the general algorithm. The start region H_1 is the edge
e. Its forward projection after Δt is the region $U \cup g$. The obstacle edges of
the forward projection are e', f, and g. Sticking must occur on f. Hence, H_2 is
$e' \cup g$.

the differential forward projection of sec. 6. The differential forward projection is a
technique for propagating the forward projection across slices, when rotations of A
and B are permitted. Recall our notation for motions θ_1 and θ_2. θ_1 is a commanded
pure translation of A, and may be viewed as unit vector $v_{\theta_1}^*$ in the plane. θ_2 is a
commanded pure rotation of A, and may be viewed as a member of $\{ +d\alpha_1, -d\alpha_1 \}$,
for positive and negative commanded rotations.

Differential and Propagated Forward Projections

Pure Translations. Forward projections must be propagated between slices
even when a pure translation is commanded, since a pure translation θ_1 can alter
the orientation of B, and hence the slice-value, through pushing. Recall how the
differential forward projection is constructed for a pure translation θ_1 (sec. 6).

Let $(x, y, \alpha_1, \alpha_2)$ denote a configuration in the generalized configuration space for the gears, $\Re^2 \times S^1 \times S^1$. (x, y, α_1) denotes a configuration of A. α_2 denotes the configuration of B. Hence, we regard the orientation of B (the "last" S^1 in the product) as J. Now, H_1 is a set in generalized configuration space. Let $H_1|_{\alpha_1, \alpha_2}$ denote a particular x-y slice of H_1 for orientation α_1 of A and α_2 of B.

Motion θ_1 commands a pure translation of A. Now, for each edge in $H_1|_{\alpha_1, \alpha_2}$, LIMITED performs a quasi-static analysis to determine the possible impending motions of A and B. That is, it determines which way(s) A and B can rotate. These directions may be viewed as tangent vectors to the pure rotational dimensions of generalized configuration space. The set of possible directions may be identified with a set of pairs

$$\{ -d\alpha_1, 0, +d\alpha_1 \} \times \{ -d\alpha_2, 0, +d\alpha_2 \} \tag{9}$$

in the tangent space to $(S^1 \times S^1)$. By performing this analysis for all edges, we obtain a set of directions,

$$dF_{\theta_1}(H_1|_{\alpha_1, \alpha_2}),$$

which is called the *differential forward projection of* $H_1|_{\alpha_1, \alpha_2}$ *under* θ_1. It is assumed that commanding θ_1 from region $H_1|_{\alpha_1, \alpha_2}$ can result in any motion direction in this set.

Suppose (α_1', α_2') is a slice taken in the direction of some tangent vector $\mathbf{v}$ in the differential forward projection. For example, if $\mathbf{v} = (+d\alpha_1, -d\alpha_2)$, then $\alpha_1' = \alpha_1 + \epsilon_1$ and $\alpha_2' = \alpha_2 - \epsilon_2$ for some small positive scalars ϵ_1 and ϵ_2.

Now, the forward projection may be propagated to the adjacent slice (α_1', α_2') as follows. An edge e_i in $H_1|_{\alpha_1, \alpha_2}$ corresponds to the intersection of an algebraic surface V in generalized configuration space with the "plane" $\Re^2 \times \{ (\alpha_1, \alpha_2) \}$. V is followed into (α_1', α_2'), and the forward projection of e_i is taken to be the intersection of V with the "plane" $\Re^2 \times \{ (\alpha_1', \alpha_2') \}$. In this manner, we obtain a set of edges $\{ e_i' \}$ in the new slice. The pure translational forward projection of these edges under θ_1 is then computed within this slice, so the propagated forward projection is $F_{\theta_1}(\{ e_i' \})$. This propagated forward projection is computed at a fixed orientation of A and B. Ideally, the planner should decide whether the sliding characteristics change along V while moving through rotation space. The rotational values which are sliding-critical are discussed in the critical slice section, 6.3.[4] The propagated forward projection increases in accuracy as the slices are taken closer together.

Pure Rotations. Consider the problem of computing forward projections across slices for a commanded pure rotation $\theta_2 \in \{ +d\alpha_1, -d\alpha_1 \}$. For simplicity, we first

---

[4]Detecting sliding critical orientation parameters along the algebraic surface V has not been implemented in LIMITED. Thus the propagated forward projection may be larger than it need be.

consider the case where H_1 consists of a single point. Let $\mathbf{x}$ be a point in the plane, and $(\mathbf{x}, \alpha_1, \alpha_2)$ be a configuration where A and B are in contact. Then the differential forward projection of $\mathbf{x}$ under θ_2 will consist of vectors in the set of eq. (9). The differential forward projection has the same structure as in the pure translational case. It may be computed using quasi-static analysis. (see the next subsection below).

Suppose for the sake of development that the differential forward projection consists of *exactly one* direction $\mathbf{v}$, and that (α_1', α_2') is an adjacent slice in that direction, as above. Now we ask, what is the propagated forward projection of $\mathbf{x}$ into the adjacent slice, (α_1', α_2')? Well, it can be one of two things: either it is $\mathbf{x}$, or it is empty. The reason is that x-y position is invariant[5] under θ_2. Thus, an upper bound on the propagated forward projection of $H_1|_{\alpha_1,\alpha_2}$ into an adjacent slice (α_1', α_2') is found by simply "copying"[6] $H_1|_{\alpha_1,\alpha_2}$ into slice (α_1', α_2').

Now, consider the propagated forward projection of $(\mathbf{x}, \alpha_1, \alpha_2)$, under motion θ_2, into slice α_1', α_2'. It is simply the point $(\mathbf{x}, \alpha_1', \alpha_2')$. There are three possible qualitative outcomes:

1. $\mathbf{x}$ is inside a generalized configuration space obstacle in slice (α_1', α_2').
2. $\mathbf{x}$ is in free space in slice (α_1', α_2').
3. $\mathbf{x}$ is on the boundary of a generalized configuration space obstacle in slice (α_1', α_2').

Obviously, (2) implies that contact has been broken. (1) corresponds to a physically impossible situation. Since the configuration $(\mathbf{x}, \alpha_1', \alpha_2')$ is physically unattainable, this means that the commanded motion θ_2 must result in sticking (no actual motion) before (α_1', α_2') can be reached. Now, if we have either outcome (1) or (2) then we have proven that, under θ_2, any path for the robot starting at $(\mathbf{x}, \alpha_1, \alpha_2)$ must stick (1) or break contact (2).

Suppose, however, we have outcome (3). This outcome is not inconsistent with the negation of (F1). That is, it has not yet been shown that any path from $(\mathbf{x}, \alpha_1, \alpha_2)$ will stick or break contact. In this case, in the new slice (α_1', α_2') we again perform the quasi-static analysis and forward project again into yet another slice. This process continues until either outcomes (1) or (2) are obtained.

More generally, the differential forward projection of $(\mathbf{x}, \alpha_1, \alpha_2)$ could consist of more than one vector. In this case, each must be taken as a forward projection direction, and in each direction we must show that outcomes (1) or (2) eventually occur. That is, the computation above must performed for each direction predicted

---

[5] See below for more on this assumption.
[6] We use the awkward term "copying" instead of "translating", since while the latter is precise mathematically it is confusing robotically.

by the quasi-static analysis, and *all* directions must terminate in sticking or breaking contact.

We have described how the failure mode analysis proceeds when the push-forward H_1 of the first motion θ_1 is simply a point. It remains to generalize the discussion to the case where H_1 is a region in generalized configuration space, represented by slices. We first introduce some notation. If CO denotes the generalized configuration space obstacle for A due to B, then let $CO|_{\alpha_1,\alpha_2}$ denote the x-y slice of CO at orientations (α_1,α_2). As usual, let ∂ denote the obstacle edges of a set. ϵ is the slice resolution parameter. The input to this procedure is a stack Q of x-y-slices of H_1. An entry in Q is a triple, consisting of an x-y slice $H_1|_{\alpha_1,\alpha_2}$, and (α_1,α_2), the orientations at which the slice was computed.

Algorithm Spec

1.   *Do until $Q = \emptyset$:*
2.   *Pop the triple $\langle H_1|_{\alpha_1,\alpha_2}, \alpha_1, \alpha_2 \rangle$ off Q. Let $H_2 \leftarrow H_1|_{\alpha_1,\alpha_2}$.*
3.   *Let $dF \leftarrow dF_{\theta_2}(H_2)$.*
4.   *For each $\mathbf{v}$ in dF do:*
5.   *Let $(\alpha'_1, \alpha'_2) \leftarrow \epsilon \mathbf{v} + (\alpha_1, \alpha_2)$.*
6.   *Compute $CO|_{\alpha'_1,\alpha'_2}$.*
7.   *Let $H_3 \leftarrow H_2 \cap \partial CO|_{\alpha'_1,\alpha'_2}$.*
8.   *If $H_3 \neq \emptyset$, push the triple $\langle H_3, \alpha'_1, \alpha'_2 \rangle$ onto Q.*

Note that this is a semi-decision procedure. This is the algorithm that is actually implemented in LIMITED. The key step is of course the iteration step (7), which we think of as

$$\text{``}H_2 \leftarrow H_2 \cap \partial CO|_{\alpha'_1,\alpha'_2}\text{''}$$

which is repeated "until H_2 is null." $CO|_{\alpha'_1,\alpha'_2}$ is computed using the plane sweep union algorithm, as is the intersection.

11.4.3 On the Invariance Assumption

We have assumed that x-y position of A is invariant under a commanded pure rotation θ_2. That is, commanding a pure rotation cannot result in an induced translation. On the other hand, we allow a commanded pure translation of A to induce a rotation of B (but not of A). These assumptions are realistic if, for example, the robot has gripped A by its center shaft, and the manipulator is very stiff in the x-y directions when commanding a pure rotation. In future work, relaxing this asymmetry should be explored. See chapter VI for suggestions.

11.4.4 Quasi-Static Analysis

We now show how the quasi-static analysis is computed. It is quite simple. We view the commanded velocity to A as $\omega = (0, 0, \pm 1)$. When the gears are in contact, this defines a moving constraint in the configuration space of B, which is a one-dimensional space. Given a contact configuration, we compute the moment arm in order to determine the direction of the constraint. The moment arm on B (resp., A) is simply the vector from B's (resp. A's) center of mass to the contact point in real space. The contact point in real space can be recovered from the contact point in configuration space.

Let r_a and r_b denote the moment arms on A and B, resp. Then the instantaneous velocity v_a of the contact point on A, given ω, is $\omega \times r_a$. B's direction of impending motion is given by the sign of the expression

$$r_b \times \pi_2 v_a = r_b \times \pi_2(\omega \times r_a),$$

where π_2 denotes the projection of $\Re^3$ onto $\Re^2$.

We now discuss recovery of the moment arms from the contact configuration. Let COM_A and COM_B denote the centers of mass of A and B. In these experiments, they are simply the centers of the gears. Suppose $(\mathbf{x}, \alpha_1, \alpha_2)$ is a contact configuration. Then it lies on an algebraic surface in the generalized configuration space $\Re^2 \times S^1 \times S^1$. This surface is one of two types [Lozano-Pérez]. Let $-A$ denote the reflection of A about its reference point. A type (A) surface is generated by an edge e_a of $-A$ and a vertex b_j of B. A type (B) surface is generated by a vertex a_i of $-A$ and an edge e_b of B. Each edge-vertex or vertex-edge pair is called the *generator pair* of the constraint surface [Donald]. The edges and vertices of $-A$ (resp. B) rotate with α_1 (resp., α_2). An (α_1, α_2)-slice of the surface is found by rotating its generators by (α_1, α_2), and taking their Minkowski sum. Hence the surface may be viewed as a parameterized line-equation, by (α_1, α_2). The table below gives the details for recovering the moment arms from the contact configuration, contact surface in generalized configuration space, and centers of mass. We employ the following notation. For an edge e or a vertex v, $e(\alpha)$ and $v(\alpha)$ respectively denote e and v rotated to orientation α. $\oplus$ denotes *convolution* (sometimes known as the *Minkowski sum*). For two sets U and V, $U \oplus V = \{\, v + u \mid u \in U,\ v \in V \,\}$.

Type	Surface	Moment arm on B r_b	Moment arm on A r_a
A	$e_a(\alpha_1) \oplus b_j(\alpha_2)$	$b_j(\alpha_2) - COM_B$	$b_j(\alpha_2) - \mathbf{x} - COM_A$
B	$a_i(\alpha_1) \oplus e_b(\alpha_2)$	$\mathbf{x} - a_i(\alpha_1) - COM_B$	$-a_i(\alpha_1) - COM_A$

11.4.5 Stiction

What the *Spec* algorithm does is this: it tries to show that from any slice of H_1, all paths that could possibly evolve from commanding a rotation of A either (1) remain in the first slice, or (2) in some subsequent slice, stick or break contact. We have described how (2) is detected. (1) is a form of stiction; the gears do not turn. Note that (1) is a form of sticking behavior, since no motion occurs. Staying in the same slice means that (α_1, α_2) are fixed, and x and y are fixed *a priori*. Hence events (1) or (2) satisfy (F1). That is, (1) is also a form of sticking, and can be detected at run-time by the termination predicate.

Now, suppose B sticks but A continues to turn? This type of stiction is also no problem, since it corresponds to a differential motion $(\pm d\alpha_1, 0)$, which can be predicted by the differential forward projection.

11.4.6 Failures Outside the EDR Framework

We will momentarily digress to a practical question. It would appear that for failure mode analysis to work, non-uniform stiction would be required in our physical model of the gears. That is, it would seem that stiction would have to be impossible in the goal, but possible in H_1. This is not the assumption made in the geometrical EDR analysis and implementation. We now show that uniform stiction is in fact not an impediment to failure mode analysis, either.

It is the responsibility of the user, or of some external inference system, to ensure that (F2) holds. Suppose, however, that this inference is incorrect, and that at run-time stiction does, in fact, occur in the goal, and that the gears jam. In this case the run-time executive will signal failure, *even though the geometrical goal has been achieved*. At first glance it appears that this is incorrect. However, when we regard the goal as a combined geometrical *and functional* specification, it is clear that this is actually the correct termination diagnosis. That is, even though the geometrical goal has been achieved, stiction prevents the quantified difference equation (DE) on paths, $goal(\cdot)$, from being satisfied. Since *something* (specifically, stiction) has prevented achievement of the functional goal, it is completely correct for the run-time executive to signal failure in this case. However, note that we regard this as serendipitous failure detection, and not as inherent in the EDR framework.

11.4.7 Generalizations

The specialized algorithm *Spec* may be generalized. The properties it exploits are (1) that certain degrees of freedom in C and J can be held fixed, while others may be commanded, (2) that "slices" of CO can be computed, (3) set intersections can be computed, and (4) differential motion across the non-fixed degrees of freedom can be predicted using quasi-static analysis.

More precisely, the specialized algorithm generalizes to cases where we fix certain degrees of freedom C_f and J_f, command C_c, and permit J_c to vary (through pushing). Hence $\mathcal{G}$ is decomposed into

$$C_f \times C_c \times J_c \times J_f,$$

$B_{ec}(v_{\theta_2}^*)$ lies in the tangent space to C_c, and all motion lies in the subspace $C_c \times J_c$. Using quasi-static analysis, we predict the impending motion direction, $\mathbf{v}$ which lies in the tangent space to $C_c \times J_c$. If $\boldsymbol{\alpha}$ is in $C_c \times J_c$, let $H_1|_{\boldsymbol{\alpha}}$ denote a slice of H_1 at $(\boldsymbol{\alpha})$. Thus $C_f \times J_f$ are the dimensions of the slice (like x, y in the gear example). Then we let $\boldsymbol{\alpha}' \leftarrow \boldsymbol{\alpha} + \epsilon \mathbf{v}$. Finally, the iteration step is

$$H_3 \leftarrow H_1|_{\boldsymbol{\alpha}} \cap \partial CO|_{\boldsymbol{\alpha}'}.$$

The rest of the algorithm goes through *mutatis mutandis*. This generalization is somewhat theoretical, in that in practice the CO-slices, set intersections, and quasi-static analysis may be difficult to compute for higher-dimensional problems.

∗11.4.8 Discussion: General vs. Specialized Algorithm for Failure-Mode Analysis

This starred subsection may be skipped at first reading. It contains a detailed proof.

The problem with implementing algorithm *Gen* directly is that arbitrary time-indexed forward projections are difficult to compute. For this reason we introduced a specialized algorithm for the gear planning. While algorithms *Spec* and *Gen* appear quite different, in fact, *Spec* is simply a special case of *Gen*. The motivation behind this viewpoint is to find a uniform framework for characterizing algorithms for failure mode analysis. That is, algorithm *Gen* can be viewed as a high-level computational approach to failure mode analysis, while *Spec* is an implementation of *Gen* in a restricted domain. We now discuss this view of the algorithms.

Recall the definition of $stick_{\theta_2}(\cdot)$. We now define $stick_{\theta_2}^*(R)$ to be all points x in R such that any feasible path from x consistent with the control uncertainty $B_{ec}(v_{\theta_2}^*)$, eventually sticks.

We employ the following topological notions. $\overline{U}$ denotes the closure of a set U. U^c denotes its complement. $i(U)$ denotes its interior. $\overline{U}^c$ denotes the complement of the closure.

Now, consider the following step of the *Spec* algorithm,

7. $H_3 \leftarrow H_2 \cap \partial CO|_{\alpha_1', \alpha_2'}$,

where $H_2 = H_1|_{\alpha_1, \alpha_2}$. This step is equivalent to

$$H_3 \leftarrow H_2 - i(CO|_{\alpha'_1,\alpha'_2}) - \overline{CO|_{\alpha'_1,\alpha'_2}}^c, \tag{10}$$

where the set difference operator $-$ associates to the left. Now, the set

$$H_2 \cap i(CO|_{\alpha'_1,\alpha'_2})$$

corresponds to all configurations $(\mathbf{x}, \alpha_1, \alpha_2)$ in the planar slice (α_1, α_2) such that under θ_2, any path from $(\mathbf{x}, \alpha_1, \alpha_2)$ will stick before reaching (α'_1, α'_2) if $\mathbf{x}$ is kept fixed. That is, it is configurations such that sticking will occur from $(\mathbf{x}, \alpha_1, \alpha_2)$ *between* (α_1, α_2) and (α'_1, α'_2).

Below, we argue that the set $H_2 \cap i(CO|_{\alpha'_1,\alpha'_2})$ in algorithm *Spec* corresponds in a quite precise fashion to $stick_{\theta_2}(\partial F)$ in algorithm *Gen*. We see this as follows:

The following step of the *Gen* algorithm,[7]

2. $\quad H_3 \leftarrow \partial F - stick_{\theta_2}(\partial F)$.

is equivalent to

$$H_3 \leftarrow F - \overline{CO}^c - stick_{\theta_2}(\partial F). \tag{11}$$

Now, it is possible to modify *Gen* as follows. Let

$$F_2 = F_{\theta_2,\Delta t}(H_1 - stick^*_{\theta_2}(H_1)).$$

Then we can replace the assignment (11) by eq. (12) and still have *Gen* be correct:

$$H_3 \leftarrow F_2 - \overline{CO}^c, \tag{12}$$

We wish to compare the step (12) of the thus modified *Gen* with the step of *Spec* given in eq. (10). In essence, we wish to show that eq. (10) is in some sense a "conservative" approximation to eq. (12), and hence conclude that algorithm *Spec* is simply a special case of algorithm *Gen*.

We must introduce some notation to compare eqs. (10) and (12). For a set V in $\Re^2$, we denote the set

$$V \times \{(\alpha_1, \alpha_2)\}$$

by

$$V \times (\alpha_1, \alpha_2).$$

---

[7] We have lexicographically substituted H_3 for H_2 throughout algorithm *Gen* to facilitate the comparison with *Spec*.

Now, H_1 is a subset of $\mathcal{G}$. A slice of it $H_1|_{\alpha_1,\alpha_2}$ lies in the "plane" $\Re^2 \times (\alpha_1,\alpha_2)$. Let us denote its projection into $\Re^2$ by $\pi_2 H_1|_{\alpha_1,\alpha_2}$. Finally, for an arbitrary set U in generalized configuration space, let $U|_{\alpha_1,\alpha_2}$ denote an (α_1,α_2)-slice of it, that is,

$$U|_{\alpha_1,\alpha_2} = U \cap (\Re^2 \times (\alpha_1,\alpha_2)).$$

Claim: *Eq. (10) is a conservative approximation to eq. (12) in each slice.*
Proof: First, we obviously have

$$CO|_{\alpha_1',\alpha_2'} \subset CO. \tag{13}$$

Next, we need only show that

$$\left(F_{\theta_2,\Delta t}(H_1|_{\alpha_1,\alpha_2}) \right)\Big|_{\alpha_1',\alpha_2'} \subset \pi_2(H_1|_{\alpha_1,\alpha_2}) \times (\alpha_1',\alpha_2') \tag{14}$$

and

$$H_1|_{\alpha_1,\alpha_2} \cap \pi_2\left(i(CO|_{\alpha_1',\alpha_2'}) \right) \times (\alpha_1,\alpha_2) \subset stick^*_{\theta_2}(H_1|_{\alpha_1,\alpha_2}). \tag{15}$$

Eqs. (14) and (15) are definitional. Now, suppose that configuration $z \in i(CO|_{\alpha_1',\alpha_2'})$. Then clearly $z \notin F|_{\alpha_1',\alpha_2'}$. Hence we have

$$
\begin{array}{ccccc}
H_{3,Gen}\Big|_{\alpha_1',\alpha_2'} & = & \underbrace{\left(F_{\theta_2,\Delta t}(H_1 - stick^*_{\theta_2}(H_1)) \right)\Big|_{\alpha_1',\alpha_2'}} & - & \overline{CO|_{\alpha_1',\alpha_2'}}^c \\
\cap & & \cap & & \| \\
H_{3,Spec} & = & \overbrace{\left(\pi_2 H_2 \times (\alpha_1',\alpha_2') \right) - i(CO|_{\alpha_1',\alpha_2'})} & - & \overline{CO|_{\alpha_1',\alpha_2'}}^c.
\end{array}
$$

$\Box$

Note that as a consequence, we may expect that *Spec* is less likely than *Gen* to terminate.

12. Weak EDR Theory, Strategy Equivalence, and the Linking Condition

12.1. Reachability and Recognizability Diagrams

We now introduce a type of diagram which permits notation of reachability and recognizability. These diagrams are a powerful tool for compactly expressing motion strategies. They greatly aid the development of concise and readable proofs.

Suppose we are given a start region R, a goal G, and a motion θ. We construct the EDR region H. Then under sticking termination, all motions from R will terminate in G or H. That is, the push-forward of the motion θ from R is contained in $G \cup H$:

$$\mathrm{push}_\theta(F_\theta(R)) \subset G \cup H. \tag{16}$$

Whenever (16) is true, we write this by the following *reachability diagram*,

$$
\begin{array}{ccc}
 & & G \\
 & \overset{\theta}{\nearrow} & \\
R & & \\
 & \searrow & \\
 & \theta & H.
\end{array} \tag{17}
$$

Suppose that G and H are distinguishable using sensors. Then θ is an EDR strategy from R, and we have

$$R = P_{\theta,R}(\{\,G, H\,\}). \tag{18}$$

Whenever (18) holds, we write this by the following *recognizability diagram*,

$$
\begin{array}{ccc}
 & & G \\
 & \overset{\theta}{\Longrightarrow} & \\
R & & \\
 & \searrow & \\
 & \theta & H.
\end{array} \tag{19}
$$

The reachability diagram (17) is an equivalent notation for the reachability termination condition (16). The recognizability diagram (19) is equivalent notation for the recognizability termination condition (18). Single arrows ($\longrightarrow$) denote reachability whereas double arrows ($\Longrightarrow$) denote recognizability. If and only if (16) is true, we say that the correspondingly reachability diagram (17) *holds*. If and only if (18) is true, we say that the correspondingly recognizability diagram (19) *holds*. A diagram is said to hold *tautologously* when it is true without additional conditions or suppositions.

The nice thing about sticking termination, as discussed in chapter II, is the following property:

Theorem: *Let R be a start region, θ a motion, and G a goal. Construct the EDR region H for R, θ, and G. Then with sticking termination the reachability diagram (17) holds tautologously.*

Now, in diagrams (17) and (19) we have labeled all the arrows. In the future, when this would clutter the diagrams, we will label only the top arrow and adopt the convention that all arrows aligned below it have the same label.

12.2. More General Push-Forwards

Hence the chief advantage with sticking termination is that (17) is always true. In this chapter, we will generally assume that either sticking termination is employed, or, if more general termination predicates are allowed, then the truth of the reachability diagram (17) can be determined through restrictions on time and history, as described in chap. II. We now digress briefly, however, to describe how this discussion generalizes for more general termination predicates.

In an appendix, we define a more general push-forward, $F_{*\theta}(R)$, which denotes all configurations at which the motion θ can terminate given more general termination predicates. When more general termination predicates than sticking are considered, then the condition (16) must be replaced by

$$F_{*\theta}(R) \subset G \cup H. \tag{20}$$

When (20) holds, we may then write the equivalent reachability diagram (17).

However, with more general termination conditions, (17) does not hold tautologously. For example, with time-termination and the approximate push-forward described in sec. 10.3, a motion could (*a priori*) terminate without sticking yet within the weak preimage. In such cases, it must be the responsibility of the planner to verify that all motions terminate in $G \cup H$.

The first difference between the sticking push-forward push($\cdot$) and the general push-forward $F_*(\cdot)$ is that $F_*(\cdot)$ depends on the start region for the motion, while push($\cdot$) does not. That is, $F_*(\cdot)$ depends on history (and possibly time) whereas push($\cdot$) does not.

Now, a *motion sequence* is a reachability or recognizability diagram of the form:

$$R_n \xrightarrow{\theta_n} R_{n-1} \xrightarrow{\theta_{n-1}} \cdots \xrightarrow{\theta_2} R_1 \xrightarrow{\theta_1} R_0 = G. \tag{21}$$

The second chief difference between the *a priori* sticking push-forward push($\cdot$) and the general push-forward $F_*(\cdot)$ is that the action of push($\cdot$) on a motion sequence

(21) is *functorial*, while $F_*(\cdot)$ is not. The non-functoriality of $F_*(\cdot)$ is a consequence of its history dependence.

12.3. Weak EDR Theory

We now make the following natural refinement of our termination predicate. Suppose the termination predicate is given some *finite* collection of goals $\{G_\beta\}$ in a distinguishable union. Then the goals $\{G_\beta\}$ are of course partially ordered by containment. We assume that the termination predicate returns the smallest goal (with respect to containment) if at termination time the actual configuration of the robot is known to lie within two or more goals. (A technical point: if two or more goals overlap, we augment the collection with a new goal which is their intersection).

Now, whenever the reachability diagram (17) holds (which it always does with sticking termination), then we have the following:

$$R = P_{\theta, R}(\{\,G, H, G \cup H\,\}). \tag{22}$$

This is trivial to show; on termination, the termination predicate will return G or H if it can, otherwise it will return $G \cup H$. In particular, it will return G or H in preference to $G \cup H$.

Thus we can write the following recognizability diagram, which is equivalent to (22):

$$
\begin{array}{ccc}
 & & G \\
 & \nearrow^{\theta} & \\
R & \overset{\theta}{\Longrightarrow} & H \\
 & \searrow_{\theta} & \\
 & & G \cup H.
\end{array}
\tag{23}
$$

(23) is called the *Weak EDR Recognizability Diagram for G, H, and θ.* (19) is called the *Strong EDR Recognizability Diagram.* (17) is called the *Reachability Diagram.*

Theorem: *Let R be a start region, θ a motion, and G a goal. Construct the EDR region H for R, θ, and G. Then with sticking termination the weak EDR diagram (23) holds tautologously.*

Up to now, in previous chapters, we have described the *strong EDR* theory. This section has introduced the weak EDR theory. It may not appear useful at first glance. However, in the next section we will see that these one-step weak EDR strategies—which are in effect always available—may under certain conditions be chained together to make a multi-step plan very like a strong EDR strategy.

The key idea behind the weak EDR theory is: given a collection of goals $\{G_\beta\}$ (possibly including H), we consider all unions of the subcollections to get some measure of weakest recognizability.

12.4. Strategy Equivalence

A one-step weak EDR strategy is not very interesting. In particular, we can always obtain one! Surprisingly, it is possible to define a way of coupling two weak, one-step EDR strategies together to make a two step strategy which has many of the characteristics of strong EDR. In particular, we will develop a way of making precise the idea that the two weak EDR steps can be combined to make a two-step strategy that is "equivalent" to a one-step strong EDR strategy.

Suppose the commanded motions of the two weak EDR steps are θ_1 and θ_2. The essence of this "equivalence" lies in disambiguating a previous motion's (θ_1's) result without destroying the goal state.

Now, let R be the start region, and G the goal as usual. Assume without loss of generality that G is contained within the forward projection of R under θ_1 (see sec. 7.3 for justification). Let

$$R_1 = R \cap P_{\theta_1, F_{\theta_1}(R)}(G). \tag{24}$$

Now, we have the recognizability diagrams

$$
\underbrace{
\begin{array}{ccc}
R_1 & \overset{\theta_1}{\Longrightarrow} & G \\
 & \nearrow & \\
R - R_1 & \Longrightarrow & H \\
 & \searrow & \\
 & & H \cup G
\end{array}
}_{\text{recog } \theta_1}
\qquad
\underbrace{
\begin{array}{ccc}
 & & G \\
 & \overset{\theta_2}{\nearrow} & \\
\text{push}_{\theta_1}(G \cup H) & \Longrightarrow & H' \\
 & \searrow & \\
 & & H' \cup G
\end{array}
}_{\text{recog } \theta_2}
\tag{25}
$$

where H' is the EDR region for motion θ_2.

The question is, how can we link together motions θ_1 and θ_2 into a two-step EDR strategy? The first condition we require of such a two-step strategy is as follows: once θ_1 has reached G, θ_2 should preserve this state and "add" recognizability. That is, G is a "fixed-point" under θ_2. This is given by the following diagram:

Definition: *The* fixed-point diagram *is*

$$\text{push}_{\theta_1}(G) \overset{\theta_2}{\Longrightarrow} G. \tag{26}$$

When the fixed-point diagram (26) holds, (25) admits the following reachability and recognizability diagram:

$$\text{push}_{\theta_1}(G) \overset{\theta_2}{\Longrightarrow} G$$

$$R \nearrow^{\theta_1}$$

$$\searrow$$

$$\text{push}_{\theta_1}(H).$$

(27)

It remains to ensure that good EDR behavior occurs when θ_2 is executed from $\text{push}_{\theta_1}(H)$. Now, think of $\theta_1 * \theta_2$ as the composite strategy formed by executing motion θ_1 followed by θ_2. We wish to find additional conditions which, together with (25), will admit both the fixed-point diagram (26) and a strong EDR diagram,

$$G$$

$$\nearrow^{\theta_1 * \theta_2}$$

$$R$$

$$\searrow^{\theta_1 * \theta_2}$$

$$H'',$$

(28)

for some H'' (see below). Together with the weak EDR diagram (25) (which is tautologously true for sticking termination), the additional conditions below, which we will call the *linking conditions*, are necessary and sufficient for defining an equivalence between two "linked" weak EDR strategies and a single-step strong EDR strategy, whose recognizability diagram is given by (19), (substituting θ_1 for θ). Henceforth, let $\theta = \theta_1$.

Definition: *If the fixed-point diagram (26) holds and if (25) admits a strong EDR diagram (28) in which*

$$H'' = \{ H' \}, \tag{29}$$

then the motion strategy $\theta_1 * \theta_2$ is said to be strongly equivalent *to a strong EDR strategy with recognizability diagram (19).*

An example of such a strategy is the two-step peg-in-hole insertion plan with model error, figs. 4–66.

Definition: *If the fixed-point diagram (26) holds and if (25) admits a strong EDR diagram (28) in which*

$$H'' = \{ H', H' \cup G \}, \tag{30}$$

then the motion strategy $\theta_1 * \theta_2$ is said to be weakly equivalent *to a strong EDR strategy with recognizability diagram (19).*

Note that we define (strong or weak) equivalence using (19) with $\theta = \theta_1$, not with $\theta = \theta_1 * \theta_2$. The reason for this is as follows. If $\theta_1 * \theta_2$ satisfies the weak equivalence condition (30) and the fixed-point diagram (26), then after termination, we are assured that the outcome of θ_1 has been completely diagnosed. That is, the run-time executor knows whether or not θ_1 terminated in success or failure. However, it is not necessarily true that the outcome of θ_2 is completely diagnosed. This occurs in the worst case, if $H' \cup G$ is recognizably attained. We discuss this point in some detail below.

The following gives an implicit definition of linking conditions:

Definition: *Let H'' be chosen for either strong or weak equivalence, as in (29) or (30). The* linking conditions *are necessary and sufficient conditions for (25) to admit a fixed-point diagram (26) and a strong EDR diagram (28).*

It remains to show, of course, that linking conditions exist for strong or weak equivalence. We will momentarily postpone the derivation of the linking conditions in order to describe what the linking should effect.

Once "linked," two one-step weak EDR plans should admit the strong EDR diagram (28). The claim is that (28) is in some sense "equivalent" to the strong EDR diagram (19). How is this possible?

(19) indicates that the run-time executor can disambiguate the success or failure of motion θ_1. The same is true of strategy $\theta_1 * \theta_2$ in (28). Here are the possible results of executing $\theta_1 * \theta_2$ when the steps θ_1 and θ_2 are properly "linked:"

1. G is achieved and recognized at termination. In this case, either (i) θ_1 achieved G and the run-time executive may not have recognized it, but θ_2 disambiguated the result while still terminating within G. Alternatively, (ii) θ_1 failed, reaching H, and θ_2 subsequently achieved G from H.

2. H' is achieved and recognized at termination. In this case, θ_1 is *known to have failed*, and the robot is known to be outside G.

(1) and (2) are the only outcomes given strong equivalence. With weak equivalence, a third outcome in also possible:

3. $G \cup H'$ is achieved and recognized at termination. In this case, θ_1 is *known to have failed*.

Thus the key is that θ_2 does not corrupt the goal state; that is, G is a fixed point under θ_2. The desirability of outcomes (1) and (2) are clear. One might ask, what good is weak equivalence? Why would anyone want outcome (3)? The answer is: in one-step strong EDR (19), the run-time executor can (a) disambiguate the result of motion θ_1, and (b) in case of failure, know that the robot is not in the goal. In weak equivalence, we have (a) but not (b). That is, in outcome (3), we have completely diagnosed the result of motion θ_1, although in the process, we may have accidentally moved into the goal. That is, we may indicate failure when we have, in fact, succeeded. However, we will never indicate success unless it is certain. In short, when linked, $\theta_1 * \theta_2$ is "conservative" about declaring success.

12.5. The Linking Conditions

We now derive the linking conditions. Let

$$F_{\theta_1} = F_{\theta_1}(R)$$
$$R_1 = R \cap P_{\theta_1, F_{\theta_1}}(G)$$
$$\text{push}_{\theta_1} = \text{push}_{\theta_1}(G \cup H)$$
$$F_{\theta_2} = F_{\theta_2}(\text{push}_{\theta_1})$$
$$R_2 = \text{push}_{\theta_1} \cap P_{\theta_2, F_{\theta_2}}(G).$$

The overloading notation for push_{θ_1} is symmetric with that for preimages and forward projections: both the map and its image are denoted by the same symbol. The discussion of linking conditions assumes sticking termination. However, the derivation goes through *mutatis mutandis* for more general termination conditions, if we let[1]

$$\text{push}_{\theta_1} = F_{*\theta_1}(R).$$

It remains, however, to extend the linking-conditions for time-indexed forward projections.

We now demonstrate our claim that linking conditions exist.

Definition: *The condition (L0) is*

$$G \cap \text{push}_{\theta_1} \subset R_2. \tag{L0}$$

Here is the motivation behind (L0). (L0) says that whenever motion θ_1 terminates in the goal G, then the state is inside the preimage of G under the next motion θ_2. The intent of (L0) is to admit the fixed-point diagram (26).

Claim: *(L0) implies the fixed-point diagram (26).*
Proof: The preimage equation for (26) is

---

[1] F_* is defined in the appendix. See also sec. 12.2.

$$P_{\theta_2, \text{push}_{\theta_1}(G)}(G) = \text{push}_{\theta_1}(G).$$

This preimage is taken with respect to a smaller start region than R_2. $\square$

Note however that the converse is false. (L0) is stronger than the fixed-point diagram (26), since the preimage R_2 is taken with respect to the entire forward projection under θ_2.

Claim: *Linking conditions exist, and, in particular, (L0) is a linking condition.*
Proof: Suppose (L0) holds. This yields the following reachability and recognizability diagram:

$$(31)$$

To see that diagram (31) demonstrates weak equivalence, we use a technique like "diagram chasing" (see, eg., [Hungerford]). Assume (L0) holds. Starting from R_1, θ_1 effects a motion reaching G. This motion in fact terminates in $G \cap \text{push}_{\theta_1}$. Since by (L0) $G \cap \text{push}_{\theta_1}$ is within R_2, θ_2 then effects recognizable termination in G.

On the other hand, if the motion begins in $R - R_1$, then θ_1 effects a motion reaching either G or H. If G is reached, then θ_2 will eventually effect recognizable termination in G, by the argument immediately above. If H has been reached, then the motion θ_1 will in fact terminate at some point z in $H \cap \text{push}_{\theta_1}$. Then there are two cases. Case (i): $z \in R_2$. Since the preimage R_2 is constructed with respect to the entire forward projection of push_{θ_1}, motion θ_2 will next effect recognizable termination in G. Case (ii): $z \notin R_2$. In this case, motion θ_2 will effect recognizable termination in one of $\{ G, H, H' \cup G \}$.

We conclude the process by "forgetting" all the intermediate steps, and renaming them to $\theta_1 * \theta_2$. First, observe that the fixed-point diagram (26) holds. Next, to see that (31) admits an EDR diagram (28) in which (30) holds, we remember only the start region R and the "results" G, H', and $H' \cup G$. Diagram chasing shows that these may be joined with recognizability arrows as in (28).

Thus the diagram (31) demonstrates weak equivalence. For strong equivalence, we remove $H' \cup G$ as an outcome of θ_2. Note that the linking condition is not a tautology. However, note that all the other subset relations and the equality in (31) are tautologous. $\square$

In the future, we will leave similar diagram-chasing arguments to the reader. We may thus conclude that

Theorem: *The linking condition (L0) is a necessary and sufficient condition for weak equivalence of $\theta_1 * \theta_2$ to a one-step strong EDR strategy.*
Proof: The claims above have demonstrated sufficiency. It remains to show (L0) is necessary. Suppose (L0) is false, but (26) still holds. (This is the interesting case, for if (26) does not hold, then equivalence cannot possibly follow). (26) says that when the motion is known to start within $\text{push}_{\theta_1}(G)$, then it can be guaranteed to terminate recognizably in G. The antecedent is a precondition for success of the motion. After θ_1, however, this precondition may be false: even if θ_1 reaches G, it is only *known* to have reached push_{θ_1}. In particular, (26) says nothing about what happens when θ_2 is executed from H. (L0), on the other hand, says that termination in G can be recognized no matter where θ_2 originates in push_{θ_1}. $\square$

Now, we can derive some equivalent linking conditions that are somewhat simpler in form. Let

$$R_2^* = R_2 \cap G.$$

Definition: *The* linking conditions **(L1)** *and* **(L2)** *are*

$$G \cap \text{push}_{\theta_1} = R_2^* \qquad (L1)$$
$$H \cap \text{push}_{\theta_1} = \text{push}_{\theta_1} - R_2^* \qquad (L2)$$

These linking conditions admit the reachability and recognizability diagram

$$
\begin{array}{ccccccccc}
& & & & \overbrace{\text{linking conditions (L1), (L2)}} & & & & \\
R_1 & \xrightarrow{\theta_1} & G & \supset & G \cap \text{push}_{\theta_1} & = & R_2^* & \overset{\theta_2}{\Rightarrow} & G \\
& \nearrow & & & & & & \nnearrow & \\
R - R_1 & \longrightarrow & H & \supset & H \cap \text{push}_{\theta_1} & = & \text{push}_{\theta_1} - R_2^* & \Longrightarrow & H' \\
& & & & & & & \searrow & \\
& & & & & & & & H' \cup G \\
\underbrace{\phantom{R_1 \xrightarrow{\theta_1} G \supset}}_{\text{reachability}} & & & & & & \underbrace{\phantom{\text{push} - R_2^*}}_{\text{recognizability}} & &
\end{array} \qquad (32)
$$

Comments: Let

$$P_{\theta_2} = P_{\theta_2, F_{\theta_2}(\text{push}_{\theta_1}(G))}(G),$$

so $R_2 = \text{push}_{\theta_1} \cap P_{\theta_2}$. Note that (L2) is not tautologous, for we can have $x \in G$, $x \notin P_{\theta_2}$ if (L1) is false. Therefore $x \in \text{push}_{\theta_1} - R_2^*$ and $x \notin \text{push}_{\theta_1} \cap H$.

Lemma. *The linking conditions (L1) and (L2) are equivalent.*

Proof. (L1) implies (L2). Suppose (L1). Let $x \in H \cap \text{push}_{\theta_1}$. $x \in R_2^*$ implies $x \in G$. Therefore $x \notin H$ is a contradiction. Therefore $x \in \text{push}_{\theta_1} - R_2^*$.

Now let $x \in \text{push}_{\theta_1} - R_2^*$. Therefore $x \notin G \cap \text{push}_{\theta_1} \cap P_{\theta_2}$. Therefore $x \notin G$ or $x \notin P_{\theta_2}$. In the former case, $x \in H$. In the latter, suppose that $x \in \text{push}_{\theta_1}$ and $x \in G$ and $x \notin P_{\theta_2}$. But by (L1), $x \in G \cap \text{push}_{\theta_1}$ implies $x \in P_{\theta_2}$, a contradiction.

(L1) if (L2). Let $x \in G \cap \text{push}_{\theta_1}$. Show $x \in R_2^*$. We need only show that $x \in P_{\theta_2}$. Now, $x \notin P_{\theta_2}$ implies $x \in H \cap \text{push}_{\theta_1}$, a contradiction. Now let $x \in R_2^*$. Therefore, $x \in G \cap \text{push}_{\theta_1}$. □

Lemma: *The linking conditions (L0) and (L1) are equivalent.*

Proof: (L0) implies (L1). Suppose (L0), i.e., $G \cap \text{push}_{\theta_1} \subset R_2$. Show $G \cap \text{push}_{\theta_1} = R_2^* = G \cap R_2$.

Let $x \in G \cap \text{push}_{\theta_1}$. Now, (L0) implies that $x \in R_2$. Therefore $x \in G$ and $x \in R_2$. Hence $x \in R_2^*$.

Let $x \in R_2^*$. Therefore $x \in G \cap R_2$. Hence $x \in G \cap \text{push}_{\theta_1} \cap P_{\theta_2}$, i.e., $x \in G \cap \text{push}_{\theta_1}$.

(L0) if (L1) is trivial. □

Theorem: *The following linking conditions are equivalent:*

$$
\begin{aligned}
G \cap \text{push}_{\theta_1} &\subset R_2 & (L0) \\
G \cap \text{push}_{\theta_1} &= R_2^* & (L1) \\
H \cap \text{push}_{\theta_1} &= \text{push}_{\theta_1} - R_2^* & (L2)
\end{aligned}
$$

∗12.6. Beyond the Fixed-Point Restriction

In the discussion above, we have required that the goal was a fixed point under motion θ_2. We now discuss how to relax this restriction. In particular, it is possible to extend the notions of strategy equivalence, and the linking conditions, to the case where a subgoal G_1 is in fact the preimage of the actual, or final goal, G_0, under θ_2. Thus G_1 is no longer the fixed point of θ_2, but rather the *preimage* of G_0. This section is somewhat technical and may be skipped at first reading. We regard relaxing the fixed-point restriction as a digression. The subsequent material may be understood even if this section is omitted, however, the reader may wish to bear in mind that such a generalization does, in fact, exist.

We consider the situation where from R, θ_1 may attain G_0 or G_1, where "$G_1 = P_{\theta_2}(G_0)$." However, G_1 may not be distinguishable from G_0 under θ_1. Thus the three reachability results of θ_1 are G_0, G_1, or H_1, where H_1 is the EDR region for θ_1 when we view the goal as $G_0 \cup G_1$.

To define strategy equivalence in the non-fixed-point case, we first generalize the fixed-point diagram (26) as follows.

Definition: *The* generalized fixed-point diagram *is*

$$\text{push}_{\theta_1}(G_0 \cup G_1) \overset{\theta_2}{\implies} G_0. \tag{33}$$

Next, we modify the definitions of strategy equivalence and the linking conditions to require that the generalized fixed-point diagram (33) hold in place of the old fixed-point diagram (26). To avoid confusion, we will call (26) the *simple* fixed-point condition.

Now, we let

$$R_1 = R \cap P_{\theta_1, F_{\theta_1}}(G_0 \cup G_1)$$
$$\text{push}_{\theta_1} = F_{*\theta_1}(R)$$
$$F_{\theta_2} = F_{\theta_2}(\text{push}_{\theta_1})$$
$$P_{\theta_2} = P_{\theta_2, F_{\theta_2}}(G_0)$$
$$R_2 = \text{push}_{\theta_1} \cap P_{\theta_2}$$

Next, define

$$R_2^j = G_j \cap R_2, \qquad (j = 0, 1)$$

It is possible to generalize the definition of R_2^j and the linking conditions to more than two subgoals $\{G_j\}$. We would do this by writing $(\forall j)$ in place of $(j = 0, 1)$.

We already know one linking condition:

$$P_{\theta_2} \supset G_0 \cup G_1. \tag{L3}$$

In addition, we can derive the following linking conditions. Recall H_1 is the EDR region for motion θ_1, viewing the goal of θ_1 as $G_0 \cup G_1$.

$$\text{push}_{\theta_1} \cap G_j = R_2^j \qquad (\forall j) \quad (L1')$$
$$\text{push}_{\theta_1} \cap H_1 = \text{push}_{\theta_1} - \bigcup_j R_2^j. \qquad (L2')$$

Comments: Clearly we have $(L1')$ implies $(L2')$. However I have not been able to prove the converse true. I suspect it is false, since G_0 may intersect G_1, and H_2, the EDR region for θ_2, may intersect G_1, etc.

Finally, note that all *three* linking conditions, $(L1', L2', L3)$ are required for the composition $\theta_1 * \theta_2$ to admit an equivalent strong EDR diagram. This points out the chief theoretical advantage of strategy equivalence with the simple fixed-point condition (26). With the *simple* fixed-point condition, the linking conditions (L0), (L1) and (L2) were found to be equivalent. With the *generalized* fixed point condition (33), not only do the corresponding linking conditions $(L1')$ and $(L2')$ appear to be inequivalent, but we also require the additional independent condition $(L3)$. While it is gratifying that our key concept—composing two weak EDR strategies via linking conditions to admit strategy equivalence—in fact generalized to the non-fixed-point case, the generalization, unfortunately, is correspondingly more complicated.

12.7. What Good is Weak Equivalence?

We now pose the following question. Why is

$$
\begin{array}{ccc}
R_1 & \overset{\theta_1 * \theta_2}{\Longrightarrow} & G \\
 & \nearrow & \\
R - R_1 & \Longrightarrow & H' \\
 & \searrow & \\
 & & G \cup H'
\end{array}
\tag{34}
$$

any better than

$$
\begin{array}{ccc}
R_1 & \overset{\theta_1}{\Longrightarrow} & G \\
 & \nearrow & \\
R - R_1 & \Longrightarrow & H \\
 & \searrow & \\
 & & G \cup H
\end{array}
\tag{35}
$$

$$?$$

(35) is simply the weak EDR diagram for motion θ_1. It always holds (given the reachability diagram). (34) is the equivalent recognizability diagram for $\theta_1 * \theta_2$ when a linking condition is satisfied. That is, (34) is obtained through weak equivalence. Why is (34) stronger than (35), and would one prefer (34) to (35)?

Here is our answer. $\mathrm{push}_{\theta_1}(G)$ is a fixed-point of θ_2. Therefore, nothing is "lost" by θ_2. θ_2 serves to disambiguate the result of θ_1, without polluting the state. Second, note that $\theta_1 * \theta_2$ is "conservative" about declaring success. It is as if we used θ_2 to convert the reachability diagram

$$R_1 \xrightarrow{\theta_1} G$$
$$\nearrow \qquad\qquad\qquad (36)$$
$$R - R_1 \longrightarrow H$$

into the recognizability diagram

$$R_1 \overset{\theta_1 * \theta_2}{\Longrightarrow} \qquad G \text{ "Win"}$$
$$\nearrow \qquad\qquad\qquad\qquad\qquad (37)$$
$$R - R_1 \implies \text{"Lose, but knowing } \theta_1 \text{ did not achieve } G.\text{"}$$

More precisely, the "lose" states are

$H' \approx \theta_1$ did not achieve G, and now the robot is outside of G.

$G \cup H' \approx \theta_1$ did not achieve G, and now we might be in H', but can't guarantee that we're outside of G.

On the other hand (35), achieving $G \cup H$ after θ_1 only tells us that we started in $R - R_1$, and does not tell us the result of motion θ_1.

12.8. Application: Failure Mode Analysis in the Gear Experiment

We now discuss how the failure mode analysis used to generate motion θ_2 in the gear domain may be viewed using the weak EDR theory.

In the gear meshing plan, θ_1 is a pure translation, and θ_2 is a pure rotation. The goal is a fixed point under θ_2. Consider (32). In the gear plan, the reachability arc

$$\overset{\theta_1}{\nearrow} \quad G \qquad\qquad\qquad (38)$$
$$R - R_1$$

is present, but the arc

$$\overset{\theta_2}{\nearrow\!\!\!\!/} \quad G \qquad\qquad\qquad (39)$$
$$\text{push}_{\theta_1} - R_2^*$$

is not. That is, it is possible to serendipitously achieve the goal under translation but not rotation. The linking conditions are satisfied. Now, is the outcome $G \cup H'$ possible? Failure mode analysis yields the answer: No. In this case, $\theta_1 * \theta_2$ is *strongly* equivalent to a one-step strong EDR strategy

$$R_1 \overset{\theta_1 * \theta_2}{\Longrightarrow} G$$
$$\nearrow\!\!\!\!/$$
$$R - R_1 \implies H'.$$

The full reachability and recognizability diagram for the gear plan is given by

$$\begin{array}{ccccccc}
 & & & \overbrace{\text{linking conditions (L1), (L2)}} & & & \\
R_1 & \xrightarrow{\theta_1} & G \supset & G \cap \text{push}_{\theta_1} & = & R_2^* & \xRightarrow{\theta_2} & G \\
 & \nearrow & & & & & \\
R - R_1 & \longrightarrow & H \supset & H \cap \text{push}_{\theta_1} & = & \text{push}_{\theta_1} - R_2^* & \Longrightarrow & H' \quad (40)
\end{array}$$

$$\underbrace{\qquad\qquad\qquad}_{\text{reachability}} \qquad\qquad\qquad \underbrace{\qquad}_{\text{recognizability}}$$

12.9. Discussion and Review

We now discuss the relationship between push-forward algorithms, failure-mode analysis, and the weak EDR theory. Recall the diagram (32):

$$\begin{array}{ccccccc}
 & & & \overbrace{\text{linking conditions (L1), (L2)}} & & & \\
R_1 & \xrightarrow{\theta_1} & G \supset & G \cap \text{push}_{\theta_1} & = & R_2^* & \xRightarrow[b]{a} & G \\
 & \nearrow & & & & & \\
R - R_1 & \longrightarrow & H \supset & H \cap \text{push}_{\theta_1} & = & \text{push}_{\theta_1} - R_2^* & \xRightarrow{c} & H' \quad (41) \\
 & & & & & & \searrow_d & H' \cup G
\end{array}$$

$$\underbrace{\qquad\qquad\qquad}_{\text{reachability}} \qquad\qquad \underbrace{\qquad}_{\text{recognizability } \theta_2}$$

(41) is the full reachability and recognizability diagram for weak equivalence. The arrows (a)-(d) all correspond to motion θ_2; we have labeled them so as to be able to refer to them in the discussion.

Failure Mode Analysis. The reachability and recognizability diagram for failure mode analysis (40) is found by deleting arcs (b) and (d) from (41). In LIMITED, arc (a) is essentially a user input[2] (see sec. 11.3). The failure mode analysis algorithms *Spec* and *Gen* decide arc (c). Thus, in sec. 11.3, (c) corresponds to (F1). Failure mode analysis links a weak EDR strategy θ_1 followed by a strong EDR strategy θ_2. (a) warrants that G is a fixed-point under θ_2. (b) ensures that failure is preserved under θ_2: no serendipitous goal achievement from H is possible. Thus such plans are pure *disambiguation* strategies.

Push-Forward Algorithms. Plans found by push-forward algorithms such as *Multi* admit a diagram from (41) containing arcs (a), (b), and (c), but not containing

---

[2] Although we have discussed methods for inferring (a) computationally, this is really a direction for future work rather than a focus of this research.

(d). The arc (b) (which is shown in detail in eq. (39)) permits serendipitous goal achievement from H under θ_2. The absence of arc (d) yields strong equivalence. Again, push-forward algorithms link a weak EDR strategy followed by a strong one. They differ from failure mode analysis plans in that the arc (b) is permissible, and (a) is not a user input. The peg-in-hole plan with model error (figs. 4–66) is an example of such a plan.

2-Step Weak EDR. A plan admitting the diagram (41) with all four arcs (a)–(d) demonstrates weak equivalence. It is formed by linking together two weak EDR strategies into a 2-Step plan. We have discussed the semantics of such plans above. The key differences between 2-step weak EDR plans and push-forward or failure-mode plans are (1) the existence of arc (d), and (2) the linking of 2 weak (as opposed to a weak and a strong) EDR strategies.

In all cases, note that the linking conditions are required. Thus the linking conditions have somewhat surprisingly turned out to be the underlying characterization for multi-step EDR strategies. That is, since they are necessary and sufficient conditions for constructing multi-step EDR plans, the linking conditions may, in fact, be taken as the *definition* of multi-step EDR strategies.

Hence in considering LIMITED's techniques for multi-step strategy generation, we find that both failure model analysis and push-forward algorithms are essentially special cases of the Weak EDR theory. This is summarized in the table below:

Method	Arcs in (41)	Strategy Type	Comments
Failure Mode Analysis	a,c	weak*strong	Pure Disambiguation. (a) is user input, (c) is computed.
Push-Forwards	a,b,c	weak*strong	(b) permits serendipitous goal achievement.
Weak EDR	a,b,c,d	weak*weak	2-Step Weak EDR.

12.9.1 Algebraic Considerations

Let us pause and review the key points in this development. Weak EDR theory, strategy equivalence, and the linking conditions were introduced as a unifying framework for planning multi-step strategies.

1. The linking conditions are necessary and sufficient criteria for admitting the composition of two weak EDR strategies $\theta_1{}^w$ and $\theta_2{}^w$ into a two-step strategy which

is weakly equivalent to a one-step strong EDR strategy from θ_1. We may write this as

$$\theta_1{}^w * \theta_2{}^w \overset{w}{\simeq} \theta_1{}^s \qquad (42)$$

2.   The linking conditions are necessary and sufficient criteria for admitting the composition of a weak EDR strategy $\theta_1{}^w$ and a strong EDR strategy $\theta_2{}^s$ into a two-step strategy which is strongly equivalent to a one-step strong EDR strategy from θ_1. We may write this as

$$\theta_1{}^w * \theta_2{}^s \overset{s}{\simeq} \theta_1{}^s \qquad (43)$$

3.   The gear plan is a special case of (2). In particular:

4.   Failure mode analysis is a special case of satisfying the linking conditions to render a two-step EDR strategy strongly equivalent to a one-step strong EDR strategy.

5.   Multi-step strategies may also be planned, by repeatedly pushing forward. This was the gist of algorithm *Multi* in the beginning of this chapter. *Multi* may be viewed as chaining together weak EDR strategies followed by a strong EDR strategy. *Multi* is also essentially a special case of (2), with the goal fixed-point condition relaxed.[3]

We can view the set all strategies Φ as a monoid under the composition operation $*$. The generators of the monoid are $\{\theta_i^w\} \cup \{\theta_i^s\}$. Strategy equivalence is a way of defining certain relations between products of these generators. When the linking conditions are satisfied, then these relations take the form of (42) for weak equivalence or (43) for strong equivalence.

However, we cannot directly define a new monoid by taking the quotient of Φ by these relations. This is because the relations are not always true, that is, they only hold when the linking conditions are satisfied. We can remedy this by viewing Φ as "a groupoid without inverses." We call such a structure a *monoidoid*. That is, the operation $*$ turns out to satisfy properties that look very much like the axioms for a monoid. These are called the *monoidoid* properties of $*$. The only difference from the properties of a monoid is that $\theta_1 * \theta_2$ is not defined for every pair of classes, but only for those pairs θ_1, θ_2 for which the linking conditions hold.

---

[3] Relaxing this restriction was discussed in the section "Beyond the Fixed Point Restriction," above.

IV. Planning Sensing and Motion for a Mobile Robot

We now consider an application of the EDR theory to planning sensing and motion for a mobile robot amidst partially-known obstacles. A partial "map" of the environment is represented using generalized configuration space. We assume that the robot has a depth sensor which it can use to interrogate the environment. We call this process *active sensing*.

Applying EDR to the mobile robot domain yields certain insights into the structure of the EDR theory. Conversely, this chapter obtains a technique for planning motions and active sensing for a mobile robot in a partially known environment. This technique provides a principled approach to motion planning with active sensing. It shows how to incorporate a more fine-grained model of sensing into the EDR planning framework.

Much work remains to be done. In particular, the EDR framework for active sensing is still fairly theoretical. Mobile robot environments are often highly unstructured [Brooks, 85], and representing this geometric uncertainty using generalized configuration space presents a non-trivial problem. Furthermore, it may be impractical to model more general vision or sonar sensors without further enhancements to the EDR theory. More study is required; hopefully this theory of EDR planning with active sensing can provide a starting point.

13. Planning Sensing and Motion for a Mobile Robot

Model error is a key theme in this thesis. One important domain in which there is uncertainty in the geometry of the environment arises in planning motions for a mobile robot. Typically, such a robot must plan motions amidst partially known obstacles. Since this partial knowledge can be represented as model error in our generalized configuration space framework, it is natural to consider EDR planning in this domain.

The use of sensing in [LMT] plans might be characterized as "passive." In each step of the plan, a nominal applied force is commanded, and the position and force sensors are monitored until some termination conditions are satisfied. At this time a new motion is selected, and so forth. This model of sensing and action arises quite naturally in developing compliant motion plans for assemblies.

A mobile robot plan, however, is typically not limited to motion commands. The vision or sonar sensors on a mobile robot may be pointed in a direction and information gathered about the environment. This is a more fine-grained model of sensing than is currently available within the EDR planning framework. In this chapter, our goal is to extend the EDR framework to planning both motion and sensing actions. We develop the extension in the mobile robot domain, although it is applicable to any domain where the robot has a choice of sensing modalities and directions to interrogate. The basic difference is that in the [LMT] framework, motion and sensing are inextricable. In the active sensing framework described here, we assume it is possible to sense without moving. In particular, we assume the following model of sensing and motion:

Motions of the mobile robot are modeled in the standard way, using generalized configuration space with sensing and control error:

- The mobile robot is represented by a polygon moving with three degrees of freedom x, y, θ in the plane. There are partially known obstacles in the plane, and they are represented using the space of geometric variations J. $\mathcal{G}$ is of course the product of the Euclidean group acting on the plane, and J. Pushing of the obstacles across J can also be represented. The mobile robot has *a priori* position sensing of accuracy ϵ_{ep}, control accuracy of ϵ_{ec}, and force-sensing accuracy of ϵ_{ev}. We assume that the robot can slide on surfaces as subject to the coefficient of friction μ.

Next, we assume the following additional sensing capability:

- The robot has a *sensor* similar to a laser range-finder. It can be pointed in any direction ϕ to ascertain, approximately, the distance to an obstacle in that direction. The sensor also gives the approximate surface normal of the obstacle patch. The aim of the sensor is inaccurate; however, it is bounded by a cone. The aiming inaccuracy cone is defined by ϵ_{aim}. The error in the distance measurement by the sensor is bounded by ϵ_{dist}. The error in normal measurement is bounded by ϵ_n.

The sensor can be pointed and aimed to ascertain the distance and orientation of a partially-known obstacle surface. The idea is that by choosing where and when to point the sensor, the robot can gather information about the geometry of the environment. This information, in turn, can be used to infer both the position of robot and bounds on the possible geometries of the environment. That is, the action of pointing the sensor and taking a "view" provides constraint on the current position both in C and in J.

Of course, it is possible to model such a sensor naively within the [LMT] preimage framework. For example, one could assume that the sensor continuously takes views of the environment, in all directions at once. Then one could, in principle, obtain upper bounds on the position sensing accuracy that can be inferred from these views. These upper bounds could then be incorporated into ϵ_{ep}, the position sensing accuracy of the robot.

We refine this model as follows. We assume that it is not feasible to take continuous views in all directions at once. In particular, we assume that only a discrete number of views may be taken, and that the robot must choose where (in the plan) to take them, and in what (relative) direction. Thus the primitive operations available to the robot are of two types:

- **Motion Commands**, of the form "Move in heading (x, y, θ) until (termination condition)." These are the standard kinds of motion commands discussed in the development of the [LMT] and EDR framework. The termination condition is the usual termination predicate.

- **Sensing Commands**, of the form "Point the sensor in direction ϕ and take a view." This returns an approximate distance and surface normal reading.

Sensing commands are always executed at rest. We define a *motion plan with active sensing* to be a sequence of motion commands interspersed with sensing commands. As usual, conditional branches are possible. An *EDR plan with active sensing* is a motion plan with active sensing that is an EDR plan. The question is: how can active sensing be incorporated into the EDR framework? We will answer this question by showing how to generate EDR plans with active sensing. As a corollary, we obtain a technique for generating guaranteed plans with active sensing.

The key idea is to define a kind of "equivalence" between sensing and motion. Informally speaking, active sensing is like moving up to an obstacle, measuring the distance traversed and the normal there, and then moving back to one's original position. At that point, by consulting an approximate "map" of the environment and using dead reckoning, a better estimate both of one's position and a revised "map" can be obtained. Using this "equivalence" between sensing and motion, we then can represent both motion and active sensing in a single generalized configuration space. In this space, both motion and active sensing are represented as kinds of "generalized motions." This representation permits the planner to treat sensing and motion uniformly. More precisely:

- *We describe a reduction of the problem of EDR planning with active sensing to (ordinary) EDR planning in a larger generalized configuration space, that represents both motion commands and sensing commands as "generalized motions."*

This reduction is computational; it is similar in flavor to the reduction of planning with model error to computing preimages in a higher-dimensional generalized configuration space.

It is now our task to make precise this notion of the "equivalence" between sensing and motion. To develop this notion without clutter, we will initially simplify the problem as follows. Assume that the robot is a *point* robot, and that rotations need not be considered. Furthermore, we prohibit pushing across J, the space of model uncertainty. Hence the robot's configuration space C is simply the plane. The reduction of the robot to a point is of course justified by existing configuration space formalisms. We will reintroduce rotations later after describing the basic idea.

First, we introduce the definition of a generalized configuration space *planning universe*. A planning universe is a tuple

$$\langle \mathcal{G}, \mathcal{O}, \epsilon_p, \epsilon_v, \epsilon_c, \mu, tp \rangle$$

consisting of

a generalized configuration space $\mathcal{G} = C \times J$,

a set of generalized configuration space obstacles $\mathcal{O} = \{ O_\beta \}$,

the position sensing, velocity sensing, and control uncertainties, $\epsilon_p, \epsilon_v, \epsilon_c$.

the coefficient of friction μ,

and the termination predicate tp.

The planner can plan motions in this universe using the EDR framework described earlier. tp represents the termination predicate available to the run-time executive. For example, we might have the [LMT] termination predicate, which uses position- and force- sensing, as well as time and history. Other termination predicates include that of [Mason], which remembers a continuous history of sensed positions and velocities, and *stick*, which terminates based on sticking.

Now, we assume that our initial planning problem is given by the tuple

$$U_M = \langle \mathcal{G}, \mathcal{O}, \epsilon_{ep}, \epsilon_{ev}, \epsilon_{ec}, \mu, tp \rangle \tag{1}$$

where $\mathcal{G}$ is simply $\Re^2 \times J$ as described above to define the space of motions for the mobile robot. This may be thought of as the "motion universe." We wish to extend

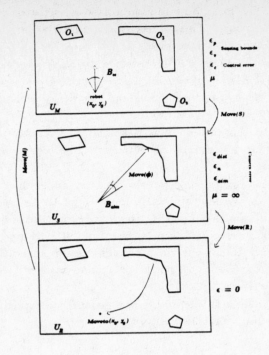

Fig. 1. Schematic illustration of the framework for EDR planning with active sensing.

this universe to incorporate active sensing. We can do this by "adjoining" a "sensing universe." Motions planned in the motion universe U_M correspond to physical motions of the robot, like "Move in heading (x, y)." "Generalized motions" in the sensing universe correspond to active sensing commands, like "Look in direction ϕ and take a view." In addition, the planner needs some special actions that move between the sensing and motion universes. While these actions have no real physical significance, they may be thought of as "preparing to move" or "preparing to sense." We must now define the "sensing universe."

The sensing universe, which we call U_S, contains the same obstacles as the motion universe (1). The sensor can be aimed in this universe. Once the sensor is aimed, we imagine that a "line of sight" motion $Move(\phi)$ is commanded. This motion terminates on the first surface it hits.[1] Here is the idea: this line of sight motion can be modeled as a generalized damper motion with control error ϵ_{aim}, the

---

[1] Assuming no mirrors!

aiming accuracy of the sensor. That is, if the nominal sensor aiming direction is ϕ, then the effective line of sight motion is actually in some direction in the angular interval $(\phi - \epsilon_{aim}, \phi + \epsilon_{aim})$. Once the motion terminates, the distance traversed can be measured with accuracy ϵ_{dist}. The normal on the surface at the point of "contact" can be measured with accuracy ϵ_n. The uncertainty bounds ϵ_{dist} and ϵ_n will be taken to be the position- and force- sensing uncertainties, resp., in the sensing universe.

Thus we construct a sensing universe whose uncertainties are given by the error characteristics of the sensor. We next provide the planner with the primitive command $Move(S)$, which moves from the motion universe into the sensing universe, retaining the same position (in $\mathcal{G}$) relative to the obstacles $\mathcal{O}$. Once in the sensing universe, it is then possible for the planner to command the generalized motion $Move(\phi)$.

We have said that active sensing was like "moving to an obstacle, measuring its distance and normal, and then moving back to the original position." So far we have sketched how the sensing universe models the motion *up to* the obstacle. Now we must describe a "return universe" which models the motion *back to* the original position. The return universe is perfect: there is no control error. However, the only termination predicate available is pure position-sensing associated with the command $Moveto(x_0, y_0)$, where (x_0, y_0) indicates the *actual* position of the robot before the $Move(S)$ command. That is, in the return universe, there is perfect position control, but the only position that can be commanded is the original position.

Thus we can define the following commands which are available to the planner to use in its motion strategies.

List of Generalized Motions Commands

1. **Physical Motion Commands.** Same as "Motion Commands" above. Applicable at any time in universe U_M.

2. **Move(S).** Applicable at any time in universe U_M. First, record the *actual* position of the robot in the variable (x_0, y_0). Next, move from the motion universe into the sensing universe, retaining the same position (x_0, y_0) relative to the obstacles $\mathcal{O}$.

3. **Move(ϕ).** This commands a straight line motion in relative direction ϕ, subject to aiming inaccuracy ϵ_{aim}. When the motion terminates on the first surface struck, the sensing uncertainty bounds ϵ_{dist} and ϵ_n provide a characterization of how accurately the distance to the obstacle and its normal may be measured. Note that the line of sight motion effected by $Move(\phi)$ does not move across J. It moves in C and retains the same position in J. Applicable *only* after a $Move(S)$ command.

4. **Move(R).** Move from the sensing universe into the return universe, retaining the same position relative to the obstacles $\mathcal{O}$. Applicable *only* after a $Move(\phi)$ command.

5. **Moveto(x_0, y_0).** Move with perfect accuracy from wherever the robot is to (x_0, y_0), where (x_0, y_0) is the value stored by the last $Move(S)$ command. That is, (x_0, y_0) is a literal here, and may not be chosen by the planner. Applicable *only* after a $Move(\phi)$ command.

6. **Move(M).** Move from the return universe into the motion universe, retaining the same position (x_0, y_0) relative to the obstacles $\mathcal{O}$. Applicable *only* after a $Moveto(x_0, y_0)$ command.

We now make the construction somewhat more formal.

The sensing universe U_S is defined to have the same obstacles as U_M. However, the uncertainties in U_S correspond to the error bounds in aiming the sensor, and in measuring the distance and normal to an obstacle. To construct U_S, first assume that $\epsilon_{dist} = 0$ and $\epsilon_n = 0$ that is, assume a perfect sensor which is aimed inaccurately. Then we could construct U_S as

$$U_{S,perfect} = \langle \mathcal{G}, \mathcal{O}, 0, 0, \epsilon_{aim}, \infty, stick \rangle.$$

In the sensing universe, the coefficient of friction is infinite. Hence the line of sight motions which terminate on the first obstacle they strike are exactly modeled by damper motions which stick on any surface. The termination predicate halts such motions as soon as they stick, that it, as soon as they make contact.

The point is that with a *perfect* sensor, the motion $Move(\phi)$ terminates exactly on the surface W it strikes. However, for an imperfect sensor, this motion must be modeled as terminating within ϵ_{dist} of this surface. That is, the motion terminates within the set $W \oplus B_{dist}$, where B_{dist} is a ball of radius ϵ_{dist}. We can model this termination via a "jerky" termination predicate which stops on the first surface it hits (using sticking), and then "jerks" away some distance no greater than ϵ_{dist} before halting. We denote this termination predicate as $stick \pm \epsilon_{dist}$. Hence, in general,

$$U_S = \langle \mathcal{G}, \mathcal{O}, \epsilon_{dist}, \epsilon_n, \epsilon_{aim}, \infty, stick \pm \epsilon_{dist} \rangle. \tag{2}$$

Recall that $push_\theta(\cdot)$ denotes the *a priori* push-forward based on sticking. Suppose that the initial position of the robot is known to lie in some start region R. Then with a perfect sensor, $Move(\phi)$ simply terminates within $push_\phi(R)$. $push_\phi(R)$ is identical to the obstacle edges of the forward projection of R under ϕ subject to control uncertainty ϵ_{aim} and $\mu = \infty$. With an imperfect sensor, $Move(\phi)$ terminates within the set

$$\mathrm{push}_\phi(R) \oplus B_{dist}.$$

The return universe U_R also has the same obstacles. In it we have perfect control and sensing:

$$U_R = \langle \mathcal{G}, \mathcal{O}, 0, -, 0, -, \text{pure position control}\rangle. \tag{3}$$

Of course, in U_R we are only permitted to command one motion; the motion returning to (x_0, y_0). In both the sensing and the return universes, $\mathcal{G}$ is again $\Re^2 \times J$.

EDR planning with active sensing may be regarded as a planning problem in the larger generalized configuration space

$$U_M \cup U_S \cup U_R. \tag{4}$$

We regard this generalized configuration space as endowed with a special "physics" that governs motions in the three universes it comprises, and how the robot can in fact move between universes. In addition, of course, the planner must satisfy certain compositional constraints in constructing plans. That is, certain steps are only applicable, or valid, when preceded by other steps. This is a constraint on the *type* of operators available to the planner when it chooses commanded generalized motions. For example, in the physical motion universe U_M, there is a choice between a physical motion command (in U_M) and a $Move(S)$ command to enter the sensing universe. But once the sensing universe has been entered, there are no choices in the type of operator to apply, but merely in their parameterization (specifically, the choice of ϕ).

For this reason, any implementation of EDR planning with active sensing should combine operators (2–6) into a single operator

(2–6). **Sensor(ϕ).** Command the sequence of generalized motions: $Move(S)$, $Move(\phi)$, $Move(R)$, $Moveto(x_0, y_0)$, $Move(M)$.

The operator $Sensor(\phi)$ is the formal model for Sensing Commands (as defined above in boldface). The reason we decomposed this operator into steps (2–6) was to illustrate the structure of the problem, and to show how active sensing could be integrated into motion planning with uncertainty, using familiar tools in the EDR framework.

This completes the reduction for the special case of point robots in the plane. We will now provide an example, and then return to generalize the reduction to non-point robots with rotational degrees of freedom.

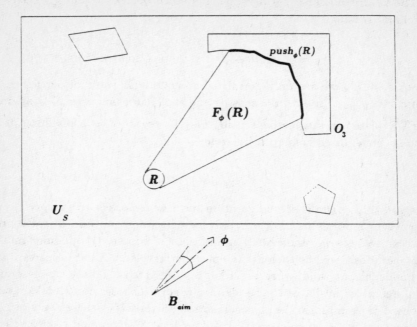

Fig. 2. Detail of the generalized motion $Move(\phi)$ in U_S. The start region is R. The forward projection is the outer envelope of all possible lines of sight, given the aiming error of the sensor. The push-forward is the wall of O_3 the sensor can see.

13.1. Using Information Provided by Active Sensing

In this section we clarify how the additional information provided by active sensing is used by the planner to further constrain the position of the robot in generalized configuration space. While the incorporation of this constraint is implicit in the reduction above, it helps to see an explicit construction in an example. This example builds on fig. 1. The development here is somewhat informal.

Suppose that the robot is known to lie in some region R in generalized configuration space. For example, in fig. 2, R is the same size as the position sensing uncertainty ball B_{ep}. We wish to calculate explicitly how taking a view in direction ϕ can further constrain the possible positions of the robot. For example, by pointing the sensor at a wall of obstacle O_3 in fig. 2, the robot may be able to further localize its position, given some information about the distance and orientation of

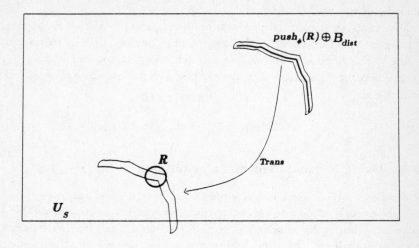

Fig. 3. After the generalized motion $Move(\phi)$ terminates, the robot is known to lie within distance ϵ_{dist} of the sticking push-forward. This defines a tube in generalized configuration space. The information effect of the perfect "return" motion $Moveto(x_0, y_0)$ is to translate this tube back to the original position. The run-time executive now has better localized the position of the robot.

the wall.

A line of sight in direction ϕ is considered to be like a straight line motion. We must consider all lines of sight that are possible, given the aiming inaccuracy of the sensor. We view all possible lines of sight as a region in generalized configuration space. This region is the forward projection $F_\phi(R)$. No sliding is possible in the forward projection, since the coefficient of friction is infinite. The push-forward (based on sticking) of the generalized motion $Move(\phi)$ is part of the wall of obstacle O_3. This region is denoted $push_\phi(R)$ in fig. 2.

An upper bound on the run-time executor's knowledge of the wall's position is found as follows. Let B_{dist} denote the size of the position sensing uncertainty ball in U_S. This ball is an upper bound on the sensor's ability to localize distances. The knowledge of the wall's position will lie within the convolution of the push-forward of the generalized motion $Move(\phi)$ by B_{dist}, that is,

$$\text{push}_\phi(R) \oplus B_{dist}. \tag{5}$$

Hence, after executing motion ϕ, the virtual robot is guaranteed to lie within distance ϵ_{dist} of the wall O_3.

Now suppose the actual position of the physical robot is (x_0, y_0), as in fig. 2. Then the information effect of the command $Moveto(x_0, y_0)$ is to translate the set (5) back to the original position. We denote this operation by[2] $\text{trans}_{(x_0, y_0)}(\cdot)$. Thus after the sensing operation $Sensor(\phi)$, the position of the robot is known to lie within the set

$$R \cap \text{trans}_{(x_0, y_0)}(\text{push}_\phi(R) \oplus B_{dist}). \tag{6}$$

*13.1.1 Using Normal-Sensing Information

The detailed starred sections below may be skipped at first reading.

The sensor's ability to detect surface normal orientation provides additional constraint. That is, by sensing the normal, the sensor can further localize the point of contact within eq. (5). Recall that π denotes the canonical projection of phase space onto position space. Then the localization provided with combined distance-sensing and normal-sensing is found as follows. Let B_n denote the normal-sensing error ball of radius ϵ_n in phase space. Now, let $\tilde{F}_\phi(\cdot)$ denote the forward projection in phase space. From the phase-space forward projection, we derive the *a priori phase-space push-forward based on sticking*, $\widetilde{\text{push}}_\phi(\cdot)$. We can view an element of $\widetilde{\text{push}}_\phi(R)$ as a pair, consisting of a point and a tangent vector. Suppose that $\mathbf{n}^*$ denotes the normal as sensed by the sensor at execution time, and let $\mathbf{n}^{*\perp}$ be its orthogonal complement. Thus $B_n \oplus \mathbf{n}^{*\perp}$ represents the set of all possible actual tangent vectors consistent with $\mathbf{n}^*$. Then after termination, the motion $Move(\phi)$ is known to be within the set[3]

$$B_{dist} \oplus \pi\left(\widetilde{\text{push}}_\phi(R) \cap \left(\mathcal{G} \times (B_n \oplus \mathbf{n}^{*\perp}))\right)\right). \tag{7}$$

Eq. (7) replaces (5) when normal sensing is available to the sensor.

*13.2. Generalizations

We now relax some of the initial simplifying assumptions adopted above. In particular, we generalize the framework for EDR planning with active sensing to

---

[2] The definition of trans is informal.

[3] Formally, the notation in eq. (7) assumes that $\mathcal{G}$ is parallelizable.

the case of a polygonal robot moving with three degrees of freedom in the plane, amidst partially-known obstacles. Some of the obstacles may be pushed by the robot, which may change their position and orientation.

*13.2.1 Pushing

First, we incorporate pushing in the model, as follows. Physical motion commands (in the physical universe U_M) are permitted to cause pushing of movable obstacles, resulting in cross-coupled motions in C and J. However, the operator $Move(\phi)$ can of course cause no motion in J, since it corresponds to vision sensing. Hence we must simply restrict the effect of the straight-line motion $Move(\phi)$ to motion exclusively in C.

*13.2.2 Non-Point Robots

Next, we wish to consider robots which are not points, for example, polygonal robots in the plane. Assume without loss of generality that the sensor is mounted on the robot at the reference point. Then we must simply replace the generalized configuration space obstacles in the construction of U_S and U_R by the set of generalized *real space* obstacles, $\mathcal{B}$. $\mathcal{B}$ represents a variational family of real-space obstacles. Intuitively, $\mathcal{O}$ represents the $\mathcal{B}$ "grown" by the shape of the robot. That is, $\mathcal{O}$ is constructed by convolving each generalized real-space obstacle with the robot geometry.

More precisely, let $B_\beta(\alpha)$ denote a particular shape of an obstacle in the environment for α in J. β indexes the set of all such obstacles. Then

$$\mathcal{B} = \left\{ \{(B_\beta(\alpha), \alpha)\}_{\alpha \in J} \right\}_\beta .$$

Now, assume for simplicity that the shape A of the robot is exactly known. If $\ominus$ denotes convolution with the reflection as in [Lozano-Pérez], then

$$\mathcal{O} = \left\{ \{(B_\beta(\alpha) \ominus A, \alpha)\}_{\alpha \in J} \right\}_\beta .$$

Thus of course, for point robots, $\mathcal{O}$ and $\mathcal{B}$ are identical.

*13.2.3 Rotations

We now incorporate rotations into the planning framework for active sensing. First, in the construction of the physical motion universe U_M (1), we construct $\mathcal{G}$ as $\Re^2 \times S^1 \times J$, using the Euclidean group on the plane for C. The generalized configuration space obstacles $\mathcal{O}$ are constructed in the usual way for rotations and translations. Next, we will leave $\mathcal{G}$ as $\Re^2 \times J$ in constructing the sensing and return universes, (2) and (3). The obstacles in the sensing and return universes are the generalized real-space obstacles $\mathcal{B}$ as described above. Again, the generalized motion $Move(\phi)$ moves only in C, without changing the position in J. However, note that $Move(\phi)$ is restricted to be a pure translation in U_S, terminating on some real space obstacle in $\mathcal{B}$. This is an important difference. The physical motion commands can move with three degrees of freedom in C within U_M; however, the sensing command moves as a pure translation in U_S. Furthermore, it moves in generalized real-space, amidst generalized real-space obstacles, whereas the physical motion commands in U_M move in generalized configuration space amidst generalized configuration space obstacles.

Some technical changes are required in the $Move(S)$ and $Move(R)$ operators. When $Move(S)$ is executed from actual configuration (x, y, θ) in the physical motion universe U_M, the forward projection consists of the point (x, y) in the sensing universe U_S. The original actual position is stored in a variable (x_0, y_0, θ_0). This variable is used by the pure position control command $Moveto$ in the perfect return universe U_R. This is easy to formalize by representing the generalized configuration space in (4) as $\mathcal{G} \times 3$, where U_M, U_S, and U_R are identified with the subspaces $\mathcal{G} \times \{0\}$, $\mathcal{G} \times \{1\}$, etc. We then view the motions between universes as a combined projection and shift. For example,

$$Move(S) : U_M \to U_S \subset \mathcal{G} \times 3$$

$$((x, y, \theta), 0) \mapsto ((x, y), 1).$$

$Move(R)$ may be formalized similarly as a combined lifting and shift.

This completes the reduction of EDR planning with active sensing to EDR planning in a three-fold generalized configuration space.

13.3. Discussion

In this chapter, we described a reduction of EDR planning with active sensing to (ordinary) EDR planning in a larger generalized configuration space that represents both motion commands and sensing commands as "generalized motions." The reduction involves defining a kind of "equivalence" between sensing and motion, which permits an EDR planner to treat sensing and motion commands "uniformly." These generalized motions can be represented in a "threefold cover" of generalized configuration space. The equivalence defined relies on the similarity between visibility analysis and generalized damper motions.[4] With our tools for planning with model error—specifically, the generalized configuration space formalism—it was possible to

---

[4] This similarity was exploited extensively by [Buckley].

give a precise characterization of what it means to plan with active sensing, and to derive a formal method for constructing these plans. The generalized configuration space representation was critical not only in representing the uncertain environment, but also in defining a planning model for active sensing. It is interesting to note that while generalized configuration space was originally envisioned exclusively as a framework for representing geometric model uncertainty [D], it appears to have broader applicability in planning pushing operations and active sensing. In EDR planning with active sensing, generalized configuration space is particularly useful in developing a systematic model of the error in absolute position vs. the error in the map of the world: the first is position error in C, the second is position error in J. Both may be reduced through an appropriate choice of physical motions or active sensing. However, error in C can grow with physical motion, while error in J cannot.[5] Furthermore, active sensing can only reduce the error in C and J; it can never increase it. When viewed in this manner, it is not at all clear that there should be any unifying concept for physical motion and active sensing! It is even more surprising that the unifying tool should emerge as our familiar friend, generalized configuration space.

This reduction yields an effective technique for planning motions and active sensing for a mobile robot in a partially known environment. This technique provides a principled approach to motion planning with active sensing. It shows how to incorporate a more fine-grained model of sensing into the EDR planning framework. As a corollary, of course, we obtain a method for planning guaranteed strategies with active sensing.

Much work remains to be done. In particular, the EDR framework for active sensing is still fairly theoretical. Mobile robot environments are often highly unstructured [Brooks, 85], and representing this geometric uncertainty using generalized configuration space presents a non-trivial problem. Furthermore, it may be impractical to model more general vision or sonar sensors without further enhancements to the EDR theory. More study is required; hopefully this theory of EDR planning with active sensing can provide a starting point.

---

[5]unless pushing is allowed.

V. Implementation, Computational Issues

In this chapter, we describe the LIMITED plane-sweep algorithm. We then turn to the problem of generating motion strategies. LIMITED has a crisp algorithm for verifying EDR strategies, but to generate a strategy, it must quantize the space of commanded motions and enumerate motion strategies exhaustively. How can motion plans be generated without exhaustive quantization of the space of commanded directions? To this end we introduce the *non-directional backprojection*. It allows us to devise exact algorithms for planning guaranteed strategies, given certain restrictions. We also address generalizing such algorithms to planning multi-step strategies, and to generating EDR strategies. While the motion planning with uncertainty is known to be hard for exponential time [Canny and Reif], we are able to identify certain interesting subclasses of planning problems which are easier (polynomial or single-exponential time). These techniques for generating multi-step strategies will hopefully be useful in EDR planning as well.

14. Implementation, Computational Issues

14.1. Comments on the Plane Sweep Algorithm

Given a 2D slice of generalized configuration space, LIMITED employs a plane-sweep algorithm for computing unions, intersections, and projections. (By *projections* we mean forward projections, backprojections, and weak-backprojections in that slice). The algorithm uses exact (rational) arithmetic, and computes unions in $O((n + c) \log n)$ time, and projections in $O(n \log n)$ time.[1] The design and implementation of the 2D plane-sweep module is joint work with John Canny; the algorithm is based on [Neivergelt and Preparata] (who give a union algorithm) and related to [Erdmann] (who implemented an $O(n^2)$ backprojection algorithm, and suggested an improved $O(n \log n)$ version). In this section we briefly discuss some details of the algorithm. A full listing of the ZetaLisp code for the plane-sweep algorithm running on a Symbolics 3600 is provided in an appendix. In LIMITED there are, of course, many software layers built on top of the sweep algorithm for quasi-static analysis, EDR planning, propagation across slices, distinguishability, and so on. In EDR planning, we essentially reduce the problem of EDR verification to deciding certain set-relations. The basic sets are projection regions. Both the projections and the set operations are computed by calls to the sweep algorithm. The design and implementation of a robust geometric engine is a formidable task. In this section we share some of our experiences.

We do not go on at great length about the details of the algorithm because, first of all, it is fairly complicated, and second, from a complexity-theoretic viewpoint, the result does not improve known bounds by much. Readers interested in the details of the algorithm will find them in the appendix.

14.1.1 The Basic Idea

We now sketch the classical plane sweep approach at a high level. In plane sweep algorithms, the vertices of the input edges are sorted on planar lexicographic x-y order, eg., lower left to upper right. This is accomplished using an AVL tree. A line is swept across the plane in this order. The algorithm keeps track of the polygonal regions swept across by maintaining an ordered queue of intervals on the sweep line. This queue is also maintained using a (different) AVL tree. Each interval along the sweep line has an associated "color." The color is an integer; 0 for free space, 1 for a region inside one input polygon, 2 for a region inside two input polygons, etc. The boundaries of the intervals grow or shrink with the sweep in a

---

[1] Where n is the number of vertices in the slice, and c is the number of intersections.

known way: their change is given by the line equation of their endpoints. These line equations are taken from the line equations of the input edges.

An "event" occurs when a new vertex is encountered in the sweep. Such an event affects one or more of the intervals in the interval queue on the sweep line. For example, in a "closing" event, the "end" of a polygon has been encountered (it has closed up), so all of the polygon lies to the left of the sweep line. In this case, the interval associated with the polygon is deleted, the two surrounding intervals are merged, and the polygon loop is placed on the output queue. Other events include "start" (start a new polygon) and "crossing", when the line equations of three adjacent intervals intersect. In a crossing event, two line segments intersect and their associated interval boundaries must be merged.

In developing a sweep algorithm for projections, we proceed as follows. Consider the forward projection. We introduce two new colors, the *projection* color and the *start* region color. The sweep proceeds in the direction of the commanded motion. When the sweep encounters the start region, then intervals of color *start* region are inserted into the interval queue along the sweep line. When these intervals close, then intervals of color *projection* must be queued. The line equations of the free-space endpoints of these projection intervals are parallel to the sides of the commanded velocity uncertainty cone. This occurs when the projection intervals border free-space intervals.

When an interval of type *projection* crosses an interval of type *obstacle* (color ≥ 1), then either (1) it may be closed off, (2) the obstacle edge boundary may be taken as the projection region boundary by updating the line equation of the projection interval's endpoints, or (3) depending on sliding behavior, a new "degenerate" interval, with no width, sliding along the edge may be queued. Whether the motion can slide on an edge e is determined by intersecting the reflected ("negative") velocity cone with the friction cone on edge e. In case (3), the line equations of degenerate interval's endpoints are copied from e.

When the sweep is complete, the output is an arrangement of polygons with different colors, including the projection and the start region colors. The forward projection is simply all polygons with color projection or start region. This algorithm is correct given the following assumption:

Correctness Criterion: *The plane sweep algorithm is correct when (a) the friction cone is larger than the commanded velocity uncertainty cone and (b) there is a bounding box around the input environment.*

This criterion is necessary, because the sweep algorithm is monotonic; hence to be correct, we must ensure that motions are also monotonic and cannot back up on surfaces.

By introducing a *goal* color, backprojections and weak backprojections are computed analogously, sweeping in the opposite direction to the commanded motion. The weak backprojection is actually a conservative (under)-approximation, since it does not take into account weak backsliding [Buckley]. This is because weak backsliding is non-monotonic and so a sweep algorithm will not suffice. Actually, our plane sweep algorithm can only sweep in one fixed direction; hence we rotate the environment first so that the sweep axis coincides with the commanded motion direction, and then rotate the projections back to the canonical orientation.

For details of the sweep algorithm, please see the appendix.

14.1.2 Contrast with Previous Algorithms

We now compare our algorithm, which we call *Sweep*, with previous work.

1.   *Sweep* combines the ability to compute set operations and projections in one sweep.

2.   The plane sweep algorithm of [Neivergelt and Preparata] for computing set operations on polygonal regions assumes general position. *Sweep* does not.

3.   Note that [Erdmann] described the first backprojection algorithm in the plane. He also described slice algorithms for 2D with rotations. [Buckley] described non-slice backprojection and forward projection algorithms in 3D with no rotations. All these algorithms have been implemented.

4.   The algorithm of [Erdmann] can compute the backprojection of a single edge in time $O(n \log n)$. In *Sweep*, the goal region can be an arbitrary polygon. Similarly, in *Sweep*, the start region for forward projections can be an arbitrary polygon.

5.   *Sweep* is implemented using exact (rational) arithmetic.

6.   *Sweep* can compute forward and weak backprojections as well as strong backprojections.

14.2. Non-Directional Backprojections

14.2.1 Intuition

LIMITED is a generate-and-test planner. We have elaborated the "test" portion—verification of EDR strategies as decision problems about projection sets. Now it is time to take a more sophisticated look at the "generation" problem. How can motion strategies be generated without exhaustive quantization and search?

A significant weakness of LIMITED is its method for generating commanded motions. It simply quantizes the space of all motions. Thus to generate two-step plans $\theta_1 * \theta_2$ LIMITED must quantize the space of motions θ_1 to generate the first motion, and then quantize the space of motions for θ_2. Essentially, LIMITED implements an existential theory; the planner can verify a strategy but the strategy must be "guessed" by some oracle, or by exhaustive search. This is theoretically unsatisfying, as well as impractical. We now address this problem. In particular, we provide a method for generating two-step plans $\theta_1 * \theta_2$ which only requires "guessing" θ_1. That is, once θ_1 is provided, θ_2 can be generated.

To this end we define a combinatorial object called the *non-directional backprojection*, and give a critical slice algorithm for constructing it. The non-directional backprojection may be used to represent, in a sense, "all possible backprojections" of a fixed goal. We intend to use it to generate motion strategies.

[LMT] first defined non-directional preimages. [Erdmann] defined the non-directional backprojection as the union of all backprojections in the plane:

$$\bigcup_\theta B_\theta(G).$$

We will use a different definition. However, it is in the same spirit as [LMT,E], and so we will employ the same name. We must point out, however, that both M. Erdmann and R. Brost have considered[2] a similar construction for generating commanded velocities, and also thought about a critical slice approach to computing it.

Our definition exploits generalized configuration space. Consider the following argument.

1. Suppose we have a planar polygonal environment with no model error. In generating motion strategies, we do not know which way to point the robot— that is, we do not know which way to command the motion. Thus in some sense, there is "uncertainty" in "which way to go." This "uncertainty" is the variable θ. Thus we have a kind of three-dimensional planning problem, with degrees of freedom x, y, θ. As the reader may expect, we intend to map this uncertainty in "which way to go" into our familiar friend, generalized configuration space.

2. Now, consider a problem which is in some sense dual to generating motion strategies. In this problem, we only consider *one* commanded motion in a fixed direction v_0^*. However, there is total uncertainty in the orientation of the entire environment. We may represent this uncertainty by a variable θ also.

Clearly, both problems (1) and (2) can be represented in an generalized configuration space where x and y are the degrees of motion freedom, and θ is "model

---

[2] [Personal communication]. I am grateful to M. Erdmann for pointing out the similarity of the construction.

error." Here is the difference, however. In (2), θ is universally quantified: that is, we are required to ensure that a motion strategy succeeds for *all* θ. In (1), however, θ is existentially quantified. We merely need one θ to find a commanded motion.

The precise analogue of (1) is a problem like (2) in which we get to choose the orientation of the environment such that the v_0^*, the fixed commanded motion under consideration, will guarantee reaching G.

14.2.2 Computing the Non-Directional Backprojection

We now make the intuitive argument more precise. Let J be the space of all commanded motions, so that J is exactly the circle, S^1. We write $\theta \in J$ for a commanded motion direction.

Definition: *Let G be a goal amidst polygonal obstacles in the plane. The* Non-Directional Backprojection $B(G)$ *of G is a set in $\Re^2 \times J$,*

$$B(G) = \bigcup_\theta \Big(B_\theta(G) \times \{\theta\} \Big). \tag{1}$$

Now, recall the critical slice algorithms of sec. 6.4. These algorithms computed 3D directional backprojections in a three dimensional generalized configuration space, $\Re^2 \times S^1$. They operate by determining critical orientations at which the topology of backprojection slices change.

$B(G)$ is also a 3D backprojection-like region. We can develop critical slice algorithms for computing $B(G)$ also. They will work by finding all values of θ at which the topology of $B_\theta(G)$ can change. Then the algorithm takes slices at these critical θ's and at an intermediate non-critical θ's between each pair of adjacent critical values.

Now, $B(G)$ is bounded by developable algebraic surfaces. These surfaces are of two types, *obstacle* surfaces, and *free-space* surfaces. The obstacle surfaces are liftings into $\Re^2 \times J$ of the obstacle edges in $\Re^2$. The free-space surfaces are swept out by free-space edges of $B_\theta(G)$ as they rotate with θ. The manner in which the bounding algebraic surfaces of $B(G)$ sweep between slices is completely known— the obstacle edges stay fixed, while the free-space edges rotate with θ, remaining parallel with edges of the velocity cone. Now, each free-space edge is anchored at an obstacle vertex cobounding a possible sticking edge. As θ varies, the free-space edge rotates about that vertex. Clearly, as θ varies, the topology of $B_\theta(G)$ can change if the free space edge contacts an obstacle vertex. When this happens, there is an edge connecting two obstacle vertices which is parallel to an edge of the commanded velocity cone. Next, we note that any such edge lies in the *visibility graph* of the planar input environment. The visibility graph may be computed in time $O(n^2)$. This gives us the following lemma, which gives an upper bound on the number of critical values of θ. Here is the intuition behind the lemma:

> Consider a free-space edge $e_i(\theta)$ of $B_\theta(G)$. $e_i(\theta)$ lies in the infinite half-ray $r_i(\theta)$ which extends from $e_i(\theta)$'s anchor vertex. We call $r_i(\theta)$ a *constraint ray*; it is parallel to an edge of $B_{ec}(v_\theta^*)$. There are $O(n)$ constraint rays in each backprojection slice $B_\theta(G)$. $r_i(\theta)$ rotates with θ, and it can intersect $O(n)$ obstacle edges as θ sweeps along. Now, how many other constraint rays of the form $r_j(\theta)$ can $r_i(\theta)$ intersect as it rotates? Note that all constraint rays $\{e_j(\theta)\}$ move "with" $r_i(\theta)$, and are either parallel to it, or else intersect it always. Therefore how $r_i(\theta)$ can intersect these other constraint rays as θ sweeps is also $O(n)$.

We assume that the input polygons represent configuration space obstacles.[3] We use the boundary operator ∂ to denote the topological boundary.

Lemma. *Given a goal G of constant size and an arrangement of input polygons $\mathcal{P}$ of size $O(n)$, there are $O(n^2)$ critical values of θ in the non-directional backprojection $B(G)$.*

Proof: Let $B_{ec}(v_\theta^*)$ denote the control velocity uncertainty cone about a commanded velocity v_θ^*. We think of $B_{ec}(v_\theta^*)$ as rotating with θ. The topology of $B_\theta(G)$ can change when any of the following occur:

A. An edge of $B_{ec}(v_\theta^*)$ becomes parallel to an edge in the visibility graph of $\mathcal{P}$. Such values of θ are called *vgraph*-critical.

B. θ is a *sliding*-critical value (see sec. 6.4), where the determination of sliding vs. sticking behavior on an edge can change. Sliding-critical values occur when an edge of $B_{ec}(v_\theta^*)$ becomes parallel to the edge of a friction cone on some configuration space edge.

C. Let $e_i(\theta)$ and $e_j(\theta)$ be free-space edges of $B_\theta(G)$. They rotate with θ about their anchor vertices. Let $p_{ij}(\theta)$ denote their intersection; it is a free-space vertex of the backprojection. Then θ is *vertex*-critical when $p_{ij}(\theta) \in \partial B_\theta(G)$ and $p_{ij}(\theta)$ intersects some obstacle edge.

Now, there are $O(n^2)$ edges in the visibility graph of $\mathcal{P}$. In sec. 6.4 we showed that there are $O(n)$ sliding-critical values. Only sliding-critical values can introduce additional constraint rays.

Now, since there are $O(n)$ constraint rays in each slice, it would appear *a priori* that there could be potentially $O(n^2)$ $p_{ij}(\theta)$'s. Note, however, that each

---

[3] See sec. 6.4 for the complexity where the input is given in real space obstacles.

free-space vertex $p_{ij}(\theta)$ of the backprojection can be identified with exactly one constraint ray, say the "left" one, $r_i(\theta)$. Hence we see that there are merely $O(n)$ $p_{ij}(\theta)$'s. Each moves in a circle. Observe that in effect, each free-space vertex of the backprojection moves with θ in a piecewise-circular, possibly disconnected locus. Consider the discontinuities in the locus caused by type (A) or (B) critical values. In between discontinuities, each circular arc in the locus can intersect only a fixed number of obstacle edges. In particular, the arc cannot intersect n obstacle edges without "using up" more type (A) or (B) critical values. Hence, there are $O(n^2)$ vertex-critical values of θ.

Next we observe that the bounds for (A) (B) and (C) are additive. In particular: the bounds on vertex-critical and vgraph-critical values apply to all *possible* free-space edges; hence the vgraph-critical and vertex-critical values do not interact and their complexities do not multiply. Similarly, the sliding-critical bounds cover all possible ways that a constraint ray can be added or deleted from the backprojection boundary as θ changes. Hence this bound is also additive. Thus we obtain the $O(n^2)$ upper bound. $\square$

Corollary: *There exists a representation of size $O(n^3)$ for the non-directional backprojection $B(G)$.*
Proof: Take $O(n^2)$ slices at critical values. Compute a backprojection slice $B_\theta(G)$ of size $O(n)$ at each of the critical values of θ. $\square$

Comments: This upper bound means that $O(n^2)$ slices are required for a critical slice representation of $B(G)$. However, as in sec. 6.4, it seems that this upper bound will almost never be attained in practice. In practice we will consider only small ranges of θ. For example, for a peg-in-hole strategy, we would probably only consider directions in the lower (downward) half-plane. While these arguments do not affect the worst-case complexity, they do suggest that in practice the number of critical θ values may be smaller than $O(n^2)$.

We can now address the complexity of computing $B(G)$. By this we mean, what is the complexity of computing a precise, combinatorial description of $B(G)$. The output representation is a finite ordered set of alternating critical and non-critical slices $\{\, B_{\theta_{c_1}}(G), B_{\theta_{nc_1}}(G), \dots \,\}$, along with an algebraic description of how the free-space edges of the backprojection change between slices. (For a free-space edge, this is completely specified by the anchor vertex and an interval of θ for which the surface bounds $B(G)$).

As above, let $\mathcal{P}$ be an arrangement of input polygons representing configuration space obstacles.

Theorem: *Given a goal G of constant size and an arrangement of input polygons* $\mathcal{P}$ *of size* $O(n)$, *a representation of size* $O(n^4)$ *for the non-directional backprojection* $B(G)$ *can be computed in time* $O(n^4 \log n)$.

Proof: First, we compute the critical values of θ. Sliding-critical values can be computed in linear time. Vgraph-critical values can be computed in time $O(n^2 \log n)$. While it may be possible to compute the vertex-critical values in quadratic time, we give the following simple $O(n^3)$ algorithm: Intersect all constraint rays to obtain $O(n^2)$ points $p_{ij}(\theta)$. Each of these points is a possible free-space vertex of the backprojection, and each moves in a circle with θ. Intersect these circles with the obstacle edges to obtain $O(n^3)$ possible critical values of θ. The actual vertex-critical values will be contained in this set.

Compute $O(n^3)$ slices $B_\theta(G)$, at each the possibly-critical value θ, using *Sweep*. *Sweep* computes a 2D backprojection slice in time $O(n \log n)$, and the output has size $O(n)$. $\square$

Some comments are in order. First, our algorithm is naive, in that each backprojection slice is recomputed from scratch. In fact, this extra work is unnecessary. At a critical value of θ, very few aspects of the topology of the backprojection will change. That is, typically, only one or two free-space edges will be introduced, or disappear, or change at any critical value. We can make this notion precise as follows. If θ is a generic singularity, then exactly one edge or vertex of $B_\theta(G)$ will appear or disappear there. Hence, for example, we can ensure that all critical values are generic singularities with probability one by subjecting the input to small rational perturbations.

Suppose that a backprojection has been computed in a critical slice at θ. Then to compute a backprojection in a nearby non-critical slice at $\theta + \epsilon$, we merely need to update the portion of the backprojection boundary which was critical at θ. This requires only constant work: only one edge or vertex must be changed to derive a backprojection in the new slice! The new slice, furthermore, need not be copied in entirety. Instead, the representation for the new slice can simply indicate how it has changed from the old slice. It is reasonable to speculate that this technique would yield an algorithm of time and space complexity $O(n^2 \log n)$ for computing $B(G)$. (The log factor arises from the necessity of sorting the critical values).

14.2.3 The Non-Directional Forward Projection

The "dual" to the non-directional backprojection is the non-directional forward projection:

Definition: *Let R be a start region amidst polygonal obstacles in the plane. The* Non-Directional Forward Projection $F(R)$ of R *is a set in* $\Re^2 \times J$,

$$F(R) = \bigcup_\theta \Big(F_\theta(R) \times \{\,\theta\,\} \Big).$$

As a corollary to our bounds on the complexity of the non-directional backprojection, we obtain the following theorem which may be derived *mutatis mutandis*:

Theorem: *Given a start region R of constant size and an arrangement of input obstacle polygons $\mathcal{P}$ of size $O(n)$, let $F(R)$ be the non-directional forward-projection of R. Then*

a. *there are $O(n^2)$ critical values of θ for $F(R)$;*

b. *there exists a representation of size $O(n^3)$ for $F(R)$;*

c. *a representation of size $O(n^4)$ for $F(R)$ can be computed in time $O(n^4 \log n)$.*

$\square$

We will need the following corollary later:

Corollary: *For a constant-sized start region R and goal region G, amidst an arrangement of input obstacle polygons $\mathcal{P}$ of size $O(n)$, the non-directional forward projection $F(R)$ and non-directional backprojection $B(G)$ have representations as polynomial-sized formulae in the language of semi-algebraic (s.a.) sets. Furthermore, these formulae are quantifier-free.*

Proof: We can represent the non-directional forward projection (resp., backprojection) at a polynomial (in n) number of critical values $\{\,\theta_1, \ldots, \theta_l\,\}$ via the formula

$$A = \bigwedge_{i=1}^{l} (\theta = \theta_i \quad \Rightarrow \quad (x,y) \in F_{\theta_i}(R)).$$

Let two adjacent critical values be $\theta_i^{\min}$ and $\theta_i^{\max}$. In between adjacent critical values of θ, the non-directional projection is bounded by a fixed[4] set of $O(n)$ developable algebraic surfaces. That is, when θ is between $\theta_i^{\min}$ and $\theta_i^{\max}$, the non-directional projection is the intersection of some fixed set of $O(n)$ algebraic half-spaces. These half spaces are represented by algebraic inequalities, $\{\,g_{ij}(x,y,\theta) \leq 0\,\}$ where each g_{ij} is a polynomial. The form of the g_{ij} is discussed in 14.2.2. We define the predicate

$$C_i = \bigwedge_{j=1}^{m_i} (g_{ij}(x,y,\theta) \leq 0),$$

---

[4] i.e., fixed between $\theta_i^{\min}$ and $\theta_i^{\max}$.

where m_i is $O(n)$. We construct the non-directional projection as a s.a. set in a case statement,

$$A \wedge \bigwedge_i (\theta \in (\theta_i^{\min}, \theta_i^{\max}) \quad \Rightarrow \quad C_i).$$

$\square$

14.3. Generating Multi-Step Strategies using the Non-Directional Backprojection

We now describe how to employ the non-directional backprojection $B(G)$ to generate two-step strategies with "less quantization." More precisely: while LIMITED is required to hypothesize both the first motion θ_1 and the second motion θ_2, we can show how, given θ_1, θ_2 may be computed. Hence only θ_1 need be guessed through exhaustive quantization, and θ_2 can be computed deterministically.

Let C be the configuration space $\Re^2$, and J the space of commanded motions S^1 as above. Define the projection map

$$\pi_J : C \times J \to J$$
$$(x, y, \theta) \mapsto \theta.$$

Now, algorithm *Semi-Plan*, below, takes a first motion θ_1, the goal G, the start region R and the set $\mathcal{P}$ of input polygons representing the arrangement of configuration space obstacles. It computes the set T of all commanded motions θ_2 such that $\theta_1 * \theta_2$ reaches G.

Algorithm Semi-Plan

1. $\text{push}_{\theta_1} \leftarrow F_{*\theta_1}(R)$.
2. $R_1 \leftarrow \text{push}_{\theta_1} \times J$.
3. $T \leftarrow J - \pi_J \left(R_1 - B(G) \right)$.
4. *Return any* $\theta_2 \in T$.

To see that *Semi-Plan* is correct, we simply observe that J is *the set of all commanded motions* θ_2, and that

$$\pi_J \left(R_1 - B(G) \right) \tag{2}$$

is simply the projection onto J of where the push-forward of θ_1 lies outside the non-directional backprojection. Choosing any θ_2 in the complement of (2) results in a two step motion that is guaranteed to reach G.

Algorithm *Semi-Plan* has several advantages over exhaustive quantization of both θ_1 and θ_2 spaces of directions. First, it requires less quantization. Second, it provides *all θ_2* such that $\theta_1 * \theta_2$ reached G, instead of just one. Third, the algorithm is crisper, in that it exploits the structure of the non-directional backprojection; the algorithm is not blind. Finally, it is possible to give precise analyses of *Semi-Plan*'s combinatorial complexity, as above. Clearly, the complexity of computing $B(G)$ will dominate.

14.4. Comments and Issues

Semi-Plan represents a theoretical algorithm. It has not been implemented in LIMITED. It was described here to give some characterization for bounds on computing multi-step strategies. In particular, it gives a precise, combinatorial description for the 3D non-directional backprojection $B(G)$ for a planar polygonal configuration space environment. *Semi-Plan* directly addresses the question of planning two-step strategies. The critical slice method attempts to put the directional backprojection techniques used in LIMITED on a firm mathematical footing. It gives a principled way to choose motion θ_2 given θ_1, a bound on how many slices are required, and an algorithm which does not have to exhaustively enumerate the possible second motions θ_2.

Note that if we were merely interested in one-step strategies, then a variation on *Semi-Plan* provides a way to compute the set of all one-step motions guaranteed to reach the goal *without quantization*. Consider algorithm *One-Step* which computes the set T of all motions guaranteed to reach G from a start region R:

Algorithm One-Step

1. $R_1 \leftarrow R \times J.$
2. $T \leftarrow J - \pi_J\left(R_1 - B(G)\right).$
3. *Return any* $\theta \in T.$

In a sense, *Semi-Plan* and *One-Step* employ the non-directional backprojection to effect "quantifier elimination." That is, the decision problem for guaranteed one-step strategies is

$$\exists \theta \qquad R \subset B_\theta(G). \tag{3}$$

One-Step provides a way to eliminate the quantifier and in fact to generate all θ satisfying (3). For two step strategies, we have the decision problem

$$\exists \theta_2, \exists \theta_1 \qquad F_{*\theta_1}(R) \subset B_{\theta_2}(G). \tag{4}$$

Semi-Plan is an algorithm for eliminating the outer quantifier, and in fact, given an θ_1, to generate all θ_2 satisfying (4). Taking this view, we can characterize *One-Step* as an *exact* algorithm for planning guaranteed strategies in a planar polygonal environment. By "exact," we mean that it does not rely on quantizations or approximations, and that precise bounds are known. Similarly, we can view *Semi-Plan* as a "semi-exact" algorithm for two-step strategy generation.

This is just a start, however, much work remains:

1.   The combinatorial bounds on $B(G)$ can probably be improved. It remains to prove or disprove the following conjecture:

Conjecture: *Given a goal G of constant size and an arrangement of input polygons $\mathcal{P}$ of size $O(n)$, $B(G)$ can be computed in time $O(n^2 \log n)$ and space $O(n^2)$.*

2.   An exact version of *Semi-Plan* could lead to an exact algorithm for planning multi-step guaranteed strategies. *Semi-Plan* is merely semi-exact. We would like to eliminate the "inner quantifier" in (4), and thus avoid the task of quantizing θ_1-space. This would yield an exact algorithm for planning two-step guaranteed strategies. One approach would be to introduce a new axis to generalized configuration space, J_1, which represented the space of all possible first motions, $\{\,\theta_1\,\}$. We then might lift $B(G)$ to $B(G) \times J_1$, and construct its backprojection $B(B(G) \times J_1)$ in the space $C \times J \times J_1$. In this case, however, instead of a discrete set of critical θ_2 values, we obtain a set of critical *curves* in the θ_1-θ_2 plane. The critical slice algorithm will be correspondingly more complicated, and remains to be generalized to this case. This approach would also require incrementing the dimension of generalized configuration space (by 1) at each backchaining step. This increase in dimensionality is consistent with known lower bounds on the motion planning problem with uncertainty [Canny and Reif].

3.   The non-directional backprojection is our key tool in developing an exact algorithm for computing guaranteed strategies. Similarly, we would like to obtain exact algorithms for computing EDR strategies. The key theoretical tools here would be the non-directional *weak* backprojection and non-directional forward-projection. The same combinatorial bounds hold for these non-directional objects. It remains to develop exact algorithms for their set difference, for determining non-directional sticking, and for distinguishability. One approach to an exact algorithm for multi-step EDR planning might be as follows. Above, we suggested how an exact algorithm for multi-step guaranteed strategy generation might be devised. [Brost] has suggested a backchaining EDR planning algorithm which can generate multi-step plans, each step of which is a strong EDR strategy. (See chap. III). By using

the non-directional weak backprojection (in place of the directional weak backprojection) in such a backchaining planner, an exact algorithm for multi-step EDR planning might be constructed.

4. The exact algorithms should be extended to more general configuration spaces. Model error should be permitted. As above, the topology of the non-directional backprojection will now become critical along hypersurfaces in the resulting generalized configuration space.

Despite the apparent difficulties in these extensions, I feel that using the non-directional backprojection is a promising approach to the strategy generation problem. In particular, it is a principled, exact algorithm for generating compliant motion strategies. All previous theoretical and implemented fine-motion planners [LMT,E,Mason,D,Buckley]—including LIMITED—essentially employed or suggested an exhaustive search which quantized or enumerated the set of possible commanded motions. In order for fine-motion planners to be practical, more study of the generation problem is required.

14.5. Complexity and Theoretical Results

Above, we described a polynomial time exact algorithm for generating one-step guaranteed compliant motion strategies amidst planar polygonal obstacles. We now briefly address the general case of generating guaranteed r-step compliant motion strategies. Assume sticking termination, so that for all θ and all R,

$$F_{*\theta}(R) = \text{push}_\theta(F_\theta(R)).$$

By analogy with the non-directional backprojection, we can define the non-directional forward projection. Now, we observe that all directional projection sets are semi-algebraic (s.a.). Then by the lemma on critical values of $B(G)$, so are the non-directional projection sets. Furthermore, when R has constant size, the lemma shows that the non-directional projection sets have descriptions (as s.a. sets) that are polynomial in the size of the input arrangement $\mathcal{P}$.

In the following definition, we assume that the control uncertainty cone B_{ec} is encoded by an angular error bound $\pm\epsilon_c$.

Definition: *The planar compliant motion planning problem with sticking termination is defined as follows. Given a polygonal start region R of constant size, an integer r, a polygonal environment $\mathcal{P}$ of size n, control uncertainty ϵ_c, coefficient of friction μ, and a polygonal goal G of constant size, find a sequence of r motions $\theta_1, \ldots \theta_r$ such that each motion terminates in sticking, and the final motion θ_r terminates in the goal. Or, if no such r-step strategy exists, then say so.*

Theorem: *The planar compliant motion planning problem with sticking termination is decidable in time* $n^{r^{O(1)}}$.

Proof: Let $p_0, \ldots, p_m \in \Re^2$. We define the predicates

$$f_\theta(p_1, p_2) \quad \Longleftrightarrow \quad p_2 \in F_\theta(p_1) \tag{5}$$

and

$$f_\theta^*(p_1, p_2) \quad \Longleftrightarrow \quad p_2 \in F_{*\theta}(p_1). \tag{6}$$

Clearly, definition (6) is equivalent to

$$f_\theta^*(p_1, p_2) \quad \Longleftrightarrow \quad f_\theta(p_1, p_2) \wedge stick_\theta(p_2). \tag{7}$$

We have shown how in polynomial time to compute a quantifier-free polynomial-sized formula (in n) for the s.a. set $F(p_i)$—the non-directional forward projection of p_i. It remains to show that (5), and consequently (6) are polynomial-sized predicates. Now, $\theta \in S^1$, $p_1 \in \Re^2$, and $p_2 \in \Re^2$. Consider $f_\theta(\cdot, \cdot)$ as a predicate on a 5D space $S^1 \times \Re^2 \times \Re^2$, that is, as $f(\theta, p_1, p_2)$. We can obtain a bound on the complexity of f by enumerating all possible edges of $F_\theta(p_1)$ as θ and p_1 vary. These edges then sweep out developable algebraic surfaces in the domain of the predicate. There are four types of edges that can bound $F_\theta(p_1)$:

a. An edge e_i of a generalized configuration space obstacle. These edges sweep out n surfaces of the form $S^1 \times \Re^2 \times e_i$.

b. A free-space edge anchored at a vertex v_j of a generalized configuration space obstacle and parallel to the left or right edge of the velocity cone. Let $r(v_j, \theta)$ denote the infinite ray anchored at v_j at orientation θ. Then type (b) edges sweep out $2n$ surfaces of the form $\bigcup_\theta (\{\theta\} \times \Re^2 \times r(v_j, \theta \pm \epsilon_c))$.

c. A free-space edge anchored at p_1 and parallel to the left or right edge of the velocity cone. These edges sweep out 2 surfaces of the form

$$\bigcup_\theta \bigcup_{p_1} \Big(\{\theta\} \times \{p_1\} \times r(p_1, \theta \pm \epsilon_c) \Big).$$

d. A partial edge of a generalized configuration space obstacle. Let v_1, v_2 be the vertices of a generalized configuration space obstacle edge. A partial generalized configuration space edge can start at v_1 or v_2 and extend to v', where v' is a vertex of a type (b) or (c) free-space edge. Clearly v' simply arises as the intersection of a type (a) surface with a type (b) or (c) surface.

By enumeration, we clearly obtain a linear $(O(n))$ bound on the number of surfaces in the 5D domain of f. The arrangement of these surfaces has polynomial size; in particular, it has $O(n^5)$ critical values. Hence we may conclude that f is a predicate of polynomial size in n.

Now, define

$$\mathcal{F}(p_0,\ldots,p_m,\theta_1,\ldots,\theta_m) \iff f_{\theta_1}^*(p_0,p_1) \wedge f_{\theta_2}^*(p_1,p_2) \wedge \cdots \wedge f_{\theta_m}^*(p_{m-1},p_m). \tag{8}$$

Since (6) has polynomial size in n, clearly the predicate (8) has polynomial size in n as well. Furthermore, it is quantifier-free.

Now, we let the points p_i serve as via points (sometimes known as switch-points) for the strategy. We quantify over all possible via points achievable by the motion strategy $\theta_1,\ldots,\theta_r$. By letting m be r, this is sufficient.

We can formulate the question of the existence of an r-step strategy as a decision problem within the theory of real closed fields:

$$(\exists \theta_1,\ldots,\theta_r)$$

$$\left(\forall p_0,\ldots,p_r \quad \left((p_0 \in R) \wedge \mathcal{F}(p_0,\ldots,p_r,\theta_1,\ldots,\theta_r) \right) \Rightarrow (p_r \in G) \right). \tag{9}$$

Now, deciding sentences in the theory of real closed fields is known be doubly-exponential only in the number of quantifier alternations. More specifically, the truth of a Tarski sentence for k polynomials of degree $< d$ in r variables, where $a \leq r$ is the number of quantifier alternations in the prenex form of the formula, can be decided in time

$$(kd)^{O(r)^{4a-2}},$$

(see [Grigoryev]). We have $a = 2$, and hence (9) can be decided in time $n^{O(r)^6}$. $\square$

This theoretical result is of interest for the following reasons. First of all, the *general* compliant motion planning problem with uncertainty (in 3D) is known to be hard for non-deterministic exponential time [Canny and Reif]. This means that any algorithm for the problem takes at least doubly-exponential time in the worst case. In this section, we have introduced restrictions on the problem which make it more tractable. These restrictions are:

- The configuration space is the plane, where directional forward projections have linear size. (In 3D they can have exponential size). A key step in our construction was then to show that the non-directional backprojection $B(G)$ has polynomial size.
- Sticking termination is used.
- The maximum number of steps in the strategy is given as input to the algorithm.

With these restrictions, the problem becomes decidable in time exponential in r. In fact, we conjecture that for a great number of planning problems, r is in fact a small constant. When r may be so regarded, we effectively obtain a polynomial-time algorithm for this restricted planar motion planning problem with uncertainty.

It might have been possible to devise these restrictions *a priori*, from a strictly complexity-theoretic viewpoint. However, I believe that only after reading the previous chapters does it become clear that these restrictions are *physically* meaningful, and in fact define a useful and interesting subclass of planning problems. In a way, this thesis has been an exploration of problems solvable within these restrictions. From this perspective, I believe it is reasonable to conjecture that a large class of planning problems do fall under this rubric.

Of course, this is only a start. From the standpoint of developing theoretical, "exact" algorithms, we have only addressed the problem of planning certain restricted classes of guaranteed strategies in the plane. It remains to consider exact algorithms in higher-dimensional configuration spaces, model error, EDR, and more sophisticated termination conditions.

VI. Conclusions

15. Conclusions

15.1. Summary

This thesis offers two main contributions to the theory of manipulation. The first is a technique for planning compliant motion strategies in the presence of model error. The second is a precise, geometrical charaterization of error detection and recovery (EDR). These led to a constructive definition of EDR plans in the presence of sensing, control, and model error. These more general strategies are applicable in assembly planning where guaranteed plans do not exist, or are difficult to find. We tested the EDR theory by implementing a planner, LIMITED, and running experiments to have LIMITED automatically synthesize EDR strategies.

A number of mathematical tools were developed for the EDR theory. First, we considered compliant motion planning problems with n degrees of motion freedom, and k dimensions of variational geometric model uncertainty. We reduced this planning problem to the problem of computing preimages in an $(n+k)$-dimensional generalized configuration space, which encompasses both the motion and the model degrees of freedom, and encodes the control uncertainty as a kind of non-holonomic constraint. We also showed how pushing motions could be planned using generalized configuration space. In addition to the assembly domain, generalized configuration space was shown to serve as a "map" for planning sensing and motion strategies for a mobile robot amidst partially known obstacles.

Next, we characterized EDR strategies geometrically via the EDR region H. Determining whether a strategy satisfied the EDR axioms was reduced to a decision problem about forward projections and preimages in generalized configuration space. Making this process formal and algorithmic required a detailed investigation of the geometric and preimage structure of the EDR regions. The Weak EDR theory introduced new mathematical tools for studying multi-step strategies—reachability and recognizability diagrams, strong and weak strategy equivalence, linking conditions, and strategy composition. A variety of techniques for planning multi-step EDR strategies were investigated and unveiled as special cases of the Weak EDR theory.

Finally, we explored the complexity of EDR planning. We derived bounds both for the implemented planner LIMITED, and for theoretical extensions. While in general it is known that compliant motion planning with uncertainty is intractable, we were able to demonstrate a number of special cases where there exist efficient theoretical algorithms. In particular, we showed a case where $n = 2$, $k = 1$ and containment in the backprojection could be computed in polynomial time (note for $n = 3$, $k = 0$, this is false [CR]). We also investigated the structure of the non-directional backprojection in the plane. It led to a polynomial-time algorithm for computing one-step (guaranteed) strategies, and a singly-exponential algorithm for multi-step strategies.

15.2. Future Work

A number of research directions deserve further attention:

15.2.1 Probabilistic Strategies

The EDR framework should be extended to include probabilistic strategies. At the moment the EDR theory essentially provides a binary test for recognizing an EDR strategy. It would be useful to have a method for deciding which of two strategies was "better." We sketched a way of formalizing this generalization in sec. 7.

15.2.2 Goals and EDR Regions in Phase Space-Time

When the goal is specified in phase space-time as the product of a cylinder over a generalized configuration space goal with a compact time interval, our geometrical characterization of EDR satisfies the EDR axioms. Without time, or with goals of the form $\pi^{-1}(G) \times [t, \infty)$, the definition of $\tilde{H}$ does not completely fulfill the EDR axioms. This is because it is possible for motions sticking in H_s to eventually slide into the goal, violating the principle that no motion should be terminated as a failure when serendipitous goal achievement is still possible.

This area deserves further research. Future directions include: Relaxations of the EDR axioms, probabilistic control strategies, implementation of termination-predicates with time, computation of time-indexed forward projections, and study of the structure of phase space-time goals.

15.2.3 Algorithmic Improvements: Search and Efficiency

LIMITED currently employs a great deal of exhaustive search. The space of model error and the space of commanded directions are exhaustively quantized. We have demonstrated certain theoretical results using critical slices of the projection regions (sec. 6) and the non-directional backprojection (sec. 14) to show how exhaustive search may be avoided by examining only "relevant" constraints. This direction should be explored more extensively.

On a related note, LIMITED is slow. We have demonstrated efficient theoretical algorithms for subproblems in the EDR theory. These algorithms should be reduced to practice. EDR planning in higher-dimensional generalized configuration spaces may be prohibitive unless faster algorithms are found.

15.2.4 How Often is Planning Hard?

While compliant motion planning with uncertainty is known to be very hard in general, this does not mean that all such problem are hard. We desire some way of talking about the "space" of geometrical planning problems, and defining a kind of measure on that space. Then perhaps one could determine whether the problems which are hard for exponential time are of "measure zero", for example.

15.2.5 Provably Good Approximate Algorithms

Concomitant with our conjecture about the distribution of geometrical problems is the observation that the intractability of exact solution does not preclude the existence of fast approximate algorithms. It would be very useful to develop such algorithms and show that they are provably good approximations.

15.2.6 Different Complexity Measures

In developing good average-time algorithms for EDR planning, it would be useful to measure the complexity in the size of the output. For example, while it is true that the forward projection in 3D can have exponential size, it seems that there are many problems in which it is much smaller. Thus it would seem natural to measure the complexity of planning in 3D by the complexity of the forward projection.

15.2.7 Hardness of EDR vs. Guaranteed Planning

Since the EDR theory contains [LMT] as a subtheory, it appears *a priori* at least as hard to decide. However, consider the following "intuitionist" argument: *many "hard" problems, requiring exponential-length guaranteed plans that take doubly-exponential time to generate, may admit "short" EDR plans that can be generated easily.* For example, the peg-in-hole insertion strategy with model error, or the gear-meshing plan, may require very long plans if the plans must be guaranteed. However, we can find 2-step EDR plans for these problems. This intuition—which is a heuristic claim, so the reader is advised to proceed with caution—should be verified or disproven.

15.2.8 Weak EDR Theory

The weak EDR theory, while still in its infancy, has already yielded some interesting results and a fairly clean mathematical framework for studying multi-step strategies. The key idea behind the weak EDR theory is: given a collection of goals $\{G_\beta\}$ (possibly including H), we consider all unions of the subcollections to get some measure of weakest recognizability. This is perhaps the most exciting theoretical area for future work.

As an immediate goal, the linking conditions should be extended for time-indexed forward projections.

15.2.9 Dynamic Model

The dynamic model in the EDR theory should be tested, by trying out the EDR plans using actual robots. The dynamic model should also be extended, to incorporate second-order dynamics, impact, and deformation.

15.2.10 Computing Projection Sets

When rotations and compliant motion are allowed, we do not know of exact algorithms, even in principle, for computing projection sets. For example, the computation of forward projections is not immediately decidable within the theory of real closed fields. This is because the physics of motion are essentially specified "differentially," that is, by a mapping that sends a configuration $x \in \mathcal{G}$ and a commanded motion $\theta \in S^n$ (where $n+1$ is the dimension of C), to a cone $B_c(x, \theta)$ in the tangent space:[1]

$$\begin{aligned} \mathcal{G} \times S^n &\rightarrow \text{ cones in } T\mathcal{G} \\ (x, \theta) &\mapsto B_c(x, \theta). \end{aligned}$$

Thus we have a differential specification of the possible motions $B_c(x, \theta)$ at each point x. The cones at each point specify a parametric family of vector fields—a field of cones to be precise. The integral curves for this family, however, may not be algebraic in general. Good approximate algorithms are needed to construct bounding algebraic envelopes about the image of this family of curves. For example, assuming that an integral curve has a power series, it is possible to construct a recurrence relation for the coefficients of the series. They can be generated deterministically to the accuracy desired. Randy Brost[2] has investigated other numerical techniques for constructing integral curves corresponding to trajectories in the forward projection. This is an interesting area for future research. In particular, it could be

---

[1] The space of "cones in $T\mathcal{G}$" can be formalized as an appropriate tensor bundle over $\mathcal{G}$.
[2] [Personal Communication].

applied to the "full" 4-dimensional gear meshing problem where a commanded pure rotation of the gripped gear could induce translations or rotations of either gear. Such algorithms might also be applied to compute projection sets under different dynamics.

15.2.11 Higher-Level Primitives

The "primitives" in the EDR and [LMT,E] theories are somewhat low-level—they consist of commanded generalized damper motions. While it is easy to describe such motions, their effects can be complex. It would be useful to develop a theory of planning with higher-level primitives that was still geometrical in character.

15.2.12 Planning Paradigms

Different planning paradigms for EDR planning should be explored. LIMITED is a forward-chaining planner. [Brost] is developing a backchaining EDR planner. It would be interesting to integrate and compare these techniques.

15.2.13 Functional vs. Geometrical Descriptions of Goals

Some of the greatest and most interesting unsolved problems in geometrical robotics lie in the interaction of functional and geometrical descriptions of goals. In particular, we would like to devise algorithms for computing a geometrical goal region given a functional description—for example, a quantified difference equation—for the desired behavior in the goal state. Conversely, we would like to be able to infer a functional description of the goal from its geometrical aspects. The latter would be useful in automatically generating termination predicates to recognize the goal.

I believe that EDR is an exciting and fruitful area for future research. Many of the directions above could be taken as criticisms of the theory—for example, that it is too slow, or may require exhaustive search. However, I would rather view these as criticisms not of the EDR theory, but rather of the state of the art in EDR implementation, that is LIMITED. In particular, if five years ago one had surveyed researchers in robotics and asked them what to do about model error and EDR, I believe that the general response would have been "I don't know; it's a good problem." Now at least we have a systematic theory of model error and EDR, and are faced with the test of reducing it to practice.

APPENDICES

§A.1. A Note On Geometry

Our definitions of phase space, and phase-space goals have been primarily set-theoretic. These sets have considerable additional structure, which is a good thing, for otherwise there would be no hope of computing them. The geometry of these regions is accessible by viewing phase space as the tangent bundle to (generalized) configuration space. This gives it structure both as a differentiable manifold and a vector bundle; π is the canonical covering map. The moving object's moment of inertia tensor defines a field of inner products on the tangent bundle, providing a natural choice for a Riemannian metric. For example, to see that $Z(H_s)$ is "well-behaved", observe that it is the image of a zero-section (see below) of the tangent bundle, and so it is an embedding of H_s. This geometric point of view is crucial to a computational analysis; it is developed in more detail here, and earlier in [Erdmann].

Notation:

Some readers may still wish to continue thinking of the tangent bundle to configuration space as "Position-space × Velocity-space." This is set-theoretically correct, although it ignores its topological, algebraic, differential, and geometric structure. Set theoretically, the tangent space T_x at a configuration x may be thought of as the collection of all velocities (or forces) "at" a configuration x. That is, the tangent space at x is the cylinder $\pi^{-1}(x)$ endowed with a vector space structure. It has the same dimension as the (generalized) configuration space. The tangent bundle is set-theoretically the disjoint union of all tangent spaces. It has twice the dimension of the configuration space. If C is a configuration space and TC its tangent bundle, a *section* of the tangent bundle is a map $s : C \rightarrow TC$ such that $\pi \circ s$ is the identity on C. Of particular interest is the *zero* section, which sends a configuration to the distinguished zero-velocity in its cylinder.

§A.2. A Formal Review of Pre-Images

A motion strategy is a *commanded velocity* together with a *termination predicate* which monitors the sensors and decides when the motion has achieved the goal. The actual path followed depends on the control uncertainty, but we require that it satisfy generalized damper dynamics (see (4), below). Given a measured position p_0^* in configuration space, a set R, and a collection of goals $\{G_\beta\}$, [LMT] define $S(p_0^*, R, \{G_\beta\})$ to be the set of all commanded velocities v_0^* such that the termination predicate, knowing the initial measured position p_0^* corresponds to an actual position p in R, is guaranteed to signal success. We denote the position sensing error ball about p by $B_{ep}(p)$. A pre-image of a collection of goals $\{\, G_\beta \,\}$ relative to a set R is the set

$$P_R(\{\, G_\beta \,\}) = \{\, p \in R \mid \forall p_0^* \in B_{ep}(p), S(p_0^*, R, \{\, G_\beta \,\}) \neq \emptyset \,\},$$

that is, the set of all positions p, such that, for all measured positions p_0^* consistent with p, there is some commanded control velocity v_0^* such that the termination predicate is guaranteed to signal success.

Analogously, define the *directional pre-image* with respect to a nominal commanded velocity v_θ^* by

$$P_{R,\theta}(\{\, G_\beta \,\}) = \{\, p \in R \mid \forall p_0^* \in B_{ep}(p), v_\theta^* \in S(p_0^*, R, \{\, G_\beta \,\}) \,\}.$$

The directional pre-image is the set of points which are guaranteed to recognizably enter the goal under a *particular* commanded velocity v_θ^*. The *weak preimage* is the set of points which could possibly enter the goal recognizably, given fortuitous sensing and control events.

The *backprojection* of a goal (with respect to a commanded velocity v_θ^*) consists of those points guaranteed to enter the goal. Recognizability of the entry plays no role.

The *forward projection* of a region R (with respect to v_θ^*) is the set of positions and velocities (considered as ordered pairs) which are possibly reachable from R under v_θ^*.

For a comprehensive account, see [LMT,E]. For convenience, we summarize the notation here. While historically the subscript θ has been used to indicate the "angular direction" of a commanded motion, we will employ it as an arbitrary index for motion strategies, commanded velocities, and termination predicates.

Symbol Table:

v_0^* nominal commanded velocity.

v_0 actual commanded velocity.

v actual velocity.

v^* sensed velocity.

p actual position.

p^* sensed position.

$B_{ec}(v_0^*)$ control uncertainty.

$B_{ev}(v)$ velocity sensing uncertainty.

$B_{ep}(p)$ position sensing uncertainty.

$\tilde{F}_\theta(R)$ forward projection of R for $v_0^* = v_\theta$.

$F_\theta(R)$ natural projection $\pi\tilde{F}$ into C-space .

$B_\theta(G)$ directional backprojection of G under $v_0^* = v_\theta$.

$P_R(\{\,G_\beta\,\})$ non-directional pre-image.

$P_{R,\theta}(\{\,G_\beta\,\})$ directional pre-image.

$\hat{P}_R(\{\,G_\beta\,\})$ non-directional weak pre-image.

$\hat{P}_{R,\theta}(\{\,G_\beta\,\})$ directional weak pre-image.

For notational felicity, we will define $B_\theta(\{\,G,H\,\}) = B_\theta(G \cup H)$.

§A.3. On the Geometry and Physics of Generalized Configuration Space

We now discuss the geometry and physics of generalized configuration space somewhat more formally. Generalized Configuration Space is a smooth manifold. Intrinsically it is not different from the configuration spaces considered in, for example, [LMT, E, D, C]. We must define a system of dynamics for generalized configuration space in order to define motions. Furthermore, we must define how sensing generalizes.

Let C be a smooth configuration space. Let J be an arbitrary set which will index the possible configuration space environments. Generalized Configuration Space is $\mathcal{G} = C \times J$, and a particular "world" is simply $C \times \{\,\alpha\,\}$ for $\alpha \in J$. Thus we let $\{\,C_\alpha\,\}_{\alpha\in J}$ be a set of configuration spaces, each containing configuration space obstacles. The ambient space for each C_α is some canonical C, which is the configuration space for the degrees of freedom of the moving object. $\mathcal{G}$ is simply the natural product representing the ambient space of the disjoint union of the C_α. There is no constraint that J be finite or even countable. Now, assume that J is also a smooth manifold (with boundary), although as we shall see, this is not a serious restriction. We wish to define a "physics" on $\mathcal{G}$, that is, a set of laws that motions in generalized configuration space must obey. This physics will be expressed as a set of constraints on uncertainties and trajectories in the tangent bundle $T\mathcal{G}$. Write $\overline{x} = (x, \alpha) \in \mathcal{G}$. A particular tangent space will be written $T_{\overline{x}} = T_{x,\alpha} = T_{x,\alpha}\mathcal{G}$. We will use the convention that the analogs of mathematical objects in the pre-image framework will be written with a bar in the model error framework. Thus a velocity in $T_{x,\alpha}$ will be written $\overline{v} = (v, d_\alpha)$ where $v \in T_x C$.

(1) There is infinite position sensing uncertainty in J. This means that we will define the generalized position uncertainty as $\overline{B}_{ep}(\overline{x}) = B_{ep}(x) \times J$.

(2) Motions are possible in $\mathcal{G}$, but any motion must stay within one slice of $\mathcal{G}$, say $C \times \{\,\alpha_0\,\}$. (We call this an α_0-*slice* of $\mathcal{G}$). α_0 is the actual position in J. If $0 \in T_{\alpha_0} J$ denotes the zero velocity in the tangent space to J at α_0, then we can define the generalized velocity sensing uncertainty $\overline{B}_{ev}(\overline{v}) = B_{ev}(v) \times \{\,0\,\}$. Analogously, the generalized control uncertainty is $\overline{B}_{ec}(\overline{v_0^*}) = B_{ec}(v_0^*) \times \{\,0\,\}$. These

definitions ensure that all sensed and commanded velocities are tangent to C and have zero component along J.

(3) Define a generalized trajectory $\overline{\Phi} : [0, \infty) \to TG$ by $\overline{\Phi}(t) = (\overline{\Phi}_p(t), \overline{\Phi}_v(t))$ $= (\Phi_p(t), \alpha(t), \Phi_v(t), d_\alpha(t))$, where $(\alpha(t), d_\alpha(t)) \in TJ$.

(4) Let $\overline{f} \in TG$ be a force tangent to generalized configuration space. Then $\overline{f}$ must satisfy the damper equation $\overline{f} = B(\overline{v} - \overline{v_0})$. In truth, this is a *generalized* generalized damper constraint. B must vary smoothly, that is, B is a smooth tensor field on G. In practice, we constrain B to be diagonal on each tangent space so that it cannot cross-couple TC and TJ.

(5) Let $\overline{p} = \overline{\Phi}_p$ and $\overline{v} = \overline{\Phi}_v$. $\overline{p}$ and $\overline{v}$ must be related via the integrability constraint

$$\overline{p}(t) = \overline{p}(0) + \int_0^t \overline{v}(t) dt.$$

(6) $\overline{v}_0 \in \overline{B}_{ec}(\overline{v_0^*})$. That is, the generalized actual commanded velocity must be consistent with the error bounds on the generalized nominal commanded velocity.

If $\overline{\Phi}$ obeys these constraints (1-6) we say it is a trajectory satisfying the damper equation with uncertainty relative to a commanded velocity v_0^*. Such a trajectory is constrained to have $\alpha(t) = \alpha_0$ and $d_\alpha(t) = 0$ for all t. The latter implies that the image of any $\overline{\Phi}$ lies in the submanifold $TC \times (J \times \{0\}) \cong TC \times J$. This is why we can think of TG, the phase space of G, as being $TC \times J$ instead of $TC \times TJ$.[3] It also suggests that we may relax the constraint that J be smooth.

[Erdmann] generalizes Euclidean friction cones to arbitrary smooth C. The generalized friction cones embed in TC. Thus friction cones embed naturally in generalized configuration space. Of course, they have no non-zero component in TJ.

In this thesis, when there is no possibility of confusion we have dropped the bar notation and assume that in generalized configuration space all quantities, uncertainty balls, trajectories, etc., are barred, i.e., generalized. We have referred to generalized configuration space as G.

The definitions and results for pre-images and backprojections [LMT,E] in C-space generalize *mutatis mutandis* to G endowed with this physics. Thus this framework reduces the *guaranteed* motion strategy planning problem with model error to computing pre-images in a somewhat more complicated, and higher-dimensional configuration space.

§A.4. Derivation of the Non-Holonomic Constraints for Pushing

The previous discussion assumed that motion across J was impossible. That is,

---

[3] This is only acceptable when no motion across J is possible! See §A.4.

all motion is confined to one α-slice of generalized configuration space. In example (1), this is equivalent to the axiom that B does not move or deform under an applied force. Such an axiom makes sense for applications where B is indeed immovable, for example, if A and B are machined tabs of a connected metal part. However, suppose that B is a block that can slide on the table. See fig. II.17. Then an applied force on the surface of the block can cause the block to slide. This corresponds to motion in J. In general, the effect of an applied force will be a motion which slides or sticks on the surface of B, and which causes B to slide or stick on the table. This corresponds to a coupled motion in both C and J. When the motion maintains contact, it is tangent to a surface S in generalized configuration space.

Our goal is to generalize the description of the physics of $\mathcal{G}$ to permit a rigorous account of such motions. This model can then be employed by an automated planner. *Such a planner could construct either Guaranteed or EDR strategies whose primitives were gross motions, compliant motions, and pushing motions.*

First, we must determine what reaction forces are in generalized configuration space. By this we mean the following. Surfaces in configuration space share many properties with real-space surfaces. When pushed on, they push back. They have a normal in configuration space, and in the absence of friction can exert forces only in that normal direction. In general the configuration space normal is different from the real-space normal; see [E]. Furthermore, [E] developed a configuration space analogue of the classical Coulomb friction cone of Cartesian space. It defines the range of reaction forces the surface can exert, and may be employed to predict reaction forces, given a applied force. In addition, given either Newtonian or generalized damper dynamics, the configuration space friction cone can be used to predict whether sticking will occur on a surface, given a cone of control velocity uncertainty. Under damper dynamics, the computation at a point is especially simple: sticking can occur when the intersection of the negative velocity cone and the friction cone is non-trivial.

We wish to extend these methods to generalized configuration space. Then, given a cone of applied forces as in fig. II.17, we can predict the cone of resulting motions in $\mathcal{G}$. That is, we can predict the motion along the surface of B, and the motion of B on the table. In particular, given a control uncertainty cone, we can compute whether sticking occurs on the surface S in generalized configuration space.

In this analysis, we will consider a force exerted by the robot on an object B. This corresponds to an application of force on a surface S in $\mathcal{G}$. The analysis will apply to arbitrary smooth C, J, and S, for an arbitrary rigid object B whose configuration space is J. The reader may imagine B and S as usual in example (1). In example (1), however, the configuration space of B is one-dimensional. To make the example more interesting, let us suppose that B is free to translate and rotate on a planar table. So C is $\Re^2$ as before, but J is $\Re^2 \times S^1$.

We must determine:

- What is the normal to a surface S in generalized configuration space?
- What is the analogue of the friction cone in generalized configuration space?
- What are the applied forces which cause sticking at a point on S? What is their geometric interpretation and computation?
- How may reaction forces be computed geometrically, using the generalized friction cone in generalized configuration space?

Our analysis is applicable under the following assumption: We must have perfect knowledge of the centers of friction of B and the robot. To satisfy this assumption, it is sufficient to assume that all (real-space) contacts consist of a finite number of points. For example, we might model the contact of B on a planar table by the intersection of four one-point contacts. Alternatively, the centers of friction are known when the pressure distributions are known precisely. In the more general case where the pressure distribution is not known precisely, then the more general theory of pushing described by [Mason, 82] must be employed. More research is needed to extend this more restricted theory of pushing to the case where the centers of friction are not known precisely. One possible solution is to introduce uncertainty in the center of friction as a model error parameter in J.

This discussion represents work in progress. In particular, the method described for the computation of reaction forces is meant to be illustrative of the techniques that an EDR planner would require, if it were to competently plan pushing motions. I hope that a simpler algorithm can be found before a practical planner is constructed.

Normals to Surfaces in Generalized Configuration Space

Let C and J be the configuration spaces of the robot and of the block B, respectively. Assume that the reference points are chosen to lie at the centers of mass. Typical configuration spaces we will consider are the two and three dimensional groups of Euclidean motions, $\Re^2 \times S^1$ and $\Re^3 \times SO(3)$. The definition of normals in the tangent spaces to these configuration spaces depends on the inner product. There is a natural choice for the Riemannian metric; see [Arnold, Abraham and Marsden, E].

The moment of inertia tensor of the robot defines a field of inner products on C. On a tangent space $T_x C$, write the inner product as $\langle \cdot, \cdot \rangle_x$. This choice of inner product is "natural" in the following sense: The Riemannian metric is a quadratic form which computes the correct kinetic energy of the robot moving with generalized velocity v at configuration x:

$$E = \frac{1}{2}\langle v, v \rangle_x \quad v \in T_x C.$$

A Riemannian metric $\langle \cdot, \cdot \rangle_\alpha$ on the tangent space $T_\alpha J$ is defined in the same way. The inner products may be combined by direct sum to define an inner product on $T_x C \times T_\alpha J$. We can visualize this as follows. Since the moment of inertia operators are symmetric 2-tensors, we can view them as square matrices Φ_x and Ψ_α. In principal axis coordinates, for example, both will be diagonal matrices with unit entries for the Cartesian dimensions, and the squares of the radii of gyration in the rotational coordinates. The operation of Φ_x on two velocity vectors v, u in $T_x C$ is defined by

$$\langle v, u \rangle_x = v \Phi_x u.$$

Write $\bar{x} = (x, \alpha)$ as usual. Let w_1, w_2 be in $T_{\bar{x}} \mathcal{G}$. So the inner product on $T_{\bar{x}} \mathcal{G}$ is defined by

$$\langle w_1, w_2 \rangle_{\bar{x}} = w_1 \begin{pmatrix} \Phi_x & 0 \\ 0 & \Psi_\alpha \end{pmatrix} w_2. \tag{$*$}$$

Thus the direct sum of the inner products defines a field of inner products on $\mathcal{G}$. Since the reference points are at the centers of mass, the kinetic energies of the robot and of B simply add without cross-coupling. Therefore $(*)$ defines the natural Riemannian metric on generalized configuration space, since it describes the kinetic energy of the system.

Now, a tangent vector (v_c, v_j) in $T_{\bar{x}} \mathcal{G}$ corresponds to a (generalized) velocity of v_c of the robot and v_j of the object B. Generalized damper dynamics permits an identification of forces and velocities. Thus the pair (f_c, f_j) with

$$f_c \in T_x C$$
$$f_j \in T_\alpha J$$

corresponds to a generalized force of f_c applied at the center of mass of the robot, and a generalized force of f_j applied at the center of mass of B.

Note that the inner product $(*)$ defines the normal space to the surface S in generalized configuration space.[4] See fig. II.18. The normal, in general, can be transverse to J. Hence S can exert reaction forces across J even when the applied force lies exclusively in $T_x C$. In the figure, this implies that pushing on the side of B results in a reaction force across J, causing B to slide. In generalized configuration space this is simply viewed as applying a force to the surface S, which exerts a reaction force across J. Since the resultant force is across J, the motion in $\mathcal{G}$ will be in that direction, tangent to S.

---

[4]This is independent of the choice of generalized damper or Newtonian dynamics.

Construction of the Sticking Cone

We now derive a geometrical object called the *sticking cone*. It represents the cone of forces (f_c, f_j) that can cause sticking on a surface in $\mathcal{G}$. Under generalized damper dynamics, the sticking cone represents the commanded velocities that can result in sticking.

Henceforth, all forces are generalized forces unless otherwise indicated. Keeping the notation above, suppose the generalized force (f_c, f_j) is applied at configuration $\overline{x} = (x, \alpha)$, which lies on surface S in generalized configuration space. Now, it is clear that f_c acts on B as well as on the robot.[5] Assume for discussion that f_c contains no torque components. Then the effect of f_c on B is both f_c acting at the center of mass of B, plus the torque induced on B by f_c. Let r_x be the radius vector from the center of mass of B to the point of application of f_c in real space. Then the effect of f_c on B can be written[6]

$$f_c^\star = f_c + r_x \times f_c \in T_\alpha J.$$

The torque component of $f_c^\star$ must also be normalized relative to the inner product on $T_\alpha J$; this is not indicated above.

Now, of course it is also true that f_j induces an force on the robot. For example, if in example (1) the block B is pushed at its center of mass, then a force can be exerted on the robot when the robot is in contact with B. The induced force contributes to the reaction force of B on the robot.

Let $f_{r,c}$ denote the reaction force of B on the robot; it lies in $T_x C$. Let $f_{r,j}$ denote the reaction force of the table on B; it lies in $T_\alpha J$. The force balance equations for static equilibrium are

$$f_c + f_{r,c} = 0$$
$$f_j + f_c^\star + f_{r,j} = 0.$$

Now, let K_x be the configuration space friction cone [E] in $T_x C$, and K_α be the configuration space friction cone in $T_\alpha J$.[7] The conditions for static equilibrium are then expressible as

$$-f_c \in K_x$$
$$-f_j - f_c^\star \in K_\alpha. \tag{$\ast\ast$}$$

---

[5] Of course, this is only true when the robot and B are in contact, i.e, $\overline{x} \in S$.

[6] Under quasi-static assumptions.

[7] We do not assume that the center of friction is at the center of mass. If this is not the case, however, the friction cone must be placed at the center of friction, and then resloved relative to the center of mass by adding the resultant torques.

Thus it is clear that the range of reaction forces that the surface S can exert is exactly the direct sum of the two friction cones,

$$K_x \oplus K_\alpha$$

which is a cone in $T_{\bar{x}}\mathcal{G}$.

We are now prepared to construct the sticking cone. Informally, the idea involves twisting and tilting the friction cone in $T_\alpha J$ as a function of f_c. The amount of the twist and tilt is determined by the force $f_c^\star$. The tilted friction cone takes into account the "internal" force $f_c^\star$, and admits a geometrical calculation of sticking that considers only the applied force (f_c, f_j).

We can rewrite the sticking conditions under static equilibrium (∗∗) as:

$$-f_c \in K_x$$
$$-f_j \in K_\alpha + \{\, f_c^\star \,\}, \tag{†}$$

where the translation operation $+$ is defined by $V + \{\, w \,\} = \{\, v + w \mid v \in V \,\}$.

(†) defines a cone of forces in the tangent space to generalized configuration space at $\bar{x}$. We may write it as[8]

$$\mathcal{K} = \bigcup_{-f_c \in K_x} \{\, -f_c \,\} \oplus (K_\alpha + \{\, f_c^\star \,\}).$$

For example, in the case with no torque, $f_c^\star = f_c$.

The cone of all forces (f_c, f_j) satisfying (†) has the following geometrical interpretation. The force $f_c^\star$ causes a translation of the friction cone in $T_\alpha J$. It parameterizes a family of cones in the tangent space to J. The union of this family defines a range of applied forces (f_c, f_j) that can cause sticking at $\bar{x}$. For example, consider fig. II.19. Here we take the configuration spaces of the robot and of B to be cartesian planes ($\Re^2$). The friction cone in generalized configuration space will then be four-dimensional. This is hard to draw; we have selected a fixed, negative normal component for f_j. The 3D force space at $\bar{x}$ represents the product of the 2D forces that can be exerted by the robot on the surface of B, with the 1D tangential forces that can be applied at the center of mass of B. An applied force (f_c, f_j) in the cone in fig. II.19 represents a combination of forces that causes no motion in $\mathcal{G}$, that is, neither sliding on the surface of B, nor of B on the table. Note that the cone in $\mathcal{G}$ is skewed out of the embedded tangent space to C at x. This is because when a force is applied in the friction cone K_x, the block B can slide unless an opposing force is exerted tangentially at the center of mass of B.

There are several points of interest. Note that the new cone defined by (†), which we will denote $\mathcal{K}$, changes from point to point when torques are permitted. This is because the radius vector changes from point to point. Therefore the torque

---

[8] $\oplus$ denotes the direct sum.

components of the generalized force f_c^* will translate the friction cone in TJ by different amounts as the vector r_x to the center of mass of B varies. This effect is similar to the way that the Erdmannian friction cone changes as the contact moves in rotation space [E]. However, in generalized configuration space it changes even under pure translation.

We can now specify a geometrical computation to determine when sticking occurs at $\overline{x}$, assuming generalized damper dynamics: Simply intersect the negative velocity control uncertainty cone $-\overline{B}_{ec}(v_\theta^*)$ with $\mathcal{K}$. If the intersection is trivial, then sticking cannot occur. If the intersection is non-trivial, then sticking can occur. If the negative velocity cone lies inside $\mathcal{K}$, then sticking must occur. See fig. II.19. Assume it is impossible to apply force at the center of mass of B. Therefore, the velocity cone is two dimensional and lies entirely in the tangent space to C at x; it has no J component. This two-dimensional cone is intersected with the 3D cone $\mathcal{K}$ to determine whether sticking is possible at $\overline{x}$.

This shows that the computation to determine whether sticking is possible at a point reduces to simple geometric cone intersection.

Computation of Reaction Forces

We now provide a geometrical method for the computation of reaction forces in $\mathcal{G}$. That is, given an applied force (f_c, f_j), we show how to compute the reaction forces and hence the resulting motion. Such an algorithm is required by a planner since it is necessary to predict the effect of a commanded force on the motion of the robot and B. We will assume Newtonian mechanics in this section, for the following reasons:

- It is not clear that the interaction of B on the table[9] surface can be modeled accurately by a damper.
- Under generalized damper dynamics, it is not clear whether the robot velocity induced by a force f_c should be relative to the object B on which it slides, or relative to some global coordinate frame.
- In second-order systems, accelerating reference frames can introduce fictitious forces. Correspondingly, under generalized damper dynamics, it seems that reference frames moving at constant velocity should also introduce fictitious forces.

It remains to give a principled account of these issues; this is a fruitful area for future research.

The prediction of reaction forces under general dynamic conditions is complicated by the fact that the object B and the robot may accelerate under the resultant

---

[9] We will use the "table" as the name for the surface B is in contact with, with the understanding that the surface is arbitrary.

force. This means that the computation of reaction forces cannot be reduced to a simple projection onto the friction cone. The reason for this is that the projection must be done in an inertial frame, fixed on the object which exerts the reaction force. That is, the applied force must be expressed in a frame of reference which is non-accelerating relative to the "bottom" object which is being "slid upon."

For example, consider the case where the normal accelerations are zero. That is, assume that contact of the robot on B, and of B on the table are both maintained. We fix a reference frame L on B. Then the reaction force of B on the robot may be found by projecting the effective applied force in L onto the Erdmannian friction cone [E]. However, the effective applied force is not known *a priori*: the fictitious force due to the acceleration of B contributes to it; this acceleration is also an unknown. The projection *relation* however, still holds. In general, it adds a quadric constraint into the equations of motion. The simultaneous solution of these equations yields the reaction force and resultant acceleration. (The global coordinate system is a non-inertial frame for the table).

To summarize, we can compute the reaction forces by writing down the equations of motion of the robot and B. Then we add the constraints from the projection relations expressed in inertial frames. Their simultaneous satisfaction yields the reaction forces.

Let us derive the reaction forces for the case where C and J are both $\Re^2 \times S^1$. The analysis follows [E], and is a generalization thereof. We will assume one-point contacts between the robot and B, and between B and the table. Furthermore, we assume that neither contact is broken. Centripital accelerations and coriolis forces are not considered. This is a reasonable assumption under quasi-static conditions, or when the robot and B are only rotating slowly.

We will use the following notation:

The radii of gyration of the robot and B, respectively, are ρ_c and ρ_j.

The masses of the robot and B, respectively, are m_c and m_j.

The generalized applied force in C is $\mathbf{f_c} = (f_c^x, f_c^y, f_c^q)$. That is, the applied force is (f_c^x, f_c^y) and the applied torque is $\tau_c = \rho_c f_c^q$.

The generalized applied force in J is $\mathbf{f_j} = (f_j^x, f_j^y, f_j^q)$. That is, the applied force is (f_j^x, f_j^y) and the applied torque is $\tau_j = \rho_j f_j^q$.

The configuration space normal in C is $\mathbf{n_c} = (n_c^x, n_c^y, n_c^q)$. The unit real space normal is $\mathbf{n_c^0} = (n_c^x, n_c^y)$.

The configuration space normal in J is $\mathbf{n_j} = (n_j^x, n_j^y, n_j^q)$. The unit real space normal is $\mathbf{n_j^0} = (n_j^x, n_j^y)$.

The magnitude of the normal reaction force at the contact point between the robot and B is $f_{n,c}$.

The magnitude of the normal reaction force at the contact point between B and the table is $f_{n,j}$.

$\mathbf{r_c}$ is the vector from the point of contact of the robot on B to the reference point of the robot.

$\mathbf{r_j}$ is the vector from the point of contact of B on the table to the reference point of B.

In the absence of friction, the equations of motion are therefore

$$
\begin{aligned}
f_{n,c}n_c^x & + & f_c^x & & & = & m_c a_c^x \\
f_{n,c}n_c^y & + & f_c^y & & & = & m_c a_c^y \\
f_{n,c}n_c^q & + & \tau_c & & & = & m_c \rho_c^2 \alpha_c
\end{aligned}
$$

$$
\begin{aligned}
-f_{n,c}n_c^x & + & f_j^x & + & f_{n,j}n_j^x & = & m_j a_j^x \\
-f_{n,c}n_c^y & + & f_j^y & + & f_{n,j}n_j^y & = & m_j a_j^y \\
f_{n,c}|\mathbf{r_j} \times \mathbf{n_c^0}| & + & \tau_j & + & f_{n,j}n_j^q & = & m_j \rho_j^2 \alpha_j.
\end{aligned}
$$

In the presence of friction, there also exist tangential reaction forces. Let their magnitudes be f_c^t and f_j^t. The are subject to the restrictions

$$
\begin{aligned}
0 & \le & |f_c^t| & \le & \mu_c f_{n,c} \\
0 & \le & |f_j^t| & \le & \mu_j f_{n,j}.
\end{aligned}
$$

Observe that the sliding tangents in real space are $(n_c^y, -n_c^x)$ and $(n_j^y, -n_j^x)$. As in [E], let

$$ v_c^q = n_c^x r_c^x + n_c^y r_c^y $$

and

$$ v_j^q = n_j^x r_j^x + n_j^y r_j^y. $$

Then in the presence of friction, the equations of motion are

$$
\begin{array}{ccccccc}
\overbrace{f_{n,c}n_c^x + f_c^t n_c^y}^{\mathbf{f_{r,c}}} & + & \overbrace{f_c^x}^{\mathbf{f_c}} & & & = & \overbrace{m_c a_c^x}^{\mathbf{M_c A_c}} \\
f_{n,c}n_c^y - f_c^t n_c^x & + & f_c^y & & & = & m_c a_c^y \\
f_{n,c}n_c^q + f_c^t v_c^q & + & \tau_c & & & = & m_c \rho_c^2 \alpha_c
\end{array}
$$

$$ (R1) $$

$$
\begin{array}{ccccccc}
\overbrace{-f_{n,c}n_c^x - f_c^t n_c^y}^{\mathbf{f_c^*}} & + & \overbrace{f_j^x}^{\mathbf{f_j}} & + & \overbrace{f_{n,j}n_j^x + f_j^t n_j^y}^{\mathbf{f_{r,j}}} & = & \overbrace{m_j a_j^x}^{\mathbf{M_j A_j}} \\
-f_{n,c}n_c^y + f_c^t n_c^x & + & f_j^y & + & f_{n,j}n_j^y - f_j^t n_j^x & = & m_j a_j^y \\
|\mathbf{r_j} \times \mathbf{f_c^{*0}}| & + & \tau_j & + & f_{n,j}n_j^q + f_j^t v_j^q & = & m_j \rho_j^2 \alpha_j,
\end{array}
$$

where

$$ \mathbf{f_c^{*0}} = \begin{pmatrix} f_{n,c}n_c^x & + & f_c^t n_c^y \\ f_{n,c}n_c^y & - & f_c^t n_c^x \end{pmatrix}^T. $$

In eq. $(R1)$, we have indicated with braces which terms correspond to which generalized applied forces and accelerations. They must be normalized relative to the inner product; this is accomplished by dividing the torque equations by ρ_c and ρ_j, respectively. For example, the torque component of $\mathbf{f_c}$ is of course actually $f_c^q = \frac{1}{\rho_c}\tau_c$. $\mathbf{M_c}$ and $\mathbf{M_j}$ are generalized mass matrices, combining the mass and the moment of inertia of the moving objects.

We will consider the case where contact is not broken. That is, the normal accelerations are zero. Henceforth, we will adopt the standard dot notation for the inner product on the tangent space. Writing this out,

$$\mathbf{A_c} \cdot \mathbf{n_c} = 0$$
$$\mathbf{A_j} \cdot \mathbf{n_j} = 0. \qquad (R2)$$

Now, attach an inertial reference frame L to B at the reference point. L accelerates by $\mathbf{A_j}$. The robot accelerates at $\mathbf{A_c}$; therefore in L it accelerates at "the sum[10] of" $\mathbf{A_c}$ and $-\mathbf{A_j}$. The acceleration of L generates a fictitious force $\mathbf{h}$; we can write the effective applied force in C relative to L by adding the ficticious force $\mathbf{h}$ arising from the acceleration of L:

$$\mathbf{f'_c} = \mathbf{f_c} + \mathbf{h} \qquad (R3a)$$

In general, $\mathbf{h}$ will be complicated, since L is a rotating coordinate system. It is conceptually simple, however. For example, in the case of no rotations, we simply have $\mathbf{h} = -\mathbf{M_c}\mathbf{A_j}$.

The reaction force $\mathbf{f_{r,c}}$ may be found by projecting the effective applied force $\mathbf{f'_c}$ onto the Erdmannian friction cone K_x. The global reference frame serves as a non-inertial frame for the table; hence the effective applied force on B is simply

$$\mathbf{f'_j} = \mathbf{f_j} + \mathbf{f_c^*}. \qquad (R3b)$$

The reaction force $\mathbf{f_{r,j}}$ may be found by projecting the effective applied force $\mathbf{f'_j}$ onto the Erdmannian friction cone K_α.

[E] derives two canonical tangent vectors $\mathbf{t_r}$ and $\mathbf{t_r^\perp}$. $\mathbf{t_r}$ is the tangent in the direction of pure rotation about the point of contact. It is normal to the plane of the Erdmannian friction cone. The reaction force may be found by projecting the effective applied force along $\mathbf{t_r}$ onto the plane of the friction cone. If the projection lies inside the friction cone, then the projection is the reaction force. If not, then we must project perpendicularly along $\mathbf{t_r^\perp}$, in the plane, onto the edge of the friction cone. The second projection, then, is the reaction force.

Now, let $\mathbf{t_1}$ and $\mathbf{t_2}$ be two orthogonal vectors in the plane of K_x, such that $\mathbf{t_1} = -\mathbf{t_r^\perp}$. Then the projection onto the plane of K_x is given by

---

[10] Before adding the generalized forces, the angular accelerations must be resolved relative to the different rotating coordinate systems.

$$\tilde{\mathbf{f}}_c = -(\mathbf{f}'_c \cdot \mathbf{t_1})\mathbf{t_1} - (\mathbf{f}'_c \cdot \mathbf{t_2})\mathbf{t_2}. \tag{R4}$$

This yields two cases. In the first, the projection lies in the friction cone, so

$$\mathbf{f}_{r,c} = \tilde{\mathbf{f}}_c. \tag{R5}$$

In the second, we must project again. That is, $\mathbf{f}_{r,c}$ is the projection of $\tilde{\mathbf{f}}_c$ along $\mathbf{t}_r^\perp$ onto the boundary of K_x. In the latter case, we can express the second projection in local $(\mathbf{t_1}, \mathbf{t_2})$ coordinates as follows. Write $\tilde{\mathbf{f}}_c = -(f_1, f_2)$ in local coordinates. Call the projection $\mathbf{p} = (p_1, p_2)$. Let $\mathbf{e} = (e_1, e_2)$ be a unit vector along the edge of the friction cone K_x, expressed in local coordinates. We obtain a quadric constraint,

$$p_2 = f_2$$
$$p_1 e_1 + p_2 e_2 = \sqrt{p_1^2 + p_2^2}. \tag{R6}$$

Analogously, we have that $\mathbf{f}_{r,j}$ is related to $\mathbf{f}'_j$ by a projection in T_α onto the plane of K_α. Thus it is possible to derive three more constraints $(R4')$, $(R5')$, and $(R6')$ in precisely the same manner.

The (R) equations may then be solved simultaneously to predict the reaction forces and resulting motion.[11] In considering this analysis, note the crucial role played by the geometrical projections onto the friction cone. It remains to generalize the analysis to consider multiple points of contact, breaking contact, coriolis forces, and centripital accelerations. I expect that, given the tools developed above, the generalization should follow [E] straightforwardly. However, I also expect the resulting system of constraint equations to remain fairly complicated, as illustrated above. Since the planner must solve this system, a simpler method for computing reaction forces would be desirable. The techniques above require algebraic manipulation as well as geometrical computation. There may be simplifying assumptions which facilitate the computation. This direction must be explored in order to build a practical planning system.

Quasi-Static Analysis

One simplifying approach is quasi-static analysis. Such an analysis would proceed as follows. First, all accelerations in equations $(R1)$ could be set to zero. The reaction force $\mathbf{f}_{r,c}$ can be in one of three states: on the "left" edge of K_x, inside K_x, or on the "right" edge of K_x. The magnitude of $\mathbf{f}_{r,c}$ can be determined from the normal component of $\mathbf{f}_c$, since the accelerations are zero. Each state corresponds to different impending motions in the direction of the force imballance. (It could also correspond to sticking on the surface of B). Similarly, there are three possible

---

[11]Of course, motion ambiguities, as in [E], are still possible.

states for $\mathbf{f_{r,j}}$, yielding six qualitative states altogether. One envisions an algorithm as follows. The algorithm hypothesizes a state, say, that $\mathbf{f_{r,c}}$ lies on the left edge of K_x. This means that it can be found from $\mathbf{f_c}$ via the one or two step Erdmannian projection given in ($R4$-$R6$). Note that there are no fictitious forces, since the accelerations are zero; hence, for example, in the easy case we simply have

$$\mathbf{f_{r,c}} = -(\mathbf{f_c} \cdot \mathbf{t_1})\mathbf{t_1} - (\mathbf{f_c} \cdot \mathbf{t_2})\mathbf{t_2}. \qquad (H4)$$

Next the algorithm makes a hypothesis about the state of the reaction force $\mathbf{f_{r,j}}$. This results in one or more hypothesis equations like ($H4$). If equations ($R1$) and the hypothesis equations are consistent, then the hypothesized reaction forces are possible under quasi-static assumptions. Furthermore, associated with the hypothesized reaction forces, there is a (set of) impending motions, corresponding to the resultant of the force imballance. These impending motions may be used to predict the effects of applied forces under quasi-static assumptions.

The advantage of this method may lie not only in its simplicity, but in the fact that it gives a partition of force space into impending motion regions. Forces applied in a given motion region will result in motions in a particular (set of) direction(s). Such a technique could be very useful in a planner for pushing operations. The investigation of simplifying assumptions such as quasi-static analysis is a fruitful direction for further research.

Application to Planning

Suppose that it is impossible to exert forces at the center of mass of B. Thus the control velocity uncertainty cones lies entirely in the tangent spaces to C, and contain no component across J. Any motion of B must be effected by the transferred pushing force. Under generalized damper dynamics, the tools above are sufficient to characterize all possible resulting motions from a cone of applied forces. Thus we can define forward projections, backprojections, and preimages in $\mathcal{G}$ when motion across J due to pushing is possible. Motion across J is only posible on certain surfaces; it is impossible to move across J in free-space.

Imagine a backchaining planner in a generalized configuration space endowed with this physics. Such a planner could compute motion strategies which may be characterized as follows:

- In free space, or on surfaces generated by immovable objects, all differential motions lie within one α-slice.
- Along surfaces generated by objects that can be pushed, the differential motions are tangent to the surface in $\mathcal{G}$, and may move across J as well as C.

The resulting motion strategy consists of a sequence of gross motions, compliant motions, and pushing motions.

Generalized Control Uncertainty as a Non-holonomic Constraint

Suppose, as above, it is impossible to exert forces at the center of mass of B, so the generalized control uncertainty in $\mathcal{G}$ has no component in the tangent space to J. (See fig. II.19.) Consider example (1) when B has three degrees of freedom and the robot has two. While the tangent space to $\mathcal{G}$ is five dimensional, note that in general, the forward projection of a point will be of lower dimension. For example, from a point in free space, the forward projection will lie in a 2D slice of $\mathcal{G}$. From a point on a surface in $\mathcal{G}$, the forward projection will typically lie on the surface.

This is a subtle and deep point. The constraints in most motion planning problems [Lozano-Pérez, SS, D, E, C] are constraints on the degrees of freedom of the moving objects. Such constraints are called *holonomic* constraints; they can be expressed as constraint surfaces in the configuration space. However, the generalized control uncertainty and the characterization of friction express constraints not on the degrees of freedom of the object, but on its *differential motions*. Informally, this is clear since in fig. II.19, $\overline{B}_{ec}(v_\theta^*)$ is 2D, while the tangent space is 5D. Such constraints are called *non-holonomic* constraints; they can not in general be expressed as constraint surfaces in the configuration space. They can be characterized as constraints in the tangent bundle, as in the sticking computation employing $\mathcal{K}$. Computing backprojections under non-holonomic constraints requires enforcing the differential motion constraints as well as the usual holonomic constraints imposed by surfaces in generalized configuration space.

§A.5. A More Formal Summary of the Construction of $\tilde{H}$

We now summarize the construction of phase space EDR regions somewhat more formally. We construct $\tilde{H}$ as follows. Given a motion strategy θ, a goal region G, and a start region R in generalized configuration space , we construct:

$$F = F_\theta(R)$$
$$P = P_{F,\theta}(G)$$
$$\hat{P} = \hat{P}_{F,\theta}(G)$$
$$H_s = \{\, x \in \hat{P} - P \mid \text{sticking can occur at } x \,\}$$
$$Z(H_s) = \{\, (x,v) \in \pi^{-1}(H_s) \mid v = 0 \,\}$$
$$\tilde{H} = \pi^{-1}(F - \hat{P}) \cup Z(H_s).$$

The forward projection F is in position space, not phase space. The map Z is the zero section of generalized configuration space .

Now, given a collection of goals $\{\, G_\beta \,\}$ we denote their backprojection under a commanded velocity v_θ^* by $B_\theta(\{\, G_\beta \,\})$. Note this is equal to $B_\theta(\bigcup_\beta G_\beta)$, since backprojections do not address recognizability. From the construction of $\tilde{H}$, we have

$$B_\theta(\{\,G, \pi\tilde{H}\,\}) \supset R. \tag{7}$$

(7) is a reachability consequence only. To form an EDR strategy using $\tilde{H}$, we must add a recognizability constraint analogous to eq. (3). We allow simple goals in phase space; that is, we permit goals in phase space as arguments to $P_{R,\theta}$. The recognizability constraint is then

$$P_{R,\theta}(\{\,\pi^{-1}(G), \tilde{H}\,\}) = R. \tag{3a}$$

As written, (3a) is a reachability and recognizability constraint. But since reachability (7) follows from the construction of $\tilde{H}$, (3a) adds exactly recognizability to the construction.

More generally, we could replace G throughout by a collection of goals $\{\,G_\beta\,\}$. (3a) then becomes the obvious

$$P_{R,\theta}(\{\,\pi^{-1}(G_\beta)\,\} \cup \{\,\tilde{H}\,\}) = R.$$

§A.6. Definition of an Approximate Push-Forward

Here is the formal definition of one kind of push-forward. (There are other kinds). This push-forward is obtained by "lying" to the termination predicate about where the motion started. It captures the intuitive notion of "trying the strategy anyway, even if we're not guaranteed to be in the right initial region."

Suppose we have a motion θ from a region R which achieves some set of goals $\{\,G_\beta\,\}$. That is,

$$P_{R,\theta}(\{\,G_\beta\,\}) = R.$$

Let U be an arbitrary region in generalized configuration space . For example, we might not be guaranteed to have the initial position within R; it might lie within some region S. We let $U = S - R$, and investigate the effect of executing the strategy from U while lying to the termination predicate: we tell it we were really within R when the motion started.

We define a *push-forward of θ from U with respect to R and $\{\,G_\beta\,\}$*, denoted $F_*(\theta, U, R, \{\,G_\beta\,\})$, as follows:

We assume a termination predicate with no local history and without time; see [Erdmann]. The formulation for variations of this predicate are very similar. Forward projections in phase space are denoted with tildes. Recall π is the canonical projection of phase space onto configuration space. Given an actual position and velocity (x, v), a corresponding sensed position and velocity is denoted (x^*, v^*). (x^*, v^*) is said to be *consistent* with (x, v) iff $(x^*, v^*) \in B_{ep}(x) \times B_{ev}(v)$.

$F_*(\theta, U, R, \{ G_\beta \})$ is the set of pairs $(x, v) \in \tilde{F}_\theta(U)$ such that there is an initial position $p_0 \in U$ and a corresponding sensed position $p_0^* \in B_{ep}(p_0) \cap R \cap P_{F_\theta(R), \theta}(G)$, and some $G \in \{ G_\beta \}$, such that for all (x^*, v^*) consistent with (x, v),

$$B_{ep}(x^*) \times B_{ev}(v^*) \cap \tilde{F}_\theta(R) \subset \pi^{-1}(G). \qquad (*)$$

Note, however, that it is possible for the motion not to terminate. For the sake of discussion, however, assume it does terminate, either by using velocity thresholding or time. This requires indexing the forward projection in $(*)$ by time. These assumptions allow us to prove some lemmas that provide some intuition about this push forward.

Now, suppose further that $R \subset S$. Abbreviate $F_* = \pi F_*(\theta, S, R, \{ G_\beta \}))$. The following lemmas help characterize the push forward F_*. Let $\tilde{H}$ be the EDR region as given in (6), and let $H = \pi \tilde{H}$. F_* says exactly where the strategy θ will terminate when executed from S, if we lie to the termination predicate and tell it we really started from R.

Lemma: $B_\theta(F_*) \supset R$.

Lemma: $P_{R, \theta}(F_*) = R$.

Now, in general, maximal preimages do not exist [Mason, E]. If R is not a maximal preimage, then the equation

$$F_* \subset H \cup \left(\bigcup_\beta G_\beta \right) \qquad (**)$$

need not hold. It would be useful to prove or disprove the following:

Conjecture: $(**)$ holds when R is maximal.

In particular, if there is just one goal G, then this would imply $F_* \subset H \cup G$.

§A.7. The Formal Requirements for Push-Forwards

We now characterize the formal requirements for push-forwards. Note that the approximate push-forward, above, need not satisfy these constraints.

For notational purposes, we regard motion strategies as mappings, and so we write

$$R_i = P_{R_i, \theta_i}(R_{i-1}) \qquad (*)$$

as

$$R_i \overset{\theta_i}{\Longrightarrow} R_{i-1}.$$

If the R_i are successive subgoals in a plan whose motions are the θ_i, then (∗) is a necessary and sufficient condition for the subgoals to be suitable for back-chaining [LMT.]

Given as data strategy θ_i, a goal R_{i-1}, an actual start region R, and a region R_i from which θ_i is guaranteed, we can always construct an EDR region H_{i-1}. (H_{i-1} is $\pi\tilde{H}_{i-1}$, see (6)). Of course we may not be able to construct an EDR *strategy* from H_{i-1}. Denote the dependence of H on its data by

$$H_{i-1} = H(R, \theta_i),$$

so we imagine examining the "domain" and "range" of θ_i to obtain R_i and R_{i-1}. If there exists an EDR strategy for the EDR region H_{i-1}, we denote this by

$$R \begin{array}{c} \overset{\theta_i}{\nearrow} R_{i-1} \\ \\ \underset{\theta_i}{\searrow} H(R, \theta_i). \end{array}$$

More generally, we could replace R_{i-1} with the distinguishable union of some set of goals. As suggested in the informal exposition, we will in fact replace it with the set of unattained subgoals in an n-step plan. The motion θ_i must then achieve either some unattained subgoal, or the EDR region.

Now, suppose we are given a guaranteed n-step plan, Θ,

$$R_n \overset{\theta_n}{\Longrightarrow} R_{n-1} \overset{\theta_{n-1}}{\Longrightarrow} \cdots \overset{\theta_2}{\Longrightarrow} R_1 \overset{\theta_1}{\Longrightarrow} R_0 = G.$$

Define $\mathcal{R}_j = \{\, R_j, R_{j-1}, \ldots, R_1, R_0 \,\}$ to be the distinguishable union of all unattained subgoals (after R_j). The one step EDR strategy we seek may achieve any one of these subgoals. Suppose the start region R contains R_n. We can construct an n-step EDR strategy with start region R, (using Θ as data) if there exist *termination regions* $F_{∗n}, \ldots, F_{∗n-i}$, for some i between 1 and n, such that

$$
\begin{array}{ccccccccc}
& & & & & & & & \mathcal{R}_{n-i-1} \\
& & & & & & & \overset{\theta_{n-i}}{\nearrow} & \\
F_{∗n} & \overset{\theta_n}{\Longrightarrow} & F_{∗n-1} & \overset{\theta_{n-1}}{\Longrightarrow} & \cdots & \overset{\theta_{n-1+1}}{\Longrightarrow} & F_{∗n-i} & & \\
\| & & \cap & & & & \cap & \searrow & \\
R & & R_{n-1} \cup H_{n-1} & & \cdots & & R_{n-i} \cup H_{n-i} & \underset{\theta_{n-i}}{} & H_{n-i-1}
\end{array}
$$

where

$$H_{j-1} = H(F_{∗j}, \theta_j).$$

In other words,

$$F_{*n} = R$$
$$F_{*n-1} \subset R_{n-1} \cup H(R, \theta_n)$$
$$F_{*n-2} \subset R_{n-2} \cup H(F_{*n-1}, \theta_{n-1})$$

$$\vdots$$

$$F_{*n-i} \subset R_{n-i} \cup H(F_{*n-i+1}, \theta_{n-i+1}),$$

such that

$$F_{*j} = P_{F_{*j}, \theta_j}(F_{*j-1}) \qquad \text{for all } j,$$

and such that there exists a one-step EDR strategy

$$\begin{array}{ccc} & \theta_{n-i} \nearrow & \mathcal{R}_{n-i-1} \\ F_{*n-i} & & \\ & \theta_{n-i} \searrow & H(F_{*n-i}, \theta_{n-i}). \end{array}$$

These termination regions $\{ F_{*j} \}$ characterize the requirements for push-forwards. The push-forward should be a function satisfying these constraints, by which we mean that the push-forward is a set-valued map whose values are these termination regions. We hope that the termination regions may be approximated by push-forwards such as the example in the last section. Computing exact push-forwards appears to be at least as hard as solving n-step pre-image equations.

Note (1): When maximal preimages do not exist, for completeness it may be necessary to employ a weaker constraint on termination regions. For example, the weakest constraint would be

$$H(F_{*j}, \theta_j) = F_{\theta_j}(F_{*j}).$$

See the previous section for more details.

Note (2): As the notation suggests, it is possible to formalize the view of "motions as mappings"—this notion is implicit in the term "preimage." To develop this viewpoint, one considers motions as a certain class of morphisms between distinguishable unions in the powerset of the tangent bundle to generalized configuration space . An EDR theory, then, is a covariant functor associated with a family of quotient maps of the form

$$\pi : TC \times J \to \{ P, \hat{P} - P, \tilde{F} - \hat{P} \}.$$

While it is possible to push such a functorial viewpoint, any category-theoretic formulation of this flavor will almost certainly be exclusively descriptive.

References

Certain frequently cited references have been given shorter mnemonics, eg., [LMT].

Abraham, R. and Marsden, J. *Foundations of Mechanics,* Benjamin/Cummings, London (1978).

Arnold, V. I. *Mathematical Methods of Classical Mechanics,* Springer-Verlag, New York (1978).

[BK] Bajaj, C. and M. Kim, "Compliant Motion Planning with Geometric Models", *Proc. ACM Symposium on Computational Geometry,* Waterloo, 1987.

Ben-Or M., Kozen D., and Reif J., "The Complexity of Elementary Algebra and Geometry", J. Comp. and Sys. Sciences, Vol. 32, (1986), pp. 251-264.

Boyse J. W., "Interference Detection Among Solids and Surfaces", Comm ACM, vol 22, No 1 (1979) pp 3-9.

Brady, M. et. al. (eds). *Robot Motion: Planning and Control.,* Cambridge, Mass.: MIT Press. (1982).

Brooks, R. A. *Symbolic Error Analysis and Robot Planning,* International Journal of Robotics Research, Vol 1, no. 4, Dec., 29–68 (1982).

Brooks, R. A *A Robust Layered Control System for a Mobile Robot,* IEEE Journal of Robotics and Automation **RA-2** (1): 14–23. Also MIT A.I. Lab Memo 864 (1985).

Brooks, R., "Solving the Find-Path Problem by Good Representation of Free Space", *IEEE Transactions on Systems, Man, and Cyberbetics,* Vol. 13, 1983.

Brooks, R., and T Lozano-Pérez, "A Subdivision Algorithm in Configuration Space for Findpath with Rotation", *Eighth International Joint Conference on Artificial Intelligence,* Karlsruhe, Germany, August, 1983.

Brost, R. C. *Planning Robot Grasping Motions in the Presence of Uncertainty,* Computer Science Department and the Robotics Institute, Carnegie-Mellon University, CMU-RI-TR-85-12 (1985).

[Bro] Brost, R., "Automatic Grasp Planning in the Presence of Uncertainty", *IEEE International Conference on Robotics and Automation,* San Francisco, April, 1986.

Brost, R. *A State/Action Space Approach to Planning Robot Actions,* Forthcoming Ph.D. Thesis, Computer Science Dept., CMU (to appear).

[Buc] Buckley, S. J. *Planning and Teaching Compliant Motion Strategies,* Ph.D. Thesis. Massachusetts Institute of Technology, Department of Electrical Engineering and Computer Science, 1987. Also MIT-AI-TR-936 (1987).

[BRS] Burridge, R., Rajan, V. T., and Schwartz, J. T. *The Peg-In-Hole Problem: Statics and Dynamics of Nearly Rigid Bodies in Frictional Contact,* IEEE ICRA, Raleigh, NC (1983).

Caine, M., "Chamferless Assembly of Rectangular Parts in Two and Three Dimensions", S.M. dissertation, MIT Department of Machanical Engineering, June 1985.

Cameron S., "A Study of the Clash Detection Problem in Robotics", proc. IEEE conf. on Robotics and Automation, 1985, pp 488-493.

Canny, J.F. *A New Algebraic method for Robot Motion Planning and Real Geometry,* FOCS (1987).

[C] Canny, J. F. *Collision Detection for Moving Polyhedra,* PAMI-8(2) (1986).

[C1] Canny, J.F. *The Complexity of Robot Motion Planning,* Ph.D. Thesis, MIT Department of Electrical Engineering and Computer Science (1987).

Canny, J.F. *Computing Roadmaps of Compact Semi-Algebraic Sets,* Intl. Workshop on Geometric Reasoning, Oxford, England, June (1986).

[CD] Canny, J.F. and Donald, B. R. *Simplified Voronoi Diagrams,* Proc. 3rd ACM Symposium on Computational Geometry, Waterloo, June (1987).

[CD] Canny, J.F. and Donald, B. R. *Simplified Voronoi Diagrams,* Discrete and Computational Geometry 3 (3) pp. 219-236. (1988).

[CR] Canny, J., and J. Reif, "New Lower Bound Techniques for Robot Motion Planning Problems", *FOCS* (1987).

Chapman, D. *Planning for Conjunctive Goals,* MIT AI-TR 802 (1985).

Chistov A. L. and Grigoryev D. Y., "Complexity of quantifier elimination in the theory of algebraically closed fields", Lect. Notes Comp. Sci. 176, Springer Verlag, (1984).

Collins G. E. "Quantifier Elimination for Real Closed Fields by Cylindrical Algebraic Decomposition" Lecture Notes in Computer Science, No. 33, Springer-Verlag, New York, (1975), pp. 135-183.

Cutkosky, M., "Grasping and Fine Manipulation for Automated Manufacturing", Ph.D. dissertation, Carnegie-Mellon University, January, 1985.

Davis, E. and McDermott, D. *Planning and Executing Routes through Uncertain Territory,* Yale University, Dept. of Computer Science (1982).

Donald, B. R. *Motion Planning with Six Degrees of Freedom,* MIT AI-TR 791, Artificial Intelligence Lab. (1984).

Donald, B. R. *On Motion Planning with Six Degrees of Freedom: Solving the Intersection Problems in Configuration Space,* IEEE International Conference on Robotics and Automation, St. Louis, MO (1985).

[D] **Donald, B. R.** *Robot Motion Planning with Uncertainty in the Geometric Models of the Robot and Environment: A Formal Framework for Error Detection and Recovery,* IEEE International Conference on Robotics and Automation, San Francisco, April (1986a).

[D] **Donald, B. R.** *A Theory of Error Detection and Recovery for Robot Motion Planning with Uncertainty,* Intl. Workshop on Geometric Reasoning, Oxford, England (1986b).

Donald, B. R. *A Search Algorithm for Motion Planning with Six Degrees of Freedom,* Artificial Intelligence, 31 (3) (1987a).

Donald, B. R. *Error Detection and Recovery for Robot Motion Planning with Uncertainty,* Ph.D. Thesis, Dept. EECS, MIT Artificial Intelligence Laboratory, MIT-AI-TR 982 (1987b).

[D] **Donald, B. R.** *A Geometric Approach to Error Detection and Recovery for Robot Motion Planning with Uncertainty,* To appear in *Artificial Intelligence* (1988).

Donald, B. R. *Planning Multi-Step Error Detection and Recovery Strategies,* Proc. IEEE Int. Conf. on Robotics and Automation, Philadelphia (1988a).

Donald, B. R. *The Complexity of Planar Compliant Motion Planning Under Uncertainty,* Proc. 4th ACM Symp. on Computational Geometry, Urbana (1988b).

Draper Laboratories, Fourth Annual Seminar on Robotics and Advanced Assembly Systems, Cambridge, Massachusetts, November, 1983.

Dufay, B., and J. Latombe, "An Approach to Automatic Robot Programming Based on Inductive Learning", in Brady, M., and R. Paul, *Robotics Research: The First International Symposium*, MIT Press, 1984.

Durrant-Whyte, H. *Concerning Uncertain Geometry in Robotics,* Intl. Workshop on Geometric Reasoning, Oxford, England, June (1986).

[E] **Erdmann, M.** *Using Backprojections for Fine Motion Planning with Uncertainty,* IJRR Vol. 5 no. 1 (1986).

Erdmann, M. *On Motion Planning With Uncertainty,* MIT AI Lab, MIT-AI-TR 810 (1984).

[EM] **Erdmann, M., and M. Mason,** "An Exploration of Sensorless Manipulation", *IEEE International Conference on Robotics and Automation,* San Francisco, April, 1986.

Faltings, B., "A Theory of Qualitative Kinematics in Mechanisms", Computer Science Department, University of Illinois at Urbana-Champaign, UIUCDCS-R-86-1274; May, 1986.

Faltings, B., "Qualitative Kinematics in Mechanisms", Proc. IJCAI 87, Milano, 1987

Faverjon, B. *Obstacle Avoidance Using an Octree in the Configuration Space of a Manipulator,* Proc. IEEE Intl. Conf. Robotics, Atlanta (March 1984).

[STRIPS] **Fikes, R. and Nilsson, N.** *STRIPS: A New Approach to the Application of Theorem Proving to Problem Solving,* Artificial Intelligence vol. 2 (1971).

Fortune, S., Wilfong, G., and Yap, C. 1986 (April 7–10, San Francisco, California). Coordinated Motion of Two Robot Arms. *Proceedings of the 1986 IEEE International Conference on Robotics and Automation,* pp. 1216–1223.

Gini, M. and Gini, G. *Towards Automatic Error Recovery in Robot Programs,* IJCAI-83 (1983).

Grigoryev D. Y., "Complexity of Deciding Tarski Algebra" Jour. Symbolic Computation, special issue on decision algorithms for the theory of real closed fields, to appear (1987).

Grossman, D., and R. Taylor, "Interactive Generation of Object Models with a Manipulator", *IEEE Transactions on Systems, Man, and Cybernetics,* Vol. 8, No. 9, September, 1978.

[Gor] **Gordon, B. B.** *Intersections of Higher-Weight Cycles over Quaternionic Modular Surfaces and Modular Forms of Nebentypus,* Bull. AMS 14 (2), pp. 293-8 (1986).

Hayes, P. *A Representation for Robot Plans,* 4th IJCAI (1976).

Hopcroft, J. E., Schwartz, J. T., and Sharir, M. 1984 On the Complexity of Motion Planning for Multiple Independent Objects; *PSPACE*-Hardness of the "Warehouseman's Problem." *International Journal of Robotics Research.* 3(4):76–88.

[HW] **Hopcroft J., and Wilfong G.**, "Motion of Objects in Contact," Int. Jour. Robotics Res. vol 4, no. 4, (1986).

Hungerford, T. W. *Algebra,* Springer-Verlag, New York GTM 73 (1974).

Hogan, N., "Impedance Control of Industrial Robots", *Robotics and Computer-Integrated Manufacturing*, Vol. 1, No. 1, 1984.

Inoue, H., "Force Feedback in Precise Assembly Tasks", MIT Artificial Intelligence Laboratory, AIM-308, August, 1974.

Khatib, O. *Real-Time Obstacle Avoidance for Manipulators and Mobile Robots,* Int. Jour. Rob. Res. vol. 5, No. 1, pp. 90-99 (1986).

Koditschek, D., "Exact Robot Navigation by Means of Potential Functions: Some Topological Considerations", Proc. IEEE Intl. Conf. Robotics, Raleigh, March 1987.

[Kou] **Koutsou, A.**, "A Geometric Reasoning System for Moving an Object While Maintaining Contact with Others", *ACM Symposium on Computational Geometry*, Yorktown Heights, N.Y., 1985.

Kozen D., and Yap C. "Algebraic Cell Decomposition in NC", Proc IEEE symp. FOCS, (1985), pp. 515-521.

Laugier, C., "A Program for Automatic Grasping of Objects with a Robot Arm", *Eleventh Symposium of Industrial Robots*, Japan Society of Biomechanisms and Japan Industrial Robot Association, 1981.

Lee, D. T., and Drysdale, R. L., "Generalization of Voronoi diagrams in the plane," SIAM J. Comp. (10) (1981) pp. 73-87.

Lieberman, L., and M. Wesley, "AUTOPASS: An Automatic Programming System for Computer Controlled Mechanical Assembly", *IBM Journal of Research Development*, Vol. 21, No. 4, 1977, pp. 321-333.

Lozano-Pérez, T., "The Design of a Mechanical Assembly System", S.M. dissertation, MIT Department of Electrical Engineering and Computer Science, also AI-TR-397, MIT Artificial Intelligence Laboratory, 1976.

Lozano–Pérez, T. *Automatic Planning of Manipulator Transfer Movements,* IEEE Trans. on Systems, Man and Cybernetics (SMC–11):681–698 (1981).

Lozano–Pérez, T. *Spatial Planning: A Configuration Space Approach,* IEEE Trans. on Computers (C–32):108–120 (1983a).

Lozano-Pérez, T., "Robot Programming", *IEEE Proceedings*, 1983b.

Lozano-Pérez, T., "Motion Planning For Simple Robot Manipulators", *Third International Symposium on Robotics Research*, Paris, October, 1985.

Lozano-Pérez, "A Simple Motion Planning Algorithm for General Robot Manipulators," in Proceedings of Fifth National Conference for the American Association of Artificial Intelligence, Philadelphia, 1986, pp. 626–631.

Lozano-Pérez T., Jones J., Mazer, E., O'Donnell, P., Grimson, E., "Handey: A Robot System that Recognizes, Plans, and Manipulates", Proc. IEEE Int. Conf. on Robotics and Automation, 1987.

[LMT] Lozano-Pérez, T., Mason, M. T., and Taylor, R. H. *Automatic Synthesis of Fine-Motion Strategies for Robots,* Int. J. of Robotics Research, Vol 3, no. 1 (1984).

Lozano-Pérez, T., and Wesley, M. A. *An algorithm for planning collision-free paths among polyhedral obstacles,* Communications of the ACM (22):560-570 (1979).

Lumelsky, V. J. *Continuous Motion Planning in Unknown Environment for a 3D Cartesian Robot Arm.* , *Proceedings of the 1986 IEEE International Conference on Robotics and Automation*, pp. 1569–1574. (April 7–10, San Francisco, Calif.) (1986).

[Ma] Mason, M.T. *Compliance and force control for computer controlled manipulators,* IEEE Trans. on Systems, Man and Cybernetics (SMC-11):418-432 (1981).

[Ma2] Mason, M.T. *Manipulator Grasping and Pushing Operations,* MIT AI Lab, MIT AI-TR-690 (1982).

Mason, M. T. 1986. Mechanics and Planning of Manipulator Pushing Operations. *International Journal of Robotics Research* 5(3).

Mason, M. T. *Automatic Planning of Fine Motions: Correctness and Completeness,* 1984 IEEE International Conference on Robotics, Atlanta Ga. (1984).

Mason, M. T. 1985 (March 25–28, St. Louis, Missouri). The Mechanics of Manipulation. *Proceedings of the 1985 IEEE Int. Conf. on Robotics and Automation*, pp. 544–548.

McDermott, D. *A Temporal Logic for Reasoning about Processes and Plans,* Cog. Sci. 6, pp. 101-55 (1982).

Natarajan, B. K. 1986 (Oct. 27–29, Toronto, Ontario). An Algorithmic Approach to the Automated Design of Parts Orienters. *Proceedings of the 27th Annual IEEE Symposium on Foundations of Computer Science*, pp. 132–142.

Natarajan, B. K. 1986. On Moving and Orienting Objects. Ph.D. Thesis. Ithaca, N.Y.: Cornell University Department of Computer Science.

Neivergelt, J., and Preparata, F. P. *Plane-Sweep Algorithms for Intersecting Geometric Figures,* CACM Vol. 25, no. 10 (1982).

Ó'Dúnlaing, C., Sharir, M., and Yap C., "Generalized Voronoi diagrams for moving a ladder: I Topological Analysis," NYU-Courant Institute, Robotics Lab. Tech. report No. 32 (1984)

Ó'Dúnlaing, C., Sharir, M., and Yap C., "Generalized Voronoi diagrams for moving a ladder: II Efficient construction of the diagram," NYU-Courant Institute, Robotics Lab. Tech. report No. 33 (1984)

Ó'Dúnlaing C., and Yap C., "A retraction method for planning the motion of a disc," J. Algorithms (6) (1985) pp. 104-111

Ohwovoriole, M., and B. Roth, "A Theory of Parts Mating For Assembly Automation", *Proceedings of the Robot and Man Symposium 81,* Warsaw, Poland, September 1981.

Paul, R., *Robot Manipulators,* MIT Press, Cambridge, Massachusetts, 1981.

Peshkin, M., "Planning Robotic Manipulation Strategies for Sliding Objects", Ph.D. dissertation, Department of Physics, Carnegie-Mellon University, 1986.

Peshkin, M., and A. Sanderson, "Reachable Grasps on a Polygon: The Convex Rope Algorithm", *IEEE Journal of Robotics and Automation,* Volume 2, Number 1, March, 1986.

Raibert, M., and J. Craig, "Hybrid Position/Force Control of Manipulators", *Journal of Dynamic Systems, Measurement, and Control,* No. 102, June, 1981, pp. 126-133.

Reif J., "Complexity of the Mover's Problem and Generalizations," Proc. 20th IEEE Symp. FOCS, (1979). Also in "Planning, Geometry and Complexity of Robot Motion", ed. by J. Schwartz, J. Hopcroft and M. Sharir, , Ablex publishing corp. New Jersey, (1987), Ch. 11, pp. 267-281.

Requicha, A. A. *Representation of Tolerances in Solid Modeling: Issues and Alternative Approaches,* Solid Modeling by Computers: From Theory to Applications; Plenum, N. Y. (1984).

Salisbury, J.K., "Active Stiffness Control of a Manipulator in Cartesian Coordinates", *IEEE Conference on Decision and Control,* Albuquerque, New Mexico, November, 1980.

Salisbury, J.K., "Kinematic and Force Analysis of Articulated Hands", Ph.D. dissertation, Stanford University, Department of Mechanical Engineering, 1982.

Segre, A. M., and G. DeJong, "Explanation-Based Manipulator Learning: Acquisition of Planning Ability Through Observation", *IEEE International Conference on Robotics and Automation*, St. Louis, March, 1985.

Schwartz J., Hopcroft J., and Sharir M., "Planning, Geometry and Complexity of Robot Motion Planning", Albex Publishing Co., New Jersey, (1987).

[SS] Schwartz J. and Sharir M., "On the 'Piano Movers' Problem, II. General Techniques for Computing Topological Properties of Real Algebraic Manifolds," Comp. Sci. Dept., New York University report 41, (1982). Also in "Planning, Geometry and Complexity of Robot Motion", ed. by J. Schwartz, J. Hopcroft and M. Sharir, Ablex publishing corp. New Jersey, (1987), Ch. 5, pp. 154-186.

Schwartz J. and Yap C. K., "Advances in Robotics," Lawrence Erlbaum associates, Hillside New Jersey, (1986).

Simunovic, S. N., "An Information Approach to Parts Mating", Ph.D. dissertation, Department of Electrical Engineering, Massachusetts Institute of Technology, 1979.

Simunovic, S. N. 1975 (Sept. 22–24, Chicago, Illinois). Force Information in Assembly Processes. *Proceedings 5th International Symposium on Industrial Robots.* Bedford, U.K.: IFS Publications, pp. 415–431.

Shapiro, V. *Parametric Modeling and Analysis of Tolerances,* GM Research Lab. Rept. CS-460 (1985).

Srinivas, Sankaran *Error Recovery in Robot Systems,* Cal. Tech. Ph.D. Thesis, Computer Science (1977).

Taylor, R. H. *The Synthesis of Manipulator Control Programs from Task-level Specifications,* Stanford Artificial Intelligence Laboratory, AIM-282, July (1976).

Tarski A., "A Decision Method for Elementary Algebra and Geometry" Univ. of Calif. Press, Berkeley, (1948), second ed. 1951.

Turk, M., "A Fine-Motion Planning Algorithm", *SPIE Conference on Intelligent Robots and Computer Vision*, Cambridge, Massachusetts, September, 1985.

Udupa, S., "Collision Detection and Avoidance in Computer Controlled Manipulators", Ph.D. dissertation, Department of Electrical Engineering, California Institute of Technology, 1977.

Udupa S., "Collision Detection and Avoidance in Computer Controlled Manipulators", Proc. 5th Int. Joint. Conf. on Art. Intell., Mass. Inst. Tech. (1977) pp 737-748.

Valade, J., "Automatic Generation of Trajectories for Assembly Tasks", *Sixth European Conference on Artificial Intelligence*, Pisa, Italy, September, 1984.

Ward, B. and McCalla, G. *Error Detection and Recovery in a Dynamic Planning Environment*, AAAI (1983).

[W] Whitney, D., "Force Feedback Control of Manipulator Fine Motions", *Journal of Dynamic Systems, Measurement, and Control*, June, 1977, pp. 91-97.

Whitney, D., "Quasi-Static Assembly of Compliantly Supported Rigid Parts", *Journal of Dynamic Systems, Measurement, and Control*, Vol. 104, March 1982.

Whitney, D., "Historical Perspective and State of the Art in Robot Force Control", *IEEE International Conference on Robotics and Automation*, St. Louis, March, 1985.

Wilkins, D. E. *Domain-Independent Planning: Representation and Plan Generation*, Artificial Intelligence, Vol. 22 No. 3 (1984).

Yap, C., "Coordinating the motion of several discs," NYU-Courant Institute, Robotics Lab. No. 16 (1984)

Yap, C., "Algorithmic Motion Planning", in *Advances in Robotics: Volume 1*, edited by J. Schwartz and C. Yap, Lawrence Erlbaum Associates, 1986.

Appendix: Code for the Sweep Algorithm

```
;;;;;;;;;;;;;;-*-  mode:lisp; package:(sweep); Base: 10 -*-;;;;;;;;;;;;;;;;;;;;
;;;;;;;;;;;;;;;;;;;;;;;;;;;;;;;;;;;;;;;;;;;;;;;;;;;;;;;;;;;;;;;;;;;;;;;;;;;;;;;;;
;;;
;;; Plane sweep algorithm for computing Forward Projections,
;;; Backprojections, and Weak Backprojections in O(n log n) time,
;;; and set differences, intersections, and unions in O((n+c) log n)
;;; time. Implemented in rational arithmetic in Zetalisp,
;;; by John Canny and Bruce Donald, MIT Artificial Intelligence Laboratory,
;;; 545 Technology Square, Cambridge, MA 02139.
;;;
;;; (c) Copyright 1986
;;;

(DEFMACRO REST (X)
  '(CDR ,X))



(DEFCONST BACKPROJECTION? ())

(DEFCONST EPS 1E-4)

(DEFSTRUCT (POLYGON :NAMED :PREDICATE)
  LOOP-LIST
  LOOP-END
  COLOR)

(DEFSTRUCT (POINT (:TYPE :LIST) :NAMED :PREDICATE)
  X
  Y)

(DEFSTRUCT (EDGE (:TYPE :LIST) :NAMED :PREDICATE)
  TAIL
  HEAD
  EQN
  EDGE-PROPERTIES)

(DEFSTRUCT (EQN (:TYPE :LIST) :NAMED :PREDICATE)
  X
  Y
  D
  PROPERTIES)

(DEFSTRUCT (EVENT (:TYPE :LIST) :NAMED :PREDICATE)
  POINT
  COLOR-CHANGE
  EQN)
```

```
(DEFSTRUCT (INTERVAL (:TYPE :ARRAY) :NAMED :PREDICATE)
  TOP
  BOTTOM
  EVENT
  OUTPUT-STRUCTURE)

(DEFSTRUCT (OUTPUT-STRUCTURE (:TYPE :ARRAY) :NAMED :PREDICATE)
  TOP
  BOTTOM
  TOP-END
  BOTTOM-END
  POLYGON)

(DEFSTRUCT (QUERY-NODE :NAMED :PREDICATE)
  X-MIN
  X-MAX
  INTERVALS)

(defstruct (CO-vertex :named (:type :list) :predicate)
  X
  Y
  edge-generator
  vertex-generator
  Csurface-type)



(DEFUN NEG-EQN (EQN)
  (IF (X EQN)
      (MAKE-EQN X (- (X EQN)) Y (- (Y EQN)) D (- (D EQN)) PROPERTIES (PROPERTIES EQN))
      EQN))

(DEFUN FAST-FLOAT (A)
  (// (FLOAT (NUMERATOR A)) (FLOAT (DENOMINATOR A))))

(DEFUN EVENT-> (EVENT-1 EVENT-2)
  (LET ((DIF (- (FAST-FLOAT (X (POINT EVENT-1)))
                (FAST-FLOAT (X (POINT EVENT-2))))))
    (COND ((> DIF EPS) 1)
          ((< DIF (- EPS)) -1)
          (T (LET ((TEST (- (X (POINT EVENT-1)) (X (POINT EVENT-2)))))
               (IF (ZEROP TEST)
                   (LET ((NEXT-TEST (- (Y (POINT EVENT-1)) (Y (POINT EVENT-2)))))
                     (IF (ZEROP NEXT-TEST)
                         (SLOPE-> (EQN EVENT-1) (EQN EVENT-2))
                         NEXT-TEST))
                   TEST))))))



(DEFUN SLOPE-> (EQN-1 EQN-2)
```

```
(IF EQN-1
    (IF EQN-2
        (IF (ZEROP (Y EQN-1))
            (IF (ZEROP (Y EQN-2))
                0
                1)
            (IF (ZEROP (Y EQN-2))
                -1
                (- (CL:// (X EQN-2) (Y EQN-2))
                   (CL:// (X EQN-1) (Y EQN-1)))))
        1)
    (IF EQN-2 -1 0)))


(DEFUN INTERSECTION-POINT (TOP BOTTOM)
  (IF (MINUSP (SLOPE-> TOP BOTTOM))
      (LET ((DET (- (* (X BOTTOM) (Y TOP)) (* (X TOP) (Y BOTTOM)))))
        (MAKE-POINT X (CL:// (- (* (Y BOTTOM) (D TOP)) (* (Y TOP) (D BOTTOM)))
                            DET)
                    Y (CL:// (- (* (X TOP) (D BOTTOM)) (* (X BOTTOM) (D TOP)))
                            DET)))))


(DEFMACRO E> (A B)
  '(> (- ,A ,B) EPS))

(DEFUN IN-INTERVAL? (POINT INTERVAL F-POINT)
  (COND
    ((E> (Y F-POINT) (Y-AT-X (TOP INTERVAL) F-POINT)) 1)
    ((E> (Y-AT-X (BOTTOM INTERVAL) F-POINT) (Y F-POINT)) -1)
    ((> (Y POINT) (Y-AT-X (TOP INTERVAL) POINT)) 1)
    ((< (Y POINT) (Y-AT-X (BOTTOM INTERVAL) POINT)) -1)
    (T 0)))


(DEFUN INTERVAL-> (INT-1 INT-2 POINT F-POINT PM)
  (IF (EQ INT-1 INT-2)
      0
      (LET ((FTD (- (Y-AT-X (TOP INT-1) F-POINT)
                    (Y-AT-X (TOP INT-2) F-POINT))))
        (COND ((> FTD EPS) 1)
              ((< FTD (- EPS)) -1)
              (T (LET ((TD (- (Y-AT-X (TOP INT-1) POINT)
                              (Y-AT-X (TOP INT-2) POINT))))
                   (IF (ZEROP TD)
                       (LET ((BD (- (Y-AT-X (BOTTOM INT-1) POINT)
                                    (Y-AT-X (BOTTOM INT-2) POINT))))
                         (IF (ZEROP BD)
```

```
                              (LET ((TS (S-> (SLOPE (TOP INT-1) PM)
                                             (SLOPE (TOP INT-2) PM))))
                                (IF (ZEROP TS)
                                    (S-> (SLOPE (BOTTOM INT-1) PM)
                                         (SLOPE (BOTTOM INT-2) PM))
                                    TS))
                              BD))
                      TD)))))))


(DEFUN DOT (EQN-1 EQN-2)
  (+ (* (FLOAT (X EQN-1)) (FLOAT (X EQN-2)))
     (* (FLOAT (Y EQN-1)) (FLOAT (Y EQN-2)))))

(DEFUN Y-AT-X (EQN POINT)
  (IF (ZEROP (Y EQN))
      (Y POINT)
      (CL:// (+ (D EQN) (* (X EQN) (X POINT)))
             (- (Y EQN)))))

(DEFUN SLOPE (EQN PM)
  (IF (ZEROP (Y EQN))
      '+¡
      (* PM (CL:// (X EQN) (- (Y EQN))))))

(DEFUN S-> (A B)
  (IF (EQ A '+¡)
      (IF (EQ B '+¡) 0 1)
      (IF (EQ B '+¡) -1 (- A B))))


(DEFUN ALWAYS-> (ignore ignore)
  1)

(DEFUN IN-RANGE? (X QUERY-NODE)
  (COND ((AND (X-MAX QUERY-NODE) (> X (X-MAX QUERY-NODE))) 1)
        ((AND (X-MIN QUERY-NODE) (< X (X-MIN QUERY-NODE))) -1)
        (T 0)))


(DEFUN ENCODE (COLOR NUMBER)
  (SELECTQ COLOR
    (OBSTACLE (LOAD-BYTE NUMBER 0 9.))
    (START (DEPOSIT-BYTE 0 9. 9. NUMBER))
    (PROJECTION (DEPOSIT-BYTE 0 18. 9. NUMBER))))
```

```
(DEFCONST PROJ-COLOR (ENCODE 'PROJECTION 1))

(DEFCONST FREE-COLOR 0)

(DEFCONST CARRY-1 (ASH 1 9.))

(DEFCONST CARRY-2 (ASH 1 18.))

(DEFUN ADD-COLORS (A B)
  (LET ((SUM (- (+ A B) (LOGAND CARRY-1 (LOGXOR A B (+ A B))))))
    (- SUM (LOGAND CARRY-2 (LOGXOR A B SUM)))))

(DEFUN ADD-COLORS-CAREFULLY (A B)
  (LET ((SUM (ADD-COLORS A B)))
    (IF (PLUSP (COLOR-FIELD SUM))
        (COLOR-FIELD SUM)
        SUM)))



(DEFUN SUB-COLORS (A B)
  (LET ((DIF (+ (- A B) (LOGAND CARRY-1 (LOGXOR A B (- A B))))))
    (+ DIF (LOGAND CARRY-2 (LOGXOR A B DIF)))))



(DEFUN NEG-COLOR (A)
  (SUB-COLORS 0 A))

(DEFUN FREE? (A)
  (ZEROP A))

(DEFUN FP? (A)
  (PLUSP (LOAD-BYTE A 18. 9)))

(DEFUN COLOR-FIELD (A)
  (LOAD-BYTE A 0 18.))

(DEFUN OBST? (A)
  (PLUSP (LOAD-BYTE A 0 9.)))

(DEFUN START? (A)
  (PLUSP (LOAD-BYTE A 9. 9.)))

(DEFUN EVENT-ADD (EVENT TREE &OPTIONAL NO-MUTATION)
  (LET ((CURRENT-EVENT (AVL-ACCESS EVENT TREE #'EVENT->)))
    (COND (CURRENT-EVENT
            (SETF (COLOR-CHANGE CURRENT-EVENT) (ADD-COLORS (COLOR-CHANGE EVENT)
                                                          (COLOR-CHANGE CURRENT-EVENT)))
            (IF (FREE? (COLOR-CHANGE CURRENT-EVENT))
                (AVL-DELETE CURRENT-EVENT TREE #'EVENT-> NO-MUTATION)
```

```
                       TREE))
              (T (AVL-INSERT EVENT TREE #'EVENT-> NO-MUTATION)))))


(DEFUN EVENT-SUB (EVENT TREE &OPTIONAL NO-MUTATION)
  (EVENT-ADD (MAKE-EVENT POINT (POINT EVENT) EQN (EQN EVENT)
                         COLOR-CHANGE (NEG-COLOR (COLOR-CHANGE EVENT)))
             TREE NO-MUTATION))



(DEFUN OLD-MERGE-EVENTS (A B)
  (DO* ((START (NCONS NIL))
        (PTR START))
       ((NOT (AND A B))
        (SETF (REST PTR) (OR A B))
        (REST START))
    (LET ((SIGN (SLOPE-> (EQN (FIRST A)) (EQN (FIRST B)))))
      (COND ((PLUSP SIGN)
             (SETF (REST PTR) (NCONS (FIRST B)))
             (SETQ PTR (REST PTR))
             (SETQ B (REST B)))
            ((MINUSP SIGN)
             (SETF (REST PTR) (NCONS (FIRST A)))
             (SETQ PTR (REST PTR))
             (SETQ A (REST A)))
            (T (LET ((NEW-COLOR (ADD-COLORS (COLOR-CHANGE (FIRST A))
                                            (COLOR-CHANGE (FIRST B)))))
                 (COND ((NOT (FREE? NEW-COLOR))
                        (SETF (REST PTR) (NCONS (MAKE-EVENT POINT (POINT (FIRST A))
                                                            EQN (EQN (FIRST A))
                                                            COLOR-CHANGE NEW-COLOR)))
                        (SETQ PTR (REST PTR))))
               (SETQ A (REST A) B (REST B)))))))))


(defun merge-events (a b)
  (do* ((start (ncons nil))
        (ptr start))
       ((not (and a b))
        (setf (rest ptr) (or a b))
        (rest start))
    (let ((sign (slope-> (eqn (first a)) (eqn (first b)))))
      (cond ((plusp sign)
             (setf (rest ptr) (ncons (first b)))
             (setq ptr (rest ptr))
             (setq b (rest b)))
            ((minusp sign)
             (setf (rest ptr) (ncons (first a)))
```

```
            (setq ptr (rest ptr))
            (setq a (rest a)))
        (t (let ((new-color (add-colors (color-change (first a))
                                        (color-change (first b)))))
            (cond ((not (free? new-color))
                   (setf (rest ptr) (ncons (make-event point (point (first a))
                                                       eqn (merge-equations
                                                             (eqn (first A))
                                                             (eqn (first B)))
                                                       color-change new-color)))
                  (setq ptr (rest ptr))))
            (setq a (rest a) b (rest b))))))))


;;; Merge the generators of two events. Assume that Eqn1 and Eqn2 are equal.
;;; They must both have obstacle tags.

(defun merge-equations (Eqn1 Eqn2)
  (cond ((and (generators (properties Eqn1))
              (generators (properties Eqn2))
              (not (equal (generators (properties Eqn1))
                          (generators (properties Eqn2)))))
         (make-eqn X (x Eqn1) Y (Y Eqn1) D (D Eqn1)
                   Properties (make-edge-description Tag (tag (properties Eqn1))
                                                     Generators
                                                     (merge-generators
                                                       (generators (properties Eqn1))
                                                       (generators (properties Eqn2))))))
        (T Eqn1)))


(defun merge-generators (G1 G2)
  (append (if (CO-vertex-p G1) (list G1) G1)
          (if (CO-vertex-p G2) (list G2) G2)))



(DEFUN AVL-HEAD-ALL (EVENT-QUEUE)
  (LET (FIRST-EVENT)
    (MULTIPLE-VALUE (FIRST-EVENT EVENT-QUEUE)
      (AVL-HEAD EVENT-QUEUE))
    (IF FIRST-EVENT
        (DO* ((EVENTS (NCONS FIRST-EVENT))
              (PTR EVENTS (REST PTR)))
             ((NULL PTR) (VALUES EVENTS EVENT-QUEUE))
          (LET ((NEXT-EVENT (LEFT-MOST EVENT-QUEUE)))
            (COND ((AND NEXT-EVENT (EQUAL (POINT NEXT-EVENT) (POINT FIRST-EVENT)))
                   (MULTIPLE-VALUE (NEXT-EVENT EVENT-QUEUE)
                     (AVL-HEAD EVENT-QUEUE))
```

```
                          (SETF (REST PTR) (NCONS NEXT-EVENT))))))
                (VALUES NIL NIL))))



(DEFUN FILTER (LIST PREDICATE)
  (LET ((OUTPUT NIL))
    (DOLIST (EL LIST)
      (IF (FUNCALL PREDICATE (COLOR EL))
          (SETQ OUTPUT (CONS EL OUTPUT))))
    OUTPUT))



(DEFUN LOCATE-POINT (POINT QUERY-TREE)
  (LET ((F-POINT (MAKE-POINT X (FLOAT (X POINT)) Y (FLOAT (Y POINT)))))
    (AVL-ACCESS POINT
                (INTERVALS (AVL-ACCESS (X POINT) QUERY-TREE #'IN-RANGE?))
                #'(LAMBDA (A B) (IN-INTERVAL? A B F-POINT)))))

(DEFUN LOCATE-X-Y (X Y QUERY-TREE)
  (LOCATE-POINT (MAKE-POINT X X Y Y) QUERY-TREE))

(defun SWEEP (polys &optional query)
  (project polys nil 1\2 -1\2 0.0 query))

;;; usage: (OUTER-UNION (SWEEP INPUT)) etc

(defun outer-union (polys)
  (mapcar #'complement-poly (filter polys #'free?)))

;;; TANGENT is the slope of the v.c. edge.
;;; for backprojection, the top and bottom tangents are of the form
;;; ( minus slope , positive slope)
;;; call with args like:  (backprojection environment1 start-region1 1\10 .26)

(defun forward-projection
       (obstacles start-region tangent mu &optional query)
  (let ((top-tangent (abs tangent))
        (bottom-tangent (- (abs tangent))))
    (project obstacles start-region top-tangent bottom-tangent mu query)))

(defun weak-backprojection
       (obstacles start-region tangent mu &optional query)
  (let ((backprojection? 'weak)
        (top-tangent (abs tangent))
        (bottom-tangent (- (abs tangent))))
    (let ((*mu* mu)
          (*neg-v1* (list (float (denominator bottom-tangent))
                          (float (numerator bottom-tangent))))
          (*neg-v2* (list (float (denominator top-tangent))
```

```
                          (float  (numerator top-tangent)))))
        (project obstacles start-region top-tangent bottom-tangent mu query))))


(defvar *mu*)

(defvar *neg-v1*)

(defvar *neg-v2*)

(defun backprojection (OBSTACLES START-REGION TANGENT MU &OPTIONAL QUERY)
  (let  ((backprojection? 'strong)
         (top-tangent (- (abs tangent)))
         (bottom-tangent (abs tangent))).
    (let ((*mu* mu)
          (*neg-v1* (list (float  (denominator top-tangent))
                          (float  (numerator top-tangent))))
          (*neg-v2* (list (float  (denominator bottom-tangent))
                          (float  (numerator bottom-tangent)))))
      (project OBSTACLES START-REGION TOP-TANGENT BOTTOM-TANGENT MU QUERY))))

(defmacro backprojection? ()
  'backprojection?)



(defmacro strong-backprojection? ()
  '(eq (backprojection?) 'strong))

(defmacro weak-backprojection? ()
  '(eq (backprojection?) 'weak))

(DEFUN PROJECT (OBSTACLES START-REGION TOP-TANGENT BOTTOM-TANGENT MU &OPTIONAL QUERY)
  (LET* ((SA (WHEN MU (// MU (SQRT (1+ (* MU MU))))))
         (EVENTS NIL)
         (STRUCT (MAKE-OUTPUT-STRUCTURE POLYGON (MAKE-POLYGON COLOR 0)))
         (FREE-INTERVAL (MAKE-INTERVAL TOP (MAKE-EQN X 0 Y 1)
                                       BOTTOM (MAKE-EQN X 0 Y 1)
                                       OUTPUT-STRUCTURE STRUCT))
         (SWEEP-LINE (AVL-INSERT FREE-INTERVAL NIL NIL))
         (EVENT-QUEUE (QUEUE-INITIAL-EVENTS OBSTACLES 'OBSTACLE FREE-INTERVAL
                        (QUEUE-INITIAL-EVENTS START-REGION 'START FREE-INTERVAL NIL)))
         (OLD-STRUCTS NIL)
         (QUERY-TREE NIL))
    (SETF (TOP-END STRUCT) STRUCT)
    (SETF (BOTTOM-END STRUCT) STRUCT)
    (MULTIPLE-VALUE (EVENTS EVENT-QUEUE) (AVL-HEAD-ALL EVENT-QUEUE))
    (DO ((POLYS NIL)
         (OLD-X NIL))
        ((NULL EVENTS)
```

```
(COND (QUERY
        (SETQ QUERY-TREE
              (AVL-INSERT (MAKE-QUERY-NODE X-MIN OLD-X INTERVALS SWEEP-LINE)
                           QUERY-TREE #'ALWAYS->))
        (FIX-OLD-STRUCTS OLD-STRUCTS)))
     (VALUES (CONS (POLYGON (OUTPUT-STRUCTURE (VALUE SWEEP-LINE))) POLYS)
             QUERY-TREE))
  (LET* ((POINT (POINT (FIRST EVENTS)))
         (F-POINT (MAKE-POINT X (FLOAT (X POINT)) Y (FLOAT (Y POINT))))
         (RELEVANT-INTERVALS (AVL-ACCESS-ALL POINT SWEEP-LINE
                                              #'(LAMBDA (A B)
                                                  (IN-INTERVAL? A B F-POINT))))
         (INT->- #'(LAMBDA (A B) (INTERVAL-> A B POINT F-POINT -1)))
         (INT->+ #'(LAMBDA (A B) (INTERVAL-> A B POINT F-POINT 1))))
    (COND ((AND QUERY (OR (NULL OLD-X) (æ OLD-X (X POINT))))
           (SETQ QUERY-TREE (AVL-INSERT (MAKE-QUERY-NODE X-MIN OLD-X X-MAX (X POINT
                                                         INTERVALS SWEEP-LINE)
                                         QUERY-TREE #'ALWAYS->))
           (SETQ OLD-X (X POINT))))
    (IF (NULL (EQN (FIRST EVENTS))) (SETQ EVENTS (CDR EVENTS)))
    (SETQ EVENTS (MERGE-EVENTS EVENTS (CROSSING-EVENTS RELEVANT-INTERVALS)))
    (MULTIPLE-VALUE (POLYS OLD-STRUCTS)
      (CLOSE-INTERVALS RELEVANT-INTERVALS POINT POLYS OLD-STRUCTS QUERY))
    (MULTIPLE-VALUE (RELEVANT-INTERVALS SWEEP-LINE)
      (DELETE-INTERVALS RELEVANT-INTERVALS INT->- SWEEP-LINE QUERY))
    (MULTIPLE-VALUE (SWEEP-LINE EVENT-QUEUE EVENTS POLYS OLD-STRUCTS)
      (UPDATE-INTERVALS RELEVANT-INTERVALS EVENTS TOP-TANGENT BOTTOM-TANGENT SA
                        POINT INT->- INT->+ SWEEP-LINE EVENT-QUEUE POLYS
                        OLD-STRUCTS QUERY))
    (SETQ SWEEP-LINE (NEW-INTERVALS RELEVANT-INTERVALS EVENTS
                                     POINT INT->+ SWEEP-LINE QUERY)))
  (MULTIPLE-VALUE (EVENTS EVENT-QUEUE) (AVL-HEAD-ALL EVENT-QUEUE)))))

(DEFUN QUEUE-INITIAL-EVENTS (POLYS TYPE FREE-INTERVAL EVENT-QUEUE)
  (DO ((POLYS POLYS (REST POLYS)))
      ((NULL POLYS) EVENT-QUEUE)
    (DOLIST (LOOP (LOOP-LIST (FIRST POLYS)))
      (DOLIST (EDGE LOOP)
        (LET ((Y (Y (HEAD EDGE)))
              (EQN (IF (OR (MINUSP (Y (EQN EDGE)))
                           (AND (ZEROP (Y (EQN EDGE)))
                                (PLUSP (X (EQN EDGE)))))
                       (NEG-EQN (EQN EDGE))
                       (EQN EDGE))))
          (IF (OR (NULL (D (TOP FREE-INTERVAL)))
                  (< (- -1 Y) (D (TOP FREE-INTERVAL))))
              (SETF (D (TOP FREE-INTERVAL)) (- -1 Y)))
          (IF (OR (NULL (D (BOTTOM FREE-INTERVAL)))
                  (> (- 1 Y) (D (BOTTOM FREE-INTERVAL))))
              (SETF (D (BOTTOM FREE-INTERVAL)) (- 1 Y)))
          (SETQ EVENT-QUEUE (EVENT-ADD (MAKE-EVENT POINT (TAIL EDGE)
```

```
                                        EQN EQN
                                        COLOR-CHANGE (ENCODE TYPE 1))
                            EVENT-QUEUE #'EVENT->))
        (SETQ EVENT-QUEUE (EVENT-ADD (MAKE-EVENT POINT (HEAD EDGE)
                                        EQN EQN
                                        COLOR-CHANGE (ENCODE TYPE -1))
                            EVENT-QUEUE #'EVENT->)))))))

(DEFUN CLOSE-INTERVALS (INTERVALS POINT POLYS OLD-STRUCTS QUERY)
  (DO ((PTR (REST INTERVALS) (REST PTR)))
      ((NULL (REST PTR)) (VALUES POLYS OLD-STRUCTS))
    (UNLESS (FP? (COLOR (POLYGON (OUTPUT-STRUCTURE (FIRST PTR)))))
      (MULTIPLE-VALUE (POLYS OLD-STRUCTS)
        (CLOSE-INTERVAL (FIRST PTR) POINT POLYS OLD-STRUCTS QUERY)))))



(DEFUN CLOSE-INTERVAL (INTERVAL POINT POLYS OLD-STRUCTS QUERY)
  (LET ((STRUCT (OUTPUT-STRUCTURE INTERVAL)))
    (SETF (TAIL (FIRST (TOP STRUCT))) POINT)
    (SETF (HEAD (FIRST (BOTTOM STRUCT))) POINT)
    (COND ((EQ (BOTTOM-END STRUCT) STRUCT)
           (SETF (LOOP-LIST (POLYGON STRUCT))
                 (CONS (TOP STRUCT) (LOOP-LIST (POLYGON STRUCT))))
           (IF (NULL (LOOP-END (POLYGON STRUCT)))
               (SETF (LOOP-END (POLYGON STRUCT)) (LOOP-LIST (POLYGON STRUCT))))
           (SETQ POLYS (CONS (POLYGON STRUCT) POLYS)))
          (T (SETF (REST (BOTTOM STRUCT)) (TOP STRUCT))
             (SETF (BOTTOM-END (TOP-END STRUCT))
                   (BOTTOM-END STRUCT))
             (SETF (TOP-END (BOTTOM-END STRUCT))
                   (TOP-END STRUCT))
             (COND (QUERY
                    (SETF (POLYGON STRUCT) 'DISCARDED)
                    (SETQ OLD-STRUCTS (CONS STRUCT OLD-STRUCTS))))))))
  (VALUES POLYS OLD-STRUCTS))



(DEFUN CROSSING-EVENTS (INTERVALS)
  (DO ((THIS (REST INTERVALS) (REST THIS))
       (PREV INTERVALS THIS)
       (EVENTS NIL))
      ((NULL THIS) EVENTS)
    (LET ((COLOR1 (COLOR (POLYGON (OUTPUT-STRUCTURE (FIRST THIS)))))
          (COLOR2 (COLOR (POLYGON (OUTPUT-STRUCTURE (FIRST PREV))))))
      (IF (NOT (OR (AND (FP? COLOR1) (FREE? COLOR2))
                   (AND (FP? COLOR2) (FREE? COLOR1))))
          (SETQ EVENTS
                (CONS (MAKE-EVENT EQN (TOP (FIRST PREV))
                                  COLOR-CHANGE (COLOR-FIELD (SUB-COLORS COLOR1 COLOR2)))
```

```
                      EVENTS))))))


(DEFUN DELETE-INTERVALS (INTERVALS INT->- SWEEP-LINE QUERY)
  (DO ((PTR (REST INTERVALS) (REST PTR))
       (PREV INTERVALS))
      ((NULL (REST PTR)) (VALUES INTERVALS SWEEP-LINE))
    (COND ((OR (EQ 'DISCARDED (POLYGON (OUTPUT-STRUCTURE (FIRST PTR))))
               (NOT (FP? (COLOR (POLYGON (OUTPUT-STRUCTURE (FIRST PTR)))))))
           (SETQ SWEEP-LINE (AVL-DELETE (FIRST PTR) SWEEP-LINE INT->- QUERY))
           (SETF (REST PREV) (REST PTR)))
          (T (SETQ PREV PTR)))))



(DEFUN UPDATE-INTERVALS (INTERVALS EVENTS TOP-TANGENT BOTTOM-TANGENT SA
                         POINT INT->- INT->+ SWEEP-LINE EVENT-QUEUE POLYS OLD-STRUCTS QUERY)
  (LET* ((TOP-INTERVAL (FIRST (LAST INTERVALS)))
         (MIDDLE-INTERVAL (SECOND INTERVALS))
         (BOTTOM-INTERVAL (FIRST INTERVALS))
         (TOP-TANGENT-EQN (MAKE-EQN X (- TOP-TANGENT) Y 1
                                    D (- (* (X POINT) TOP-TANGENT) (Y POINT))))
         (BOTTOM-TANGENT-EQN (MAKE-EQN X (- BOTTOM-TANGENT) Y 1
                                    D (- (* (X POINT) BOTTOM-TANGENT) (Y POINT)))))
    (SETQ EVENTS (PROJECTION-EVENTS (COLOR (POLYGON (OUTPUT-STRUCTURE TOP-INTERVAL)))
                                    (COLOR (POLYGON (OUTPUT-STRUCTURE BOTTOM-INTERVAL)))
                                    TOP-TANGENT-EQN BOTTOM-TANGENT-EQN EVENTS SA))
    (LET ((TEMP-EVENTS EVENTS))
      (COND ((REST2 INTERVALS)
             (MULTIPLE-VALUE (SWEEP-LINE EVENT-QUEUE TEMP-EVENTS POLYS OLD-STRUCTS)
               (UPDATE-MIDDLE-INTERVAL TOP-INTERVAL MIDDLE-INTERVAL BOTTOM-INTERVAL
                                       EVENTS TOP-TANGENT-EQN BOTTOM-TANGENT-EQN SA
                                       POINT INT->- INT->+ EVENT-QUEUE SWEEP-LINE
                                       POLYS OLD-STRUCTS QUERY))))
      (IF (REST INTERVALS)
          (COND (TEMP-EVENTS
                 (MULTIPLE-VALUE (SWEEP-LINE EVENT-QUEUE)
                   (CHANGE-INTERVAL TOP-INTERVAL (TOP TOP-INTERVAL)
                                    (EQN (FIRST (LAST TEMP-EVENTS)))
                                    POINT INT->- INT->+ SWEEP-LINE EVENT-QUEUE QUERY))
                 (MULTIPLE-VALUE (SWEEP-LINE EVENT-QUEUE)
                   (CHANGE-INTERVAL BOTTOM-INTERVAL (EQN (FIRST TEMP-EVENTS))
                                    (BOTTOM BOTTOM-INTERVAL)
                                    POINT INT->- INT->+ SWEEP-LINE EVENT-QUEUE QUERY)))
                (T (MULTIPLE-VALUE (SWEEP-LINE EVENT-QUEUE OLD-STRUCTS)
                     (JOIN-INTERVALS TOP-INTERVAL BOTTOM-INTERVAL POINT INT->- INT->+
                                     SWEEP-LINE EVENT-QUEUE OLD-STRUCTS QUERY))))
          (IF TEMP-EVENTS (MULTIPLE-VALUE (SWEEP-LINE EVENT-QUEUE)
                            (SPLIT-INTERVAL BOTTOM-INTERVAL (EQN (FIRST (LAST TEMP-EVENTS)))
                                            (EQN (FIRST TEMP-EVENTS)) POINT
```

```
                                    INT->- INT->+ SWEEP-LINE EVENT-QUEUE QUERY))))))
    (VALUES SWEEP-LINE EVENT-QUEUE EVENTS POLYS OLD-STRUCTS))


(DEFUN IN-BETWEEN (BOTTOM-EVENT MIDDLE TOP-EVENT)
  (AND (OR (NULL TOP-EVENT)
           (PLUSP (SLOPE-> (EQN TOP-EVENT) MIDDLE)))
       (OR (NULL BOTTOM-EVENT)
           (PLUSP (SLOPE-> MIDDLE (EQN BOTTOM-EVENT))))))



;; modified for Backprojection and Weak backprojection

(DEFUN PROJECTION-EVENTS (TOP-COLOR BOTTOM-COLOR TOP-TANGENT-EQN BOTTOM-TANGENT-EQN EVENTS SA)
  (DO* ((NEW-EVENTS (CONS NIL EVENTS))
        (PTR NEW-EVENTS (REST PTR))
        (COLOR BOTTOM-COLOR)
        (OLD-COLOR BOTTOM-COLOR))
       ((NULL PTR) (REST NEW-EVENTS))
    (LET* ((PREV-EVENT (FIRST PTR))
           (THIS-EVENT (SECOND PTR))
           (NEW-COLOR (IF THIS-EVENT
                          (ADD-COLORS-CAREFULLY COLOR (COLOR-CHANGE THIS-EVENT))
                          TOP-COLOR))
           (NEXT-COLOR (IF THIS-EVENT
                           (COND ((AND (FREE? COLOR) (START? NEW-COLOR)) PROJ-COLOR)
                                 ((AND (FP? COLOR) (OBST? NEW-COLOR)) FREE-COLOR)
                                 (T COLOR))
                           TOP-COLOR))
           (PREV-COLOR (IF (AND (FREE? COLOR) (START? OLD-COLOR)) PROJ-COLOR COLOR)))
      (COND ((AND PREV-EVENT
                  (OR (AND (FP? NEXT-COLOR)
                           (PLUSP (SLOPE-> (EQN PREV-EVENT) BOTTOM-TANGENT-EQN)))
                      (AND (FP? PREV-COLOR)
                           (PLUSP (SLOPE-> TOP-TANGENT-EQN (EQN PREV-EVENT))))))
             (SETF (COLOR-CHANGE PREV-EVENT) (ADD-COLORS (COLOR-CHANGE PREV-EVENT)
                                                         PROJ-COLOR))))
      (COND ((AND (FREE? PREV-COLOR)
                  (FP? NEXT-COLOR)
                  (IN-BETWEEN PREV-EVENT BOTTOM-TANGENT-EQN THIS-EVENT))
             (cond ((compute-backprojection-sliding  prev-event top-tangent-eqn
                                            bottom-tangent-eqn SA 'bottom)
                    (SETF (REST PTR)
                          (CONS (MAKE-EVENT EQN BOTTOM-TANGENT-EQN COLOR-CHANGE PROJ-COLOR)
                                (REST PTR)))
                    (SETQ PTR (REST PTR)))
                   (prev-event
                    (setf (color-change prev-event) (add-colors (color-change prev-event)
                                                       proj-color)))))))))
```

```
      (COND ((AND (FREE? NEXT-COLOR)
                  (FP? PREV-COLOR)
                  (IN-BETWEEN PREV-EVENT TOP-TANGENT-EQN THIS-EVENT)
                  (compute-backprojection-sliding this-event top-tangent-eqn
                                          bottom-tangent-eqn SA ()))
             (SETF (REST PTR) (CONS (MAKE-EVENT EQN TOP-TANGENT-EQN
                                     COLOR-CHANGE (NEG-COLOR PROJ-COLOR))
                              (REST PTR)))
             (SETQ PTR (REST PTR))))
        (SETQ OLD-COLOR COLOR)
        (SETQ COLOR NEW-COLOR))))


;;; should return T if we should erect a velocity constraint

(defun compute-backprojection-sliding (event top-tangent-eqn bottom-tangent-eqn SA bottom?)
  (cond ((Not (backprojection?)) T)
        ((null event) T)
        (T (let ((edge-eqn (eqn event)))
             (cond ;;; ((start? (color-change event)) nil)
                   (T
                    (selectq (backprojection?)
                      (Weak
                       (not (weak-can-slide? (orient-edge-equation edge-eqn bottom?))))
                      (Strong
                       (not (must-slide? (orient-edge-equation edge-eqn bottom?))))
                      (old-weak (not (old-weak-can-slide? edge-eqn
                                                 top-tangent-eqn
                                                 bottom-tangent-eqn SA)))))))))


;;; event normals are oriented upwards, always. Except for vertical events,
;;; where the normals point to the left.

(defun orient-edge-equation (eqn bottom?)
  (when eqn
    (if (or (and (zerop (y eqn))
                 (minusp (x eqn)))
            (and bottom?        (minusp (y eqn)))
            (and (not bottom?) (plusp  (y eqn))))
        (neg-eqn eqn)
        eqn)))


;;; Decides if, using the OPPOSITE velocity cone, we can slide on the
;;; edge with eqn EDGE-EQN.
```

```
(defun old-weak-can-slide? (edge-eqn top-tangent-eqn bottom-tangent-eqn sa)
  (and edge-eqn (can-slide? edge-eqn top-tangent-eqn bottom-tangent-eqn SA)))



;; does not handle the case where mu = 0 and there's no velocity uncertainty

(defun weak-can-slide? (eqn &optional (neg-v1 *neg-v1*) (neg-v2 *neg-v2*) (mu *mu*))
  (and eqn
       (let* ((normal (list (float (x eqn))  (float (y eqn))))
              (tangent (list (* mu (cadr normal)) (* (minus mu) (car normal)))))
         (let ((e1 (vc2add normal tangent))
               (e2 (vc-sub normal tangent)))
           (or  (= mu 0.0)
                (not (In-2D-cone-p neg-v1 e1 e2))
                (not (In-2D-cone-p neg-v2 e1 e2)))))))



(DEFUN MUST-SLIDE? (EQN)
  (and eqn
       (slide-p eqn)))



;; modified to close in case of backprojection

(DEFUN UPDATE-MIDDLE-INTERVAL (TOP-INTERVAL MIDDLE-INTERVAL BOTTOM-INTERVAL
                              EVENTS TOP-TANGENT-EQN BOTTOM-TANGENT-EQN SA POINT
                              INT->- INT->+ EVENT-QUEUE SWEEP-LINE POLYS OLD-STRUCTS QUERY)
  (COND ((AND (not (backprojection?))
              (FREE? (COLOR (POLYGON (OUTPUT-STRUCTURE BOTTOM-INTERVAL))))
              (NOT (START? (COLOR (POLYGON (OUTPUT-STRUCTURE TOP-INTERVAL))))))
         (MULTIPLE-VALUE (MIDDLE-INTERVAL SWEEP-LINE EVENT-QUEUE EVENTS POLYS OLD-STRUCTS)
           (CONTINUE-MIDDLE MIDDLE-INTERVAL
                            (IF EVENTS (EQN (FIRST EVENTS)) TOP-TANGENT-EQN)
                            (IF (AND EVENTS  (PLUSP (SLOPE-> BOTTOM-TANGENT-EQN
                                                            (EQN (FIRST EVENTS)))))
                                (EQN (FIRST EVENTS))
                                BOTTOM-TANGENT-EQN)
                            TOP-TANGENT-EQN BOTTOM-TANGENT-EQN SA POINT INT->- INT->+
                            SWEEP-LINE EVENT-QUEUE EVENTS POLYS OLD-STRUCTS QUERY)))
        ((AND (not (backprojection?))
              (FREE? (COLOR (POLYGON (OUTPUT-STRUCTURE TOP-INTERVAL))))
              (NOT (START? (COLOR (POLYGON (OUTPUT-STRUCTURE BOTTOM-INTERVAL))))))
         (MULTIPLE-VALUE (MIDDLE-INTERVAL SWEEP-LINE EVENT-QUEUE EVENTS POLYS OLD-STRUCTS)
           (CONTINUE-MIDDLE MIDDLE-INTERVAL
                            (IF (AND EVENTS (PLUSP (SLOPE-> (EQN (FIRST (LAST EVENTS)))
                                                           TOP-TANGENT-EQN)))
                                (EQN (FIRST (LAST EVENTS)))
                                TOP-TANGENT-EQN)
```

```lisp
                       (IF EVENTS (EQN (FIRST (LAST EVENTS))) BOTTOM-TANGENT-EQN)
                       TOP-TANGENT-EQN BOTTOM-TANGENT-EQN SA POINT INT->- INT->+
                       SWEEP-LINE EVENT-QUEUE EVENTS POLYS OLD-STRUCTS QUERY)))
          (T (MULTIPLE-VALUE (POLYS OLD-STRUCTS)
               (CLOSE-INTERVAL MIDDLE-INTERVAL POINT POLYS OLD-STRUCTS QUERY))
             (SETQ SWEEP-LINE (AVL-DELETE MIDDLE-INTERVAL SWEEP-LINE INT->- QUERY))
             (SETQ MIDDLE-INTERVAL NIL)))
    (COND ((AND MIDDLE-INTERVAL (FP? (COLOR (POLYGON (OUTPUT-STRUCTURE BOTTOM-INTERVAL)))))
           (MULTIPLE-VALUE (SWEEP-LINE EVENT-QUEUE OLD-STRUCTS)
             (JOIN-INTERVALS MIDDLE-INTERVAL BOTTOM-INTERVAL
                     POINT INT->- INT->+ SWEEP-LINE EVENT-QUEUE OLD-STRUCTS QUERY)))
          ((AND MIDDLE-INTERVAL (FP? (COLOR (POLYGON (OUTPUT-STRUCTURE TOP-INTERVAL)))))
           (MULTIPLE-VALUE (SWEEP-LINE EVENT-QUEUE OLD-STRUCTS)
             (JOIN-INTERVALS TOP-INTERVAL MIDDLE-INTERVAL
                     POINT INT->- INT->+ SWEEP-LINE EVENT-QUEUE OLD-STRUCTS QUERY))))
    (VALUES SWEEP-LINE EVENT-QUEUE EVENTS POLYS OLD-STRUCTS))


(DEFUN CONTINUE-MIDDLE (MIDDLE-INTERVAL MIDDLE-TOP MIDDLE-BOTTOM TOP-TANGENT-EQN
                        BOTTOM-TANGENT-EQN SA POINT INT->- INT->+
                        SWEEP-LINE EVENT-QUEUE EVENTS POLYS OLD-STRUCTS QUERY)
  (COND ((AND (EQUAL MIDDLE-TOP MIDDLE-BOTTOM)
              (NOT (CAN-SLIDE? MIDDLE-TOP TOP-TANGENT-EQN BOTTOM-TANGENT-EQN SA)))
         (MULTIPLE-VALUE (POLYS OLD-STRUCTS)
           (CLOSE-INTERVAL MIDDLE-INTERVAL POINT POLYS OLD-STRUCTS QUERY))
         (SETQ SWEEP-LINE (AVL-DELETE MIDDLE-INTERVAL SWEEP-LINE INT->- QUERY))
         (SETQ MIDDLE-INTERVAL NIL))
        (T (SETQ EVENTS (MERGE-EVENTS EVENTS (LIST (MAKE-EVENT EQN MIDDLE-BOTTOM
                                                        COLOR-CHANGE PROJ-COLOR)
                                             (MAKE-EVENT EQN MIDDLE-TOP
                                                        COLOR-CHANGE
                                                        (NEG-COLOR PROJ-COLOR)))))
           (UNLESS (EQUAL MIDDLE-TOP MIDDLE-BOTTOM)
             (COND ((PLUSP (SLOPE-> MIDDLE-TOP TOP-TANGENT-EQN))
                    (SETQ SWEEP-LINE (CREATE-INTERVAL MIDDLE-TOP TOP-TANGENT-EQN FREE-COLOR
                                             POINT INT->+ SWEEP-LINE QUERY))
                    (SETQ MIDDLE-TOP TOP-TANGENT-EQN)))
             (COND ((PLUSP (SLOPE-> BOTTOM-TANGENT-EQN MIDDLE-BOTTOM))
                    (SETQ SWEEP-LINE
                          (CREATE-INTERVAL BOTTOM-TANGENT-EQN MIDDLE-BOTTOM FREE-COLOR
                                      POINT INT->+ SWEEP-LINE QUERY))
                    (SETQ MIDDLE-BOTTOM BOTTOM-TANGENT-EQN))))
           (MULTIPLE-VALUE (SWEEP-LINE EVENT-QUEUE)
             (CHANGE-INTERVAL MIDDLE-INTERVAL MIDDLE-TOP MIDDLE-BOTTOM
                     POINT INT->- INT->+ SWEEP-LINE EVENT-QUEUE QUERY))))
  (VALUES MIDDLE-INTERVAL SWEEP-LINE EVENT-QUEUE EVENTS POLYS OLD-STRUCTS))


(DEFUN CAN-SLIDE? (EQN TOP-TANGENT-EQN BOTTOM-TANGENT-EQN SA)
```

```
(> (MAX (ABS (// (DOT EQN TOP-TANGENT-EQN)
                 (SQRT (* (DOT EQN EQN) (DOT TOP-TANGENT-EQN TOP-TANGENT-EQN)))))
        (ABS (// (DOT EQN BOTTOM-TANGENT-EQN)
                 (SQRT (* (DOT EQN EQN) (DOT BOTTOM-TANGENT-EQN BOTTOM-TANGENT-EQN))))))
   SA))


(DEFUN CHANGE-INTERVAL (INTERVAL TOP BOTTOM POINT INT->- INT->+ SWEEP-LINE EVENT-QUEUE QUERY)
  (LET ((STRUCT (OUTPUT-STRUCTURE INTERVAL)))
    (COND ((NOT (AND (EQUAL (TOP INTERVAL) TOP)
                     (EQUAL (BOTTOM INTERVAL) BOTTOM)))
           (COND ((NOT (EQUAL (TOP INTERVAL) TOP))
                  (SETF (TAIL (FIRST (TOP STRUCT))) POINT)
                  (SETF (TOP STRUCT) (CONS (MAKE-EDGE HEAD POINT EQN TOP) (TOP STRUCT)))))
           (COND ((NOT (EQUAL (BOTTOM INTERVAL) BOTTOM))
                  (SETF (HEAD (FIRST (BOTTOM STRUCT))) POINT)
                  (SETF (REST (BOTTOM STRUCT))
                        (NCONS (MAKE-EDGE TAIL POINT EQN (NEG-EQN BOTTOM))))
                  (SETF (BOTTOM STRUCT) (REST (BOTTOM STRUCT)))))
           (LET ((NEW-INTERVAL  (MAKE-INTERVAL TOP TOP BOTTOM BOTTOM
                                               OUTPUT-STRUCTURE STRUCT)))
             (SETQ SWEEP-LINE (AVL-DELETE INTERVAL SWEEP-LINE INT->- QUERY))
             (SETQ SWEEP-LINE (AVL-INSERT NEW-INTERVAL SWEEP-LINE INT->+ QUERY))
             (IF (EVENT INTERVAL)
                 (SETQ EVENT-QUEUE (EVENT-SUB (EVENT INTERVAL) EVENT-QUEUE)))
             (SETQ EVENT-QUEUE (CLOSURE-EVENT? NEW-INTERVAL EVENT-QUEUE))))))
  (VALUES SWEEP-LINE EVENT-QUEUE))


(DEFUN SPLIT-INTERVAL (INTERVAL TOP BOTTOM POINT INT->- INT->+ SWEEP-LINE EVENT-QUEUE QUERY)
  (LET* ((BOTTOM-STRUCT (OUTPUT-STRUCTURE INTERVAL))
         (TOP-STRUCT (MAKE-OUTPUT-STRUCTURE POLYGON (POLYGON BOTTOM-STRUCT)
                                            TOP (TOP BOTTOM-STRUCT)
                                            TOP-END (TOP-END BOTTOM-STRUCT)
                                            BOTTOM-END BOTTOM-STRUCT)))
    (SETF (BOTTOM-END (TOP-END BOTTOM-STRUCT)) TOP-STRUCT)
    (SETF (TOP-END BOTTOM-STRUCT) TOP-STRUCT)
    (SETF (TOP BOTTOM-STRUCT) (LIST (MAKE-EDGE HEAD POINT EQN BOTTOM)
                                    (MAKE-EDGE TAIL POINT EQN (NEG-EQN TOP))))
    (SETF (BOTTOM TOP-STRUCT) (REST (TOP BOTTOM-STRUCT)))
    (SETQ SWEEP-LINE (AVL-DELETE INTERVAL SWEEP-LINE INT->- QUERY))
    (IF (EVENT INTERVAL)
        (SETQ EVENT-QUEUE (EVENT-SUB (EVENT INTERVAL) EVENT-QUEUE)))
    (LET ((TOP-INTERVAL (MAKE-INTERVAL TOP (TOP INTERVAL) BOTTOM TOP
                                       OUTPUT-STRUCTURE TOP-STRUCT))
          (BOTTOM-INTERVAL (MAKE-INTERVAL TOP BOTTOM BOTTOM (BOTTOM INTERVAL)
                                          OUTPUT-STRUCTURE BOTTOM-STRUCT)))
```

```lisp
      (SETQ SWEEP-LINE (AVL-INSERT BOTTOM-INTERVAL
                          (AVL-INSERT TOP-INTERVAL SWEEP-LINE INT->+ QUERY)
                          INT->+ QUERY))
      (SETQ EVENT-QUEUE (CLOSURE-EVENT? BOTTOM-INTERVAL
                          (CLOSURE-EVENT? TOP-INTERVAL EVENT-QUEUE)))))
   (VALUES SWEEP-LINE EVENT-QUEUE))


(DEFUN JOIN-INTERVALS (TOP-INTERVAL BOTTOM-INTERVAL
                       POINT INT->- INT->+ SWEEP-LINE EVENT-QUEUE OLD-STRUCTS QUERY)
  (LET* ((TOP-STRUCT (OUTPUT-STRUCTURE TOP-INTERVAL))
         (BOTTOM-STRUCT (OUTPUT-STRUCTURE BOTTOM-INTERVAL))
         (TOP-POLY (POLYGON TOP-STRUCT))
         (BOTTOM-POLY (POLYGON BOTTOM-STRUCT)))
    (SETF (HEAD (FIRST (BOTTOM TOP-STRUCT))) POINT)
    (SETF (TAIL (FIRST (TOP BOTTOM-STRUCT))) POINT)
    (COND ((EQ (TOP-END BOTTOM-STRUCT) TOP-STRUCT)
           (SETF (LOOP-LIST TOP-POLY)
                 (CONS (TOP BOTTOM-STRUCT) (LOOP-LIST TOP-POLY)))
           (IF (NULL (LOOP-END TOP-POLY))
               (SETF (LOOP-END TOP-POLY) (LOOP-LIST TOP-POLY)))
           (SETF (LOOP-LIST BOTTOM-POLY)
                 (LOOP-LIST TOP-POLY))
           (SETF (LOOP-END BOTTOM-POLY) (LOOP-END TOP-POLY)))
          (T (SETF (REST (BOTTOM TOP-STRUCT)) (TOP BOTTOM-STRUCT))
             (SETF (TOP-END (BOTTOM-END TOP-STRUCT)) (TOP-END BOTTOM-STRUCT))
             (SETF (BOTTOM-END (TOP-END BOTTOM-STRUCT)) (BOTTOM-END TOP-STRUCT))))
    (SETF (BOTTOM-END (TOP-END TOP-STRUCT)) BOTTOM-STRUCT)
    (SETF (TOP BOTTOM-STRUCT) (TOP TOP-STRUCT))
    (SETF (TOP-END BOTTOM-STRUCT) (TOP-END TOP-STRUCT))
    (COND (QUERY
           (SETF (BOTTOM-END TOP-STRUCT) BOTTOM-STRUCT)
           (SETF (POLYGON TOP-STRUCT) 'DISCARDED)
           (SETQ OLD-STRUCTS (CONS TOP-STRUCT OLD-STRUCTS))))
    (COND ((NOT (EQ (LOOP-LIST TOP-POLY)
                    (LOOP-LIST BOTTOM-POLY)))
           (IF (LOOP-LIST BOTTOM-POLY)
               (SETF (REST (LOOP-END BOTTOM-POLY))
                     (LOOP-LIST TOP-POLY))
               (SETF (LOOP-LIST BOTTOM-POLY) (LOOP-LIST TOP-POLY)))
           (IF (LOOP-END TOP-POLY)
               (SETF (LOOP-END BOTTOM-POLY) (LOOP-END TOP-POLY)))
           (SETF (LOOP-LIST TOP-POLY) (LOOP-LIST BOTTOM-POLY))
           (SETF (LOOP-END TOP-POLY) (LOOP-END BOTTOM-POLY))))
    (SETQ SWEEP-LINE (AVL-DELETE TOP-INTERVAL
                        (AVL-DELETE BOTTOM-INTERVAL SWEEP-LINE INT->- QUERY)
                        INT->- QUERY))
    (IF (EVENT TOP-INTERVAL)
        (SETQ EVENT-QUEUE (EVENT-SUB (EVENT TOP-INTERVAL) EVENT-QUEUE)))
    (IF (EVENT BOTTOM-INTERVAL)
```

```
              (SETQ EVENT-QUEUE (EVENT-SUB (EVENT BOTTOM-INTERVAL) EVENT-QUEUE)))
      (LET ((INTERVAL (MAKE-INTERVAL TOP (TOP TOP-INTERVAL) BOTTOM (BOTTOM BOTTOM-INTERVAL)
                                OUTPUT-STRUCTURE BOTTOM-STRUCT)))
        (SETQ SWEEP-LINE (AVL-INSERT INTERVAL SWEEP-LINE INT->+ QUERY))
        (SETQ EVENT-QUEUE (CLOSURE-EVENT? INTERVAL EVENT-QUEUE))))
    (VALUES SWEEP-LINE EVENT-QUEUE OLD-STRUCTS))


(DEFUN CLOSURE-EVENT? (INTERVAL EVENT-QUEUE)
  (LET ((NEW-POINT (INTERSECTION-POINT (TOP INTERVAL) (BOTTOM INTERVAL))))
    (COND (NEW-POINT
            (SETF (EVENT INTERVAL)
                  (MAKE-EVENT POINT NEW-POINT COLOR-CHANGE 1))
            (SETQ EVENT-QUEUE (EVENT-ADD (EVENT INTERVAL) EVENT-QUEUE)))))
  EVENT-QUEUE)


(DEFUN NEW-INTERVALS (INTERVALS EVENTS POINT INT->+ SWEEP-LINE QUERY)
  (DO ((PTR EVENTS (REST PTR))
       (COLOR (COLOR (POLYGON (OUTPUT-STRUCTURE (FIRST INTERVALS))))))
      ((NULL (REST PTR)) SWEEP-LINE)
    (LET ((TOP-EVENT (SECOND PTR))
          (BOTTOM-EVENT (FIRST PTR)))
      (SETQ COLOR (ADD-COLORS-CAREFULLY COLOR (COLOR-CHANGE BOTTOM-EVENT)))
      (SETQ SWEEP-LINE (CREATE-INTERVAL (EQN TOP-EVENT) (EQN BOTTOM-EVENT) COLOR POINT
                                    INT->+ SWEEP-LINE QUERY)))))


(DEFUN CREATE-INTERVAL (TOP BOTTOM COLOR POINT INT->+ SWEEP-LINE QUERY)
  (LET ((STRUCT (MAKE-OUTPUT-STRUCTURE
                    POLYGON (MAKE-POLYGON COLOR COLOR)
                    TOP (LIST (MAKE-EDGE HEAD POINT EQN TOP)
                              (MAKE-EDGE TAIL POINT EQN (NEG-EQN BOTTOM))))))
    (SETF (BOTTOM STRUCT) (REST (TOP STRUCT)))
    (SETF (BOTTOM-END STRUCT) STRUCT)
    (SETF (TOP-END STRUCT) STRUCT)
    (AVL-INSERT (MAKE-INTERVAL TOP TOP BOTTOM BOTTOM OUTPUT-STRUCTURE STRUCT)
                SWEEP-LINE INT->+ QUERY)))


(DEFUN FIX-OLD-STRUCTS (OLD-STRUCTS)
  (DOLIST (STRUCT OLD-STRUCTS)
    (LET ((POLY (DO ((PTR STRUCT (BOTTOM-END PTR)))
                    ((NOT (EQ 'DISCARDED (POLYGON PTR))) (POLYGON PTR)))))
      (DO ((PTR STRUCT (BOTTOM-END PTR)))
          ((NOT (EQ 'DISCARDED (POLYGON PTR))))
        (SETF (POLYGON PTR) POLY)))))
```

```
(DEFUN PROBLEM-SIZE (PROBLEM)
  (LET ((SIZE 0))
    (COND ((EDGE-P PROBLEM) 1)
          ((POLYGON-P PROBLEM)
           (DOLIST (LOOP (LOOP-LIST PROBLEM))
             (SETQ SIZE (+ SIZE (PROBLEM-SIZE LOOP))))
           SIZE)
          ((LISTP PROBLEM)
           (DOLIST (PROB PROBLEM)
             (SETQ SIZE (+ SIZE (PROBLEM-SIZE PROB))))
           SIZE))))
```

```
;;;; Sliding predicate from Mike Erdmann.

;;;;;;;;;;;;;;;;;;;;;;;;;;;;;;;;;;;;;;;;;;;;;;;;;;;;;;;;;;;;;;;;;;;;;;;;;;;;;;;;
;
; This function decides whether none of the velocity vectors in the range
; v1 through v2 cause sticking on an edge specified by "normal".
;
;;;;;;;;;;;;;;;;;;;;;;;;;;;;;;;;;;;;;;;;;;;;;;;;;;;;;;;;;;;;;;;;;;;;;;;;;;;;;;;;


(defun slide-p (eqn &optional (neg-v1 *neg-v1*) (neg-v2 *neg-v2*) (mu *mu*))
  (let* ((normal (list (float (x eqn))  (float (y eqn))))
         (tangent (list (* mu (cadr normal)) (* (minus mu) (car normal)))))
    (let ((e1 (vc2add normal tangent))
          (e2 (vc-sub normal tangent)))
      (and (not (In-2D-cone-p normal neg-v1 neg-v2))
           (or (= mu 0)
               (and (not (In-2D-cone-p neg-v1 e1 e2))
                    (not (In-2D-cone-p neg-v2 e1 e2)))))))))
```

```
;;;;;;;;;;;;;;;;;;;;;;;;;;;;;;;;;;;;;;;;;;;;;;;;;;;;;;;;;;;;;;;;;;;;;;;;;;;;;;;;
;
; Given that the two 2-D vectors e1 and e2 are independent,
; this function decides whether a third 2-D vector, v,
; lies in the cone formed by the positive span of e1 and e2.
;
;;;;;;;;;;;;;;;;;;;;;;;;;;;;;;;;;;;;;;;;;;;;;;;;;;;;;;;;;;;;;;;;;;;;;;;;;;;;;;;;

(defun In-2D-cone-p (v e1 e2)
  (let ((perp (2D-cross-product e1 e2))
        (e1-x-v (2D-cross-product e1 v))
        (v-x-e2 (2D-cross-product v e2)))
    (let ((sigperp (signum perp)))
      (and (>= (* (signum e1-x-v) sigperp) 0)
```

```
                  (>= (* (signum v-x-e2) sigperp) 0)))))

;;;;;;;;;;;;;;;;;;;;;;;;;;;;;;;;;;;;;;;;;;;;;;;;;;;;;;;;;;;;;;;;;;;;;;;;;;;;;;;;
;
; This function computes the cross-product of its two 2-D vector arguments.
;
;;;;;;;;;;;;;;;;;;;;;;;;;;;;;;;;;;;;;;;;;;;;;;;;;;;;;;;;;;;;;;;;;;;;;;;;;;;;;;;;

(defun 2D-cross-product (v1 v2)
   (let ((x1 (car v1))
         (y1 (cadr v1))
         (x2 (car v2))
         (y2 (cadr v2)))
      (- (* x1 y2) (* x2 y1))))

;;;;;;;;;;;;;;;;;;;;;;;;;;;;;;;;;;;;;;;;;;;;;;;;;;;;;;;;;;;;;;;;;;;;;;;;;;;;;;;;
;
;  This function expects two lists, representing vector.
;  It computes their vector sum.
;
;;;;;;;;;;;;;;;;;;;;;;;;;;;;;;;;;;;;;;;;;;;;;;;;;;;;;;;;;;;;;;;;;;;;;;;;;;;;;;;;

(defun vc2add (v1 v2)
   (cond ((or (atom v1)
              (atom v2))  (ferror "vector may not be an atom in vc2add"))
         (t (mapcar (function +) v1 v2))))

;;;;;;;;;;;;;;;;;;;;;;;;;;;;;;;;;;;;;;;;;;;;;;;;;;;;;;;;;;;;;;;;;;;;;;;;;;;;;;;;
;
;  This function expects two lists, representing vector.
;  It computes their vector difference.
;
;;;;;;;;;;;;;;;;;;;;;;;;;;;;;;;;;;;;;;;;;;;;;;;;;;;;;;;;;;;;;;;;;;;;;;;;;;;;;;;;

(defun vc-sub (v1 v2)
   (cond ((or (atom v1)
              (atom v2))  (ferror "vector may not be an atom in vc-sub"))
         (t (mapcar (function -) v1 v2))))
```

```lisp
;;;;;;;;;;;;;;;;;;;-*- base:10; package:sweep; mode:lisp -*-;;;;;;;;;;;;;;;;;;;

;
;; Code to build and maintain AVL trees, (c) 1986 Roger-the-AVL-shrubber, (a shrubber).
;

(DEFSTRUCT (AVL-NODE :NAMED
                     :PREDICATE
                     (:PRINT "<~s ~s ~s>" (LEFT AVL-NODE) (VALUE AVL-NODE) (RIGHT AVL-NODE))
  VALUE
  LEFT
  RIGHT
  BALANCE)

(DEFUN AVL-COPY (TREE)
  (IF (NULL TREE)
      NIL
      (MAKE-AVL-NODE BALANCE (BALANCE TREE) VALUE (VALUE TREE)
                     LEFT (AVL-COPY (LEFT TREE))
                     RIGHT (AVL-COPY (RIGHT TREE)))))

(DEFUN AVL-SIZE (TREE)
  (IF (NULL TREE)
      0
      (1+ (+ (AVL-SIZE (LEFT TREE))
             (AVL-SIZE (RIGHT TREE))))))


;
;; This determines the height of an AVL tree and also checks if your tree is
;; out of balance or "Koyaanisquatsi" in Hopi Indian. Actual height difference
;; should be the same as the balance value, and should be in the range {-1,0,1}.
;

(DEFUN AVL-HEIGHT (TREE)
  (COND ((NULL TREE) 0)
        (T (LET ((HL (AVL-HEIGHT (LEFT TREE)))
                 (HR (AVL-HEIGHT (RIGHT TREE))))
             (COND ((æ (- HR HL) (BALANCE TREE))
                    (FORMAT T "
The actual height difference ~s does not agree with the balance entry ~s for node ~s"
                            (- HR HL) (BALANCE TREE) TREE))
                   ((> (ABS (BALANCE TREE)) 1)
                    (FORMAT T "
Node ~s is Koyaanisquatsi, its balance value is ~s" TREE (BALANCE TREE))))
             (1+ (MAX HL HR))))))
```

```
;
;; Function to find an entry in an AVL tree. PREDICATE should return 0 if KEY and
;; the node value are the same, +1 if KEY is greater than the node value, -1 otherwise.
;

(DEFUN AVL-ACCESS (KEY TREE PREDICATE)
  (AND TREE
       (LET ((DIF (FUNCALL PREDICATE KEY (VALUE TREE))))
         (COND ((PLUSP DIF) (AVL-ACCESS KEY (RIGHT TREE) PREDICATE))
               ((MINUSP DIF) (AVL-ACCESS KEY (LEFT TREE) PREDICATE))
               (T (VALUE TREE))))))


;
;; Function to find all the entries in an AVL tree that are equal to KEY according to
;; PREDICATE. PREDICATE should return 0 if KEY and the node value are the same,
;; +1 if KEY is greater than the node value, -1 otherwise.
;

(DEFUN AVL-ACCESS-ALL (KEY TREE PREDICATE)
  (AND TREE
       (LET ((DIF (FUNCALL PREDICATE KEY (VALUE TREE))))
         (COND ((PLUSP DIF) (AVL-ACCESS-ALL KEY (RIGHT TREE) PREDICATE))
               ((MINUSP DIF) (AVL-ACCESS-ALL KEY (LEFT TREE) PREDICATE))
               (T (NCONC (AVL-ACCESS-ALL KEY (LEFT TREE) PREDICATE)
                         (NCONS (VALUE TREE))
                         (AVL-ACCESS-ALL KEY (RIGHT TREE) PREDICATE)))))))


;
;; Return the left-most value in an AVL tree.
;

(DEFUN LEFT-MOST (TREE)
  (COND ((NULL TREE) NIL)
        ((NULL (LEFT TREE)) (VALUE TREE))
        (T (LEFT-MOST (LEFT TREE)))))

;
;; Return the right-most value in an AVL tree.
;

(DEFUN RIGHT-MOST (TREE)
  (COND ((NULL TREE) NIL)
        ((NULL (RIGHT TREE)) (VALUE TREE))
        (T (RIGHT-MOST (RIGHT TREE)))))

;
;; Return the successor of a given node in an AVL tree. This returns the left-most
```

```
;; node in the tree whose value is greater than the value of KEY.
;

(DEFUN AVL-NEXT (KEY TREE PREDICATE)
  (AND TREE
       (COND ((MINUSP (FUNCALL PREDICATE KEY (VALUE TREE)))
              (OR (AVL-NEXT KEY (LEFT TREE) PREDICATE)
                  (VALUE TREE)))
             (T (AVL-NEXT KEY (RIGHT TREE) PREDICATE)))))

(DEFUN AVL-PREV (KEY TREE PREDICATE)
  (AND TREE
       (COND ((PLUSP (FUNCALL PREDICATE KEY (VALUE TREE)))
              (OR (AVL-PREV KEY (RIGHT TREE) PREDICATE)
                  (VALUE TREE)))
             (T (AVL-PREV KEY (LEFT TREE) PREDICATE)))))


;
;; The first interesting operation on AVL trees. This inserts THING into the tree
;; and returns a new tree and an integer which is the change in height of the tree.
;; If NO-MUTATION is T, the old tree is not changed, but a new tree is returned
;; containing the inserted element. This adds only about (AVL-HEIGHT TREE) extra nodes,
;; i.e. log(tree-size) extra space.
;

(DEFUN AVL-INSERT (THING TREE PREDICATE &OPTIONAL NO-MUTATION)
  (IF (NULL TREE)
      (VALUES (MAKE-AVL-NODE BALANCE 0 VALUE THING) 1)
      (LET ((DIF (FUNCALL PREDICATE THING (VALUE TREE))))
        (COND ((ZEROP DIF)
               (VALUES (UPDATE-NODE TREE (BALANCE TREE) THING
                                    (LEFT TREE) (RIGHT TREE) NO-MUTATION)
                       0))
              ((PLUSP DIF)
               (MULTIPLE-VALUE-BIND (SUBTREE HEIGHT-CHANGE)
                   (AVL-INSERT THING (RIGHT TREE) PREDICATE NO-MUTATION)
                 (SETQ TREE (UPDATE-NODE TREE (+ (BALANCE TREE) HEIGHT-CHANGE)
                                         (VALUE TREE) (LEFT TREE) SUBTREE NO-MUTATION))
                 (IF (> (BALANCE TREE) 1)
                     (BALANCE-RIGHT TREE 1 NO-MUTATION)
                     (VALUES TREE (IF (PLUSP (BALANCE TREE)) HEIGHT-CHANGE 0)))))
              (T (MULTIPLE-VALUE-BIND (SUBTREE HEIGHT-CHANGE)
                     (AVL-INSERT THING (LEFT TREE) PREDICATE NO-MUTATION)
                   (SETQ TREE (UPDATE-NODE TREE (- (BALANCE TREE) HEIGHT-CHANGE)
                                           (VALUE TREE) SUBTREE (RIGHT TREE) NO-MUTATION))
                   (IF (< (BALANCE TREE) -1)
                       (BALANCE-LEFT TREE 1 NO-MUTATION)
                       (VALUES TREE (IF (MINUSP (BALANCE TREE)) HEIGHT-CHANGE 0)))))))))
```

```
;
;; This deletes an entry from an AVL tree.
;; This also has a non-mutating mode for producing coherent structures.
;

(DEFUN AVL-DELETE (THING TREE PREDICATE &OPTIONAL NO-MUTATION)
  (IF (NULL TREE)
      (VALUES NIL 0)
      (LET ((DIF (FUNCALL PREDICATE THING (VALUE TREE))))
        (COND ((ZEROP DIF)
               (ERASE-NODE TREE NO-MUTATION))
              ((PLUSP DIF)
               (MULTIPLE-VALUE-BIND (SUBTREE HEIGHT-CHANGE)
                   (AVL-DELETE THING (RIGHT TREE) PREDICATE NO-MUTATION)
                 (SETQ TREE (UPDATE-NODE TREE (+ (BALANCE TREE) HEIGHT-CHANGE)
                                         (VALUE TREE) (LEFT TREE) SUBTREE NO-MUTATION))
                 (IF (< (BALANCE TREE) -1)
                     (BALANCE-LEFT TREE 0 NO-MUTATION)
                     (VALUES TREE (IF (ZEROP (BALANCE TREE)) HEIGHT-CHANGE 0)))))
              (T (MULTIPLE-VALUE-BIND (SUBTREE HEIGHT-CHANGE)
                     (AVL-DELETE THING (LEFT TREE) PREDICATE NO-MUTATION)
                   (SETQ TREE (UPDATE-NODE TREE (- (BALANCE TREE) HEIGHT-CHANGE)
                                           (VALUE TREE) SUBTREE (RIGHT TREE) NO-MUTATION))
                   (IF (> (BALANCE TREE) 1)
                       (BALANCE-RIGHT TREE 0 NO-MUTATION)
                       (VALUES TREE (IF (ZEROP (BALANCE TREE)) HEIGHT-CHANGE 0)))))))))


;
;; This gets rid of a value that has been found in the tree. NODE is the node containing
;; the value. If the right subtree of NODE is higher than its left, replace the value
;; of NODE with the value of the left-most leaf of the right subtree, and remove this
;; leaf from the right subtree. Otherwise replace  NODE's value with the value of the
;; right-most leaf of the left subtree of NODE, and remove this leaf from the left subtree.
;

(DEFUN ERASE-NODE (NODE NO-MUTATION)
  (COND ((AND (NULL (LEFT NODE)) (NULL (RIGHT NODE)))
         (VALUES NIL -1))
        ((PLUSP (BALANCE NODE))
         (MULTIPLE-VALUE-BIND (VAL SUBTREE HEIGHT-CHANGE)
             (AVL-HEAD (RIGHT NODE) NO-MUTATION)
           (SETQ NODE (UPDATE-NODE NODE (+ (BALANCE NODE) HEIGHT-CHANGE)
                                   VAL (LEFT NODE) SUBTREE NO-MUTATION))
           (VALUES NODE HEIGHT-CHANGE)))
        (T (MULTIPLE-VALUE-BIND (VAL SUBTREE HEIGHT-CHANGE)
               (AVL-TAIL (LEFT NODE) NO-MUTATION)
             (SETQ NODE (UPDATE-NODE NODE (- (BALANCE NODE) HEIGHT-CHANGE)
                                     VAL SUBTREE (RIGHT NODE) NO-MUTATION))
```

```
              (VALUES NODE (IF (ZEROP (BALANCE NODE)) HEIGHT-CHANGE 0))))))


;
;; This returns the head (leftmost element) in the tree, and removes it from the tree.
;; Useful for implementing priority queues as AVL trees.
;; Values returned are the value of the leftmost element, the modified tree, and the
;; change in height of the tree.
;

(DEFUN AVL-HEAD (TREE &OPTIONAL NO-MUTATION)
  (COND ((NULL TREE) NIL)
        ((NULL (LEFT TREE))
         (VALUES (VALUE TREE) (RIGHT TREE) -1))
        (T (MULTIPLE-VALUE-BIND (HEAD-VALUE SUBTREE HEIGHT-CHANGE)
               (AVL-HEAD (LEFT TREE) NO-MUTATION)
             (SETQ TREE (UPDATE-NODE TREE (- (BALANCE TREE) HEIGHT-CHANGE)
                                     (VALUE TREE) SUBTREE (RIGHT TREE) NO-MUTATION))
             (IF (> (BALANCE TREE) 1)
                 (MULTIPLE-VALUE (TREE HEIGHT-CHANGE)
                   (BALANCE-RIGHT TREE 0 NO-MUTATION))
                 (IF (NOT (ZEROP (BALANCE TREE))) (SETQ HEIGHT-CHANGE 0)))
             (VALUES HEAD-VALUE TREE HEIGHT-CHANGE)))))


;
;; This returns the tail (rightmost element) in the tree, and removes it from the tree.
;; Values returned are the value of the rightmost element, the modified tree, and the
;; change in height of the tree.
;

(DEFUN AVL-TAIL (TREE &OPTIONAL NO-MUTATION)
  (COND ((NULL TREE) NIL)
        ((NULL (RIGHT TREE))
         (VALUES (VALUE TREE) (LEFT TREE) -1))
        (T (MULTIPLE-VALUE-BIND (TAIL-VALUE SUBTREE HEIGHT-CHANGE)
               (AVL-TAIL (RIGHT TREE) NO-MUTATION)
             (SETQ TREE (UPDATE-NODE TREE (+ (BALANCE TREE) HEIGHT-CHANGE)
                                     (VALUE TREE) (LEFT TREE) SUBTREE NO-MUTATION))
             (IF (< (BALANCE TREE) -1)
                 (MULTIPLE-VALUE (TREE HEIGHT-CHANGE)
                   (BALANCE-LEFT TREE 0 NO-MUTATION))
                 (IF (NOT (ZEROP (BALANCE TREE))) (SETQ HEIGHT-CHANGE 0)))
             (VALUES TAIL-VALUE TREE HEIGHT-CHANGE)))))


;
;; Balance a TREE that is right-Koyaanisquatsi, i.e. the right subtree is  2 levels
;; higher than the left subtree. HEIGHT-CHANGE is the height of TREE relative to its
```

```
;; value before the delete/insert operation. Balance-right returns a node and the height
;; of that node relative to the original height of TREE.
;

(DEFUN BALANCE-RIGHT (TREE HEIGHT-CHANGE NO-MUT)
  (LET ((R (RIGHT TREE)))
    (COND ((PLUSP (BALANCE R))
           (SETQ TREE (UPDATE-NODE TREE 0 (VALUE TREE) (LEFT TREE) (LEFT R) NO-MUT))
           (SETQ R (UPDATE-NODE R 0 (VALUE R) TREE (RIGHT R) NO-MUT))
           (VALUES R (1- HEIGHT-CHANGE)))
          ((ZEROP (BALANCE R))
           (SETQ TREE (UPDATE-NODE TREE 1 (VALUE TREE) (LEFT TREE) (LEFT R) NO-MUT))
           (SETQ R (UPDATE-NODE R -1 (VALUE R) TREE (RIGHT R) NO-MUT))
           (VALUES R HEIGHT-CHANGE))
          (T (LET ((LR (LEFT R)))
               (SETQ R (UPDATE-NODE R (IF (MINUSP (BALANCE LR)) 1 0)
                                    (VALUE R) (RIGHT LR) (RIGHT R) NO-MUT))
               (SETQ TREE (UPDATE-NODE TREE (IF (PLUSP (BALANCE LR)) -1 0)
                                       (VALUE TREE) (LEFT TREE) (LEFT LR) NO-MUT))
               (SETQ LR (UPDATE-NODE LR 0 (VALUE LR) TREE R NO-MUT))
               (VALUES LR (1- HEIGHT-CHANGE)))))))


;
;; Balance a TREE that is left-Koyaanisquatsi, i.e. the left subtree is  2 levels
;; higher than the right subtree. HEIGHT-CHANGE is the height of TREE relative to its
;; value before the delete/insert operation. Balance-left returns a node and the height
;; of that node relative to the original height of TREE.
;

(DEFUN BALANCE-LEFT (TREE HEIGHT-CHANGE NO-MUT)
  (LET ((L (LEFT TREE)))
    (COND ((MINUSP (BALANCE L))
           (SETQ TREE (UPDATE-NODE TREE 0 (VALUE TREE) (RIGHT L) (RIGHT TREE) NO-MUT))
           (SETQ L (UPDATE-NODE L 0 (VALUE L) (LEFT L) TREE NO-MUT))
           (VALUES L (1- HEIGHT-CHANGE)))
          ((ZEROP (BALANCE L))
           (SETQ TREE (UPDATE-NODE TREE -1 (VALUE TREE) (RIGHT L) (RIGHT TREE) NO-MUT))
           (SETQ L (UPDATE-NODE L 1 (VALUE L) (LEFT L) TREE NO-MUT))
           (VALUES L HEIGHT-CHANGE))
          (T (LET ((RL (RIGHT L)))
               (SETQ L (UPDATE-NODE L (IF (PLUSP (BALANCE RL)) -1 0)
                                    (VALUE L) (LEFT L) (LEFT RL) NO-MUT))
               (SETQ TREE (UPDATE-NODE TREE (IF (MINUSP (BALANCE RL)) 1 0)
                                       (VALUE TREE) (RIGHT RL) (RIGHT TREE) NO-MUT))
               (SETQ RL (UPDATE-NODE RL 0 (VALUE RL) L TREE NO-MUT))
               (VALUES RL (1- HEIGHT-CHANGE)))))))
```

```
;
;; Modify an existing AVL node or create a new one, depending on the value of NO-MUTATION
;

(DEFUN UPDATE-NODE (NODE BALANCE VALUE LEFT RIGHT NO-MUTATION)
  (IF NO-MUTATION
      (MAKE-AVL-NODE BALANCE BALANCE VALUE VALUE LEFT LEFT RIGHT RIGHT)
      (PROGN (SETF (BALANCE NODE) BALANCE)
             (SETF (VALUE NODE) VALUE)
             (SETF (LEFT NODE) LEFT)
             (SETF (RIGHT NODE) RIGHT)
             NODE)))
```